192 476 3020

W9-CFV-984

SOVIET CRITICISM OF AMERICAN LITERATURE

IN THE SIXTIES

An Anthology

Edited and Translated by Carl R. Proffer

ARDIS   **ANN ARBOR**

Soviet Criticism of American Literature in the Sixties

ISBNO-88233-012-8

Copyright © 1972 by
  Ardis Publishers
  615 Watersedge
  Ann Arbor, Michigan 48105

This book is dedicated to

Russian friends and colleagues.

TABLE OF CONTENTS

PART TWO

PREFACE

A critic sits at a desk in Moscow. He has never been to America, and his English is school-learned. His knowledge of American culture is derived almost exclusively from the books he reads. What this critic finds in those books is the matter of this one.

The reader of the reviews, magazine articles and scholarly criticism translated in this anthology will find critics who have new ideas, but perhaps the main interest here is seeing ourselves as others see us. For the Soviet critics what is true of American literature is also assumed to be true of the American people, a view not unfamiliar to readers of our own relevance-oriented criticism. The last decade was a fascinating period, because there were great changes in Soviet attitudes toward American literature. Books that could never have been published before appeared regularly, and a substantial body of commentary was written about twentieth-century American authors.

The incomprehension many Russians experience when trying to understand and write about American literature will be matched by many American readers' incomprehension of the new point of view. While the selections are intended to represent a variety of Soviet opinions, critical genres and abilities, the reader who is patient will see that the writers have certain things in common. The reader himself can easily judge which of the critics is good or bad, careful or sloppy, informed or ignorant; so only a few prefatory remarks are necessary.

"Contradictions" is a common word in Soviet criticism. It derives essentially from socio-political writing, and usually it means a situation which is not easy for them to explain ("progressive" and "reactionary" trends in the same author, formal experimentation combined with leftist political views). This stems from a kind of disbelief in, mistrust of, or hate of pluralism. The general attitude seems to be that a society—or literature (a mirror of society)—characterized by the diversity which creates these "contradictions" is internally unstable, and the moment of rupture and revolution cannot therefore be far in the future. That diversity and "contradictions" could be a sign of inner strength seems an alien concept to many Soviet critics.*

The indignant remarks by various critics about Arthur Miller's plays being next door to popular musicals or "absurdist trash"—or Faulkner being sold (and outsold) by trash are also a manifestation of hostility to diversity. In this case it is harder to understand the Soviet complaint because the Soviet reader also has at his disposal "trash literature," or "popular literature" which sells alongside Tolstoy—and one is just as likely to see the second-rate literature being read on the subways and in the parks as one is to see Tolstoy being read—Rod McKuen has his counterpart in the vastly popular Eduard Asadov.

Soviet critics tend to complain that American critics (or, to use their terminology, "bourgeois critics") overlook or purposely conceal the social significance of literary works. American critics will probably be surprised to learn they are involved in a conscious ideological conspiracy. In any case anyone who reads the major literary reviews of this country will be puzzled by the Soviet view, since our reviews consistently stress social aspects to the exclusion of artistic considerations. Indeed, serious books of fiction and poetry are given much less space in our reviews than books on politics and social problems, memoirs and publicistic writing. The answer to the Soviet point of view is that the opinions expressed by American bourgeois critics do not match those of Soviet Marxist critics. The ways in which this is true are self-evident in the selections below.

---

*It is the experience of most Americans who know Soviet liberals or "dissenters," people in the Soviet civil rights movement, that even they hold this view and tend to be very disturbed by "too much freedom" in the West—so much it allows Maoists, terrorists, black revolutionaries and long-haired students to promulgate their views widely. On a lower and purely material level one finds Soviet visitors to America confused, and often indignant, at the diversity of products—why there should be twenty kinds of toothpaste in twenty different stores, or the same product with many different prices, is frustrating to them; and they consider it a waste of energy and resources. That the absolute principle that diversity or pluralism is a good thing is more important than individual "excesses" is difficult for a Russian to understand.

x

Surely the Soviet tendency to see the personal problems of literary heroes as reflections of social inequities and contradictions should be familiar. Before we raise the indignant charge of "anti-American propaganda criticism," we should remember that virtually all of the American criticism of Soviet literature does exactly the same thing in reverse. For example, recall how often the *Saturday Review* or *Time* have clumsily assured us that *Cancer Ward* is a symbol or mirror of Soviet society. Russian sociological criticism does tend to oversimplify more than ours does. For example, Soviet critics usually present the fifties as the era of literary conformity as well as social conformity, and the sixties as a period of renaissance (thus following the pattern of their own country). But this overlooks the many important ("nonconformist") books written in the fifties—from Faulkner and Hemingway to Salinger, Ellison, Baldwin, Flannery O'Connor, Styron, Bellow, Cheever, Heller and Nabokov. Soviet critics argue that the political and social revolutions of the sixties (compared to the fifties and McCarthyism) were naturally trailed by better, more "progressive" literature. At best this is a dubious generalization.

This anthology is divided into two parts. The selections in Part One, translated by the editor, range from book reviews to an entire short book. Nearly all of these are taken from periodicals. As a matter of principle, excerpts have been avoided, and items are given in full except in two cases: the section on *Couples* is from a longer article by Mendelson, and one section is omitted from Orlova's book on Hemingway. (By excerpting from scholarly criticism in books one could give examples of criticism more oriented toward formal textological analysis.) The earliest selection is from 1960, the latest from 1970. Once space was given to show a variety of opinion on individual authors and to cover the sixties chronologically, it was necessary to omit articles by numerous Soviet specialists other than those represented—for which the editor apologizes to them and the reader.

Part Two is made up of articles which appeared in Soviet English-language periodicals (sometimes after they had appeared in Russian). Here the Soviet critics survey their own criticism and translations of American literature.

Anyone interested in pursuing the subject of Soviet criticism of American literature can consult the following English-language sources:

(1) Valentina A. Libman, *Russian Studies of American Literature. A Bibliography.* Trans. R. V. Allen. Chapel Hill, 1969. [Covers the period from the beginnings to 1964.]

(2) Glenora W. Brown and Deming Brown, *A Guide to Soviet Translations of American Literature.* New York, 1954.

(3) Deming Brown, *Soviet Attitudes Toward American Writing.* Princeton, 1962. [Covers to 1960.]

(4) Charles Pomeroy, "Soviet Russian Criticism 1960-69 of Seven Twentieth Century American Novelists," Ph.D. Diss. Univ. of Southern California, 1971. [On Dreiser, Steinbeck, Hemingway, Faulkner, Fitzgerald, Salinger, Updike.]

(5) The journal *Russian Literature Triquarterly,* beginning with No. 2 (1972), regularly surveys and reviews Soviet literary journals, including those which publish criticism and translations of American literature.

Valentina Libman's bibliography of criticism is updated, in Russian only, from 1964 to 1968 in *Sovremennoe literaturovedenie v SSHA* (M. 1969), and there is a complete bibliography of Russian translations of twentieth-century American literature by Libman in *Problemy literatury SSHA XX veka* (M. 1970).

Time for the research on this topic and translations of the criticism was generously supported by a Fulbright Fellowship in 1969 and a grant from the University of Michigan's Center for Russian and East European Studies in 1971.

Also, a few kind words to Ellendea Proffer, without whose constant carping this book might not have been finished.

Passages from Hemingway's *For Whom the Bell Tolls,* first published by Scribner's in 1940, copyright 1940 by Ernest Hemingway, are quoted with permission.

August 8, 1972

INTRODUCTION

American Literature in the Soviet Union

Moby Dick was not translated into Russian until 1961. If it took Ahab's whale more than a century to reach Russia, it is a peculiar spectacle to see it arrive with closer small fish such as Faulkner and Fitzgerald, Wolfe and Wilder, Robert Penn Warren and Tennessee Williams, Mailer, Malamud, Baldwin and McCullers, Styron and Shirley Ann Grau, Capote and Cheever, Salinger and Updike, Robert Frost and Edward Arlington Robinson—all of whom were virtually unknown to Russian readers until the sixties. Until the latter part of the fifties for most Soviet readers American literature consisted of Fenimore Cooper, Jack London, Mark Twain, Mayne Reid and Theodore Dreiser. This was not a simple case of anti-Americanism. Major classics of many countries remained un- translated until the revolution of the sixties, and however inelegant stylistically, again the catalog is the most appropriate rhetorical figure to describe the period—Jane Austen arriving with Kafka; Rilke, Camus, Beckett and T. S. Eliot all made their major debuts.

The fact that a writer is not translated is a greater impediment to his popularization in the Soviet Union than it would be in most Western countries, because while English-language books are sold widely in all Western countries, there is not a single bookstore in the Soviet Union which sells Western books in the original lan- guages. Thus the only place Russians can buy American books is in the second-hand bookshops of big cities, which have haphazard selections. Russians cannot order books from stores abroad either, partly because it is unlawful to possess foreign currency and impos- sible to exchange it. However, it is possible for Russians to receive non-Russian-language books and magazines from friends in the West, and tourists are allowed to bring in foreign books not printed in Russian. Finally, Soviet publishers do a few English-language editions of such war-horses as London and Dreiser. Otherwise the Russian reader must rely on what he can borrow from friends or read in a library. Libraries have collections of American books ranging from the excellent Library of Foreign Literatures in Moscow to selections in smaller libraries which are as bad as our own small libraries would be.

But the best libraries have a system of *spetskhrany* ("special repositories") which severely limits the availability of many modern books and, especially, periodicals. For example, *The Atlantic Monthly* and *Harper's Magazine* are in a "special repository" at the Moscow Library of Foreign Literatures, and they can be read only with special permission (a document to the effect that the item is connected with the reader's scholarly work). There is no totally centralized management of special repositories, so what is or is not restricted (both Russian and non-Russian books) varies considerably from library to library even in the same city. Of course the very existence of such a system of restriction seems senseless for a stable society, and it will greatly improve the Soviet image when it is ended.* Certainly the quantity of information and the speed with which it is spread has been increasing so rapidly in the past two decades that Russian critics, let alone the informed public which must be the milieu for superior criticism, will find it more and more difficult to avoid errors and write intelligently if all kinds of literature and periodicals are not made more readily available.

Of course, translation is one way to help solve this problem, and in this area the Soviets have much to boast about—especially during the last ten or fifteen years. Soviet translators of American

---

*I say this as a simple matter of fact, and not to assume the holier than thou attitude typical of the Western press when discussing Soviet literature. Apart from special repositories for so-called pornography, the United States often suffers from the idiocyncrasies of librarians and the attempts to ban everything from Mark Twain to J. D. Salinger from high school courses and libraries—all of which are serious matters of concern.

literature are vastly superior to their American counterparts translating Russian literature. We have a monotonous series of inaccurate translations of Pasternak and mediocre ones of Solzhenitsyn by Glenny and others, with only Mirra Ginzburg's work to praise. But the Russians have a long tradition of respect for translation of literature as a responsible art—with many good translators such as Elena Golysheva, Viktor Hinkis, Evgenia Kalashnikova, Tatyana Litvinova and Rita Rait-Kovalyova. These talented translators have done a great deal for American culture over the last fifteen years or more, and some enlightened American publisher should invite them all to visit this country so that in some measure they can be given the thanks they deserve.

Several translations made during the sixties are regarded as triumphs of the art—the complete renaissance of a foreign cultural consciousness in a new Russian idiom. Andrei Sergeev's translations of Robert Frost and Viktor Golyshev's translation of *All the King's Men* are two outstanding achievements, important events in the history of the Russian literary language. Translators are greatly respected in the Soviet Union, partly due to the long Russian tradition—going back at least to Zhukovsky at the beginning of the nineteenth century—of good poets doing many translations. And most of the great twentieth-century Russian poets from Mandelstam, Akhmatova and Pasternak to contemporary writers have enriched the Russian literary heritage with translations.

One external, and somewhat capitalistic, proof of the esteem held for translation in the USSR is the royalty paid. It would be hard to find an American who could make a living solely by translating Russian literature, but many Soviets live solely on royalties from translation. Indeed, the honorariums paid by journals such as *Foreign Literature* and *New World* are almost as high for translations as for original writing. Translators are paid by the printed signature (thirty-two pages)—and the amount may range from 200 to 300 rubles (a ruble equals $1.10) per signature. A normal three-act play brings 700-800 rubles, novels of course more. When one considers that a typical academic salary for a beginning PhD is 110-125 rubles per month, one can see why most translators do not need to hold regular academic positions as they do in the United States.

How does a work of American literature get published in the USSR? Who initiates it? What are the relations between translator and publisher? Surprising as it may seem, the great majority of works are begun at the initiative of the individual translators. This is particularly true for authors who have not previously been translated, while in the case of accepted writers such as Dreiser, Hemingway, or more recently Faulkner, a publishing house may ask a translator to do a novel. The fact that it is contracted, and even paid for, does not always mean it will be printed; for example, I was told that several years ago a publisher contracted a translation of *Peyton Place,* and realized it would be unpublishable in the USSR only after it was completed. It seems safe to regard this as a serious error of judgment. Anyway, in most cases the translator himself begins things. He may discuss it with an editor or he may simply go ahead to do the translation first—either because he thinks he can persuade someone to print it, or—especially in the case of poetry—it is simply something he wants to do for his own satisfaction. Novels such as *For Whom the Bell Tolls* and *Look Homeward, Angel* were translated many years before they were published. In any case, the individual translator has to persuade an editor and the editor an editorial board—and the whole process may take a long time and be very complicated, as unpleasant as it is in any other country. While there are happy exceptions everywhere, I think editors in the USSR as in the United States are among the most hated of human beings (though some writers reasonably maintain editors are not human).

What an editor chooses to print must be fit into the regular Two or Three-Year Plan of the publishing house (all have yearly plans—and projections for varying numbers of years). Given the uneasy state of political relations between Communist USSR and capitalist US, the Soviet editors would probably be well advised not to overload the plan with American literature, particularly if it is too popular. (For example, *Foreign Literature* was reportedly criticized by other journals for publishing *Airport*—and raising their subscription rate spectacularly for the year.) Publication sometimes appears to be tied to external political events—as when a spate of publishing of American literature *(Tender Is the Night, Look Homeward, Angel,* a collection of novellas) preceded the visit of President Nixon and signing of treaties in May 1972.

What criteria are used by editors to determine if a work of American literature should be published or written about? This is harder to answer now than it would have been before 1960, because of the great variety of new authors and approaches which have become acceptable. But usually "realists" are preferred to what the Russians call "modernists"—modernism being anything from use of stream of consciousness devices to any radical experiment in form. Writers generally closer in form to Balzac, Dreiser or Mann are published more often than ones close to Robbe-Grillet, Joyce or Hesse. Thus Faulkner's more conventionally "realistic" works were translated first, and only after some fifteen years of printing Faulkner in the USSR is *The Sound and the Fury* scheduled to appear and *Light in August* being translated.

Furthermore, most Soviet editors look for "critical realism." There are exceptions, but they generally publish negative portrayals of American society (these are not hard to find in any really good national literature). In fact, the Soviet editor's attitude in considering American literature is exactly the same as the American editor's attitude in considering Soviet literature. This is a regrettable situation on both sides. Any American translator who has tried to interest a national magazine in Soviet literature, or who has approached a publisher, knows he will be told that without the "dissent angle" it will not be interesting and sell. Check any ten reviews of any translations of Soviet novels and at least nine will consist primarily of sociological commentary on dissent in the USSR. The most influential American periodicals play up the dissent angle most consistently and crudely—*The New York Times Book Review, The New York Review of Books,* and the *Saturday Review.* For example, *The New York Times Book Review* is as dominated by sociological or political criticism as

Soviet periodicals, not only in the kinds of books chosen for review, but also, when it does get around to fiction, in the kind of criticism written. *Time's* weekly snarl at the USSR is as predictable, inaccurate and self-righteous as analogous items in the Soviet journal *October*—whether dealing with literature or light bulbs. In both countries the author's socio-political stance is far more important than how he writes—thus they have Dreiser and we have Solzhenitsyn. The difference is that the Russians are quite open in their tendentiousness; there it is a matter of conscious, unapologetic public policy, while here editors and critics pretend, or believe, choices for publication are done solely on "intrinsic" criteria. —I have digressed on the subject of American treatment of Soviet literature, because it is so easy for us to be condescending to some aspects of Soviet treatment of American literature. The presumed average reader of this book will not be a professional Slavist, so he will not know how similar the situation is here with respect to Soviet literature—and one of the main uses of this book is to help make us aware that things we take for granted may be based on propaganda—which is offensive to another country. The consistent bias in American writing on Soviet literature is true not only in ephemera like newspapers and weekly magazines, but also, to a lesser extent, in professional scholarly criticism published in small scholarly journals and books. A number of well known American Slavists have made their careers on Soviet dissent, while pretending to be interested in the art of writing. Of course, even from a Soviet point of view, which demands ideological vigilance, writing about literary politics is perfectly acceptable and even useful as an activity. It is reprehensible only when written under the guise of literary criticism and when blind to exactly similar phenomena in the author's own society

Let us return to the criteria for publishing in the USSR and the last major consideration—"naturalism." If a book has too much detailed description of sex or violence, no matter how it is handled by the author, it will not be acceptable to Soviet editors. Thus, because a whole major section of *Rabbit, Run* depends on a description of sex, it has not been published in the Soviet Union—

while *Of the Farm* and *The Centaur* have. The Soviet attitude (in the press, reviews, etc.) seems to be that too much interest in sex distracts one from useful social activity—not realizing that sex is a very useful social activity. But the Soviet puritans' idea is that if there are a lot of dirty books around nobody is going to go to work. Of course, the ridiculous argument that pornography debases humanity more than censorship does is employed by petty tyrants there as it is here in America. Recalling President Nixon rejecting the report of a Presidential Commission on Pornography it strikes me that he would make a good Soviet editor, if he would work on his style a little.

Realism, dissent, and lack of naturalism are probably the Soviet editor's most important concerns, but there are many things published which do not on the face of it meet the requirements. Theoretically, the Soviets would not publish the theater of the absurd because it is *prima facie* absurd to publish something absurd—but they have published a few plays, ostensibly to show Soviet readers how absurd this "modernist" trend is *(Waiting for Godot, The Rhinocerous)*. Similarly, examples of the *nouveau roman* have been published—to show what a barren movement it is.

The situation with criticism is much the same. Indeed, most of the critical essays are written on authors who have been translated. Far more is still written about Twain and Dreiser than about any modern author.* Especially for writers since the thirties, the most important recent Russian books on American literature, listed chronologically, are: (1) Raisa Orlova, *The Descendents of Huckleberry Finn* (M. 1964, 378pp., 10,000 copies), (2) *Problems*

---

*A number of the books on authors not covered in the translations below are mentioned in the introductory notes to each section. One might also note Zasursky's *Theodore Dreiser* (M. 1964), Yury Lidsky's *Bret Harte* (Kiev, 1961), O. V. Vasilevskaya's *The Works of Stephen Crane* (M. 1967), and A. S. Mulyarchik's *The Works of John Steinbeck* (M. 1963). The reader can consult the translation of Libman's bibliography and other sources noted in the Preface above.

of the History of American Literature (M. 1964, 480pp.), (3) Moris Mendelson, *The Modern American Novel* (M. 1964, 534pp., 5500 copies), (4) Yakov Zasursky, *Twentieth-Century American Literature* (M. 1966, 440pp.), (5) Ivan Kashkin, *For the Contemporary Reader* (M. 1968, 562pp., 10,000 copies), (6) *Contemporary Literary Criticism in the United States* (M. 1969, 3700 copies), (7) *Problems of Twentieth-Century American Literature* (M. 1970, 526pp., 5800 copies). All of these contained much information on authors little known in the Soviet Union, as well as extensive studies of older writers—and Libman's excellent bibliographies of translations and Russian criticism of American literature. The size of the editions is modest by Soviet standards—but large when compared to many American scholarly books on Russian literature (2000 is a typical edition). *Questions of Literature* contained several solid scholarly articles helping to introduce new writers during this period. Writers who are not being translated, but who are so popular in the West that they cannot be ignored, are usually dismissed in reviews of American editions. Still even these reviews are valuable for the Soviet reader, because they are often the only source of information available. Thus, for example, Tugusheva's review of Henry Miller's works should not be dismissed too lightly. The same is true of the article published in *The Literary Gazette* in 1969, a survey of Nabokov's works; although he was condemned, the article provided the only substantial information on Nabokov printed in the Soviet Union, and the reader well versed in the cliches of Soviet journalism can draw useful conclusions from any such article.

Who publishes American literature in the USSR? There are several periodicals such as *New World, Moscow, The Don, The Flame (Ogonek), Youth (Iunost'), Neva, The Star, The Young Guard, Our Contemporary, Around the World, Open Space, The Urals, Crocodile, The Banner, Knowledge Is Strength,* etc. which from time to time publish poems, stories, or literary criticism—as do a variety of newspapers, particularly a weekly called, appropriately, *The Week.* But by far the most important organs are the newspaper called *The Literary Gazette* and the journal *Foreign Literature (Inostrannaia literatura)*.

The Literary Gazette is generally regarded by intelligentsia readers as the most interesting of all Soviet newspapers. It is the official organ of the Union of Soviet Writers—published weekly, most issues sixteen pages long. *The Literary Gazette* is rather more like *Boston After Dark* in content (though in the Soviet context it would have to be called *Leningrad At Dawn)*, with an obvious heavy percentage of pages given to literature—reviews, polemics, congratulations on birthdays to various writers, unpublished works from the archives of classics, travel notes, and translations of short stories or excerpts from long ones. Since *The Literary Gazette* is an establishment organ, what one finds in it is often a prediction of things to come—or not to come. For example, a generally sympathetic survey of the work of a previously untranslated author can mean a translation will soon appear (either in a magazine or in book form); thus as this book goes to print I can predict (on the basis of this week's issue of *The Literary Gazette)* that translations of Joyce Carol Oates will soon be published. On the other hand, a negative survey of a previously undiscussed writer (Nabokov in a 1969 issue) usually means one should not hold one's breath waiting for first-hand acquaintance through translation.

The Literary Gazette is the central wind vane, but the magazine *Foreign Literature* * is the most important periodical for the publication of all non-Russian literatures in the Soviet Union. It is currently edited by N. T. Fedorenko (best known in this country as the former ambassador to the UN), and at least two members of the editorial board have written on American literature—Tamara Motylyova and P. V. Palievsky. Circulation is not, as is customary in the Soviet Union, currently listed in each issue, but it is somewhere between 100,000 and 150,000 twelve times per year.

---

*The title-page reads: *"Foreign Literature*—a literary-artistic and socio-political magazine. Organ of the Union of Writers of the USSR. Izvestiia Publishers, Moscow."

Foreign Literature contains translations and criticism from the literatures of virtually every country that is literate, and some that aren't. An issue chosen at random contains a Japanese story, some French poetry and Yugoslav stories, a part of the serialization of Remarque's last novel, and recent Hindu poetry—plus criticism on Nekrasov, an article on Western films, comments on Western newspapers, five book reviews, two interviews—and the "Chronicle"—a regular department of brief notes on current artistic and political events country by country (people such as Mort Sahl or Art Buchwald are sometimes quoted here). American literature plays a moderate role in the overall plan of *Foreign Literature,* but virtually every American author new in the sixties appeared there— everything from *The Catcher in the Rye* to *Washington D. C.* Novels are frequently serialized and then published as books a year or two later *(The Centaur, To Kill a Mockingbird).* Edward Albee and Arthur Miller's plays, and a relatively small amount of poetry have also appeared in *Foreign Literature* (poetry has not fared as well as prose during the sixties). Substantial excerpts from non-literary works such as Studs Terkel's *Division Street: America* and *The Peter Principle* also appeared in *Foreign Literature.* Ordinarily they print without cuts, but occasionally, as in the case of *In Cold Blood* (1966), there is severe abridgement. *Foreign Literature's* critical reviews are rather less important, but its chronicle section and frequent polemics with the Western press make it perhaps the most important source of information on current events for the Soviet reader. All in all *Foreign Literature* is the most interesting literary magazine in the Soviet Union, and it is a testament to our provinciality that we have nothing similar in scope and influence in this country.

Most of the serious scholarship and criticism on American literature is printed either in book form or in the journal *Questions of Literature* (circulation 20,000, published monthly in Moscow as an organ of the Union of Writers and the Gorky Institute of World Literature), edited by V. Ozerov. The journal is devoted primarily to Russian literature, but almost every issue contains non-Russian items (including translations of letters and other documents). For example, major essays such as Landor's "Centaur-Novels" (translated below) and the first long essay on Thomas Wolfe (N. A. Anastasiev, "Faust Does Not Die," No. 4, 1967) appeared there. Though this oversimplifies matters somewhat, a typical pattern for the introduction of a new writer is: (1) an article in *The Literary Gazette,* (2) a longer, serious survey in *Questions of Literature,* (3) translation in *Foreign Literature* or book form. Its occasional interest in American literature aside, *Questions of Literature*—along with *Russian Literature* (published in Leningrad) is the elite scholarly journal on Russian literature.

New World, when edited by Tvardovsky, published several important things from American literature. First among these was Golyshev's translation of *All the King's Men* (serialized in 1968). Frost, Cheever, and others were translated here too. Two of the important reviews by major critics (translated below) appeared in *New World* (Landor's of *The Great Gatsby* and Levidova's of *Clock Without Hands).* In 1970 and 1971 the magazine also published *Slaughterhouse 5* and *The Bridge of San Luis Rey,* as well as short selections of Mailer and Flannery O'Connor.

Book publishing is all done by the same "company" in that it is state controlled, but there are numerous individual publishing houses. The State Publishers of Artistic Literature (fondly known as "Geekl," from its Russian initials) does most of the translations of foreign literature, especially collected works. "Soviet Writer" also does a fair amount of American literature, as does "Young Guard" Publishing (the former is more "establishment," the latter usually does lighter things). Sometimes there are astounding events in the publishing world though—as when we find *Catch 22* (abridged) put out by the conservative Military Publishing House (which also did Fletcher Nebel's *Seven Days in May)*—or *The Naked and the Dead* brought out by the "Library of Science Fiction and Adventure!" For literary criticism the publishing outlets are much the same, with the addition of the Academy of Sciences Publishing House, which along with the Gorky Institute has printed some of the most important books and bibliographies of American literature. Most publishers are centered in Moscow as ours are in New York.

Critics, like translators, can make a living doing free-lance writing of reviews and articles; but usually the critics have at least nominal connection with a university, literary institute or library. They do not usually conduct regular university classes as American academics do; they may have a number of graduate students writing dissertations under them, but they usually hold research posts which require few formal duties—other than committee work one day a week and the obligation to produce a quota of 32-page signatures for publication each year. They often give guest lectures at other institutions—everywhere from Georgia to Vladivostok (which is starting a new American Studies Program). Most of the criticism of American literature is written by people who live in or near Moscow; Leningrad is a distant second, and all other areas are of less importance. Moscow State University and Leningrad State University are far and away the most prestigious universities in the country; Moscow's Lenin Library and Leningrad's Saltykov-Shchedrin Library are the best in the country; Moscow's Central State Archives of Art and Literature, the Lenin Library Manuscript Division, and Leningrad Pushkin House (Institute of Russian Literature) hold all of the papers of important Russian writers; and the most prestigious literary institutes are all in Moscow and Leningrad. Taken together these institutions make a formidable bastion for the establishment, and all are of course ultimately dominated by the Party, which is considered to be the avant-garde of the intelligentsia as for the workers. Of course, Party membership is not required to publish (nor is membership in the Union of Soviet Writers), but presumably it does not hurt one's chances, and Party membership is a normal step in the careers of most successful critics.

What role does censorship play in translation and literary criticism? The normal American view of an ogre from *Glavlit* (the censorship board whose number appears in every Soviet book) with a small head and red pencil oversimplifies matters. The *editors* are the ones who do the great majority of crossing out, and they tend to be so cautious that *Glavlit* has little left to do. In translations censorship is of two kinds—acknowledged and unacknowledged. To the former type belong the translations of *In Cold Blood* and *Catch 22;* they are noted as being "abridged" on the title page. But where these cuts are and how substantial they are the Soviet reader cannot generally determine. For example, about fifty pages is cut from *Catch 22,* including most of the plot line involving Nately's whore, her sister and Yossarian—so the ending of the novel is quite puzzling to Russian readers ("who is this female, where does she come from, why is she trying to kill Yossarian?"). As it happens, censored translations such as these two are *not* typical in the USSR, and both editions were criticized in the Soviet press. The second kind of censorship is harder to find, but the extensive unacknowledged cuts in *For Whom the Bell Tolls* (especially Chapter 18 where the Russians are discussed) are a good example. There is no justification for this treatment of a text, but the Soviet point of view is that anything harmful or derogatory to its system and citizens should be removed. What Soviet editors cut out as a general rule is (1) naturalistic detail of sex or violence ("pornography"),* (2) references to the USSR or Russians or Communism or socialism which in context are not respectful, (3) fantastic events in otherwise realistic novels (this is done less consistently, but examples can be found in *Catch 22* and are matched by certain cuts in Russian works such as Bulgakov's *The Master and Margarita),* (4) pacifistic statements—such as those in *Catch 22*—to the effect that World War II was not worth fighting.

In the case of criticism editorial change is harder to classify, but some of the same categories work here too. As I checked passages quoted by the Soviet critics in the selections of this anthology, I found several cases of strategic hiatuses which turned out to be filled with remarks on sex or Stalin or Communism (I have noted some of these in the footnotes to the translations). Whether these deletions are made by the critics or the editors is impossible to determine in all cases. Certainly editors are responsible for some of them, and it is known that Soviet editors can be

---

*This goes so far that even things such as this are deleted: "He [Yossarian] rolled a piece of lint out of his navel."

arbitrary in cutting—and in adding things on their own. If the reader discovers seemingly irrelevant sentences of abuse in the text of an essay, he may suspect that this is an editorial interpolation. The beginnings and endings of the articles and reviews are especially susceptible to editorial revision.

However, in other cases it is clear that the critics censor themselves. While the great majority are careful with the passages which they translate into Russian as examples, some have little respect for the author's text—and the retranslation to English of what they quote beside the actual original English shows how different the effects can be. Since except in some books published by the Academy of Sciences, edition and page numbers are not given for quotes, it is easy to do this undetected. Along with the abridgment of translation by editors, this practice of critics is the least praiseworthy feature of Soviet treatment of American and other foreign literatures.

A graph of amounts of Soviet publication and criticism of American literature from 1960 to the present has no sharp ups and downs. Except possibly 1961, there was a steady increase in the early sixties, to some extent continuing a trend begun in the late fifties with the introduction of Faulkner. From 1962 to 19-68 there was continued growth as new works and new authors continued to be introduced every year.

In an article called "The Books We Still Don't Have" in the January 5 issue of *The Literary Gazette* in 1960 the respected critic Tamara Motylyova complained of Soviet ignorance of many foreign writers—few translations and little serious criticism on such major figures as Proust. The article was published along with several items on the need for peaceful coexistence and disarmament—and immediately after Khrushchev's visit to the United States. Motylyova's programmatic appeal was matched in No. 1 of *Foreign Literature* for 1960 by Elena Romanova's article "New Prospects Are Opening Up," written in connection with the American Exhibition then in Moscow. Her call to broaden and deepen Soviet knowledge of American literature marked the beginning of more liberal publication of translations and criticism. She mentioned Thomas Wolfe favorably, and said that *The Naked and the Dead* and *From Here to Eternity* should be translated; by the end of the decade Mailer, Jones and Wolfe had all been published. Two other key articles in this early period were Orlova's "Little People in a Big War" *(Questions of Literature,* No. 6, 1960), among the first serious discussions of Mailer, Jones,* Hersey and others, and Tugusheva's "The American Tragedy in 1960" *(Questions of Literature,* No. 6, 1961) with its praise of *Rabbit, Run; Set This House on Fire,* and *The Child Buyer.* The first major article-introduction on Tennessee Williams' plays also appeared in 1960—G. Zlobin's "On Stage and Backstage" *(Foreign Literature,* No. 7), in the same issue as the translation of *Orpheus Descending.* Motylyova's book *Foreign Literature and the Modern Day* followed the next year (Moscow, 1961), opening serious critical discussion of many new writers. Favorably reviewing Motylyova's book Orlova said, "In the previous period it was often accepted as axiomatic that there were only two writers in modern American literature—Theodore Dreiser and Howard Fast," but she noted that that time was passing. And fundamental changes continued all during the decade.

Some idea of the chronological development can be formed from the brief introductions to each of the critical articles translated below. The history of each author—in translation and criticism—is outlined in these introductions. The development moves from the publication of Salinger and Melville in 1960-61 to the printing of Mailer, John O'Hara, and even Arthur Hailey at the end of the sixties and beginning of the seventies. It is curious that as the American exhibition and then Vice President Nixon's visit helped spark publication of Americana at the end of the fifties and

---

*James Jones was little written about until *From Here to Eternity* was published at the end of the decade. Landor gave several pages to him in an article on post-war prose *(Questions of Literature,* No. 3, 1963), and Alvah Bessie's comments on *The Thin Red Line* were translated in *Foreign Literature* in 1963. Zverev reviewed *Go to the Widow Maker* favorably in *Foreign Literature* (No. 6, 1968), not long before the first translation of Jones.

beginning of the sixties, so his visit as President in 1972 was preceded by a flurry of publication of American literature, including *Tender Is the Night, Look Homeward, Angel, The Bridge of San Luis Rey,* and a collection of novellas.

Here is a bare chronology of important events in translation, including authors not discussed in the criticism translated below:

1960

Salinger, *The Catcher in the Rye*
Miller, *Selected Plays*
Williams, *Orpheus Descending*
Kerouac, *On the Road* (excerpts)
Langston Hughes, *Collected Poems*
Melville, *Omoo*
Listen, America Sings (anthology of poetry)
American Science Fiction Stories
Scenarios of the American Film

1961

Faulkner, *The Mansion*
Melville, *Moby Dick*
Steinbeck, *The Winter of Our Discontent*
American Theatrical Miniatures (O'Neill, Saroyan and others)

1962

Faulkner, *The Bear*
Thurber, *The Secret Life of Walter Mitty*
Cheever, *Selected Stories*
Shaw, *The Young Lions*
Richard Wright, *Selected Stories* (64pp.)
Vidal, *A Visit to a Small Planet*
Crane, *The Red Badge of Courage* (lasted printed in 1930)

1963

Lee, *To Kill a Mockingbird*

Steinbeck, *Travels with Charley* (abridged)
    "   , *The Pearl* (first pub. in 1956)
    "   , *Of Mice and Men*
    "   , *Tortilla Flat*
Frost, *From Nine Books* (144pp., anthology)
Parrington, *Main Currents of American Thought* (3 vols.)
The Modern American Novella (462pp., anthology)

1964

Faulkner, *The Hamlet*
James Baldwin, *Blues for Mr. Charlie*
Hemingway, *A Moveable Feast*
Albee, *The Death of Bessie Smith*
Fletcher Nebel, *Seven Days in May*

1965

Fitzgerald, *The Great Gatsby*
Faulkner, *The Town*
Updike, *The Centaur*
Capote, *Breakfast at Tiffany's*
Bradbury, *Fahrenheit 451*
Saroyan, *Plays* (572pp.)
Miller, *Incident at Vichy*
Salinger, *Raise High the Roofbeam, Carpenters*
    "   , *The Catcher in the Rye and Other Stories*
Hersey, *The Child Buyer*

1966

Capote, *The Grass Harp*
McCullers, *Clock Without Hands*
Capote, *In Cold Blood* (abridged)
Cheever, *Selected Stories*
Bret Harte, *Collected Works* (6 vols.)

1967

Heller, *Catch 22* (abridged)
Updike, *Of the Farm*
Styron, *The Long March*
Malamud, *Selected Stories* (270pp.)
Williams, *The Glass Menagerie and Nine Plays* (724pp.)
Hellman, *Toys in the Attic*
Capote, *Selected Stories*
Melville, *Typee*
Vonnegut, *Cat's Cradle*

1968

Warren, *All the King's Men*
Cheever, *The Wapshot Chronicle*
Faulkner, *Intruder in the Dust*
Miller, *The Price*
Vidal, *Washington D. C.*
Salinger, *Franny*
Frost, *Selected Lyrics* (48pp.)
Hemingway, *Collected Works* (4 vols., including the first publica-
    tion of *For Whom the Bell Tolls)*
Hansberry, *The Sign in Sidney Brustein's Window*

1969

Grau, *Keepers of the House*
Albee, *Everything in the Garden*
Halberstam, *One Very Hot Day*

1970

Jones, *From Here to Eternity* (abridged)
Mailer, *The Naked and the Dead* (abridged)
Vonnegut, *Slaughterhouse 5*

1971

Fitzgerald, *Tender Is the Night*
Wolfe, *Look Homeward, Angel*
Wilder, *The Bridge of San Luis Rey*
O'Hara, *The Instrument and Other Stories*
Hailey, *Airport*
T. S. Eliot, *Selected Verse*
E. A. Robinson, *Selected Verse*
O'Neill, *Plays* (2 vols.)
Van Wyck Brooks, *The Flowering of New England and Other Criticism* (2 vols.)

1972

Faulkner, *The Reivers*

For the most part I have not included in this list works by nineteenth-century writers such as Twain, Poe and Whitman—except where they are extremely important works which either had never appeared in Russian or had not been published since the twenties and thirties. Nor have I included Dos Passos, Dreiser, Caldwell, Mitchell Wilson or the proletarian writers who, it is well known, have been published quite regularly. Also generally excluded is American science fiction, which has grown to be quite popular during the sixties—Ray Bradbury, Isaac Asimov, Robert Sheckley and many others, often printed in anthologies and separately. If we were to include such things as Irving Stone's *Lust for Life* and an abridged translation of Sandburg's *Lincoln* (both published in 1961) the picture would also be somewhat fuller. Criticism and translation are for the most part coordinated, so the number of essays and reviews tends to follow the same chronological pattern.

Obviously American literature is a subject of extensive and serious study in the Soviet Union, a fact of which most Americans are not aware. A bare listing of the major translations and the few examples of criticism which now follow should be ample proof of the intensity of Russian interest in our culture. Soviet critics work with handicaps which the American reader should try to keep in mind. One of the most obvious is the lack of first-hand experience in the United States, with resulting howlers in matters of realia, everyday life. Few Soviet specialists have been to this country, or any Western country, and the results in their work are sometimes painfully apparent—this would be true of anyone studying any foreign country in the abstract, without personal experience. Indeed, it is surprising that the Union of Soviet Writers has not done more to end this purely abstract study of the United States by regularly sending both their established and younger scholars and critics on extensive visits. American scholars who read this book can help foster this interest in American literature by asking their universities to issue invitations to Soviet colleagues (which can be sent in care of the Union of Soviet Writers, 52 Vorovsky St., Moscow). Most of the Soviet scholars could lecture in English, and what they have to say would be very stimulating for students here. Since the Union of Soviet Writers will sometimes pay travel expenses for its members, the institution which issues an invitation may have to pay only an honorarium. Given the increasingly congenial spirit of cooperation between the Soviet Union and the United States, such broadened contacts can only be useful to everyone concerned. Serious scholars will be able to make more informed contributions, and if we are to be abused, we will at least be absued intelligently.

Carl R. Proffer
University of Michigan

A NOTE ON TRANSLATION AND RETRANSLATION

The translation of the essays is intended to be accurate, which means it cannot always "read smoothly." The participial constructions typical of Russian critical prose are not readily rearrangeable into English dependent clauses, and I was more interested in avoiding Russian charges of distortion than in winning approval from those who love the style and error method of translation.

The translation of quotations from works originally written in English was a greater problem. There are two basic choices: (1) quote everything in the English original, (2) retranslate everything from Russian into English. The first is impossible because Soviet critics seldom give edition and page numbers—so one could spend a lifetime searching fat novels or whole runs of journals for quotes of a few words or sentences. Moreover, the Russian translation of these quotes is sometimes revealingly different than the original. The second basic choice is impossible because Hemingway and Updike would never really be Hemingway and Updike, but one of those jokes which are translated through two or three languages and come out gibberish.

Therefore, I have done the following: (1) wherever I could find the original, I quote in the original—using footnotes or brackets to note alterations in the Russian version, or, where it is of interest, sometimes giving the complete retranslation along with the original, (2) where I could not find the original I use only retranslation—and these cases are either noted in a footnote, or marked by a cross [†], symbolizing the place where the original is buried.

All footnotes not specifically marked as the editor's belong to the authors.

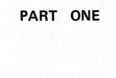

PART ONE

PANOVA ON SALINGER

Vera Panova (1905-), a Leningrader, is one of the most prominent women prose writers of the post-war period. Author of many stories, novels and plays, she has won various Soviet literary awards. Some of her works deal with the war and antisemitism, some are on historical themes. She has written sensitively about children and problems within the family. On occasion her works have been the focus of lively polemics between liberals and conservatives in the Soviet literary press.

The Catcher in the Rye was the first of Salinger's works to be translated (by Rita Rait-Kovalyova) into Russian. It appeared in *Foreign Literature* in 1960, and Panova's essay accompanied the translation. It was later published in book form (1965 and 1967, editions of 100,000 each), along with "Raise High the Roof Beam, Carpenters" and five other stories. While the adolescent bluntness of Holden Caulfield's language is often bowdlerized in the translation, enough of the original remained for the diction and frankness to come as a pleasant shock to the Soviet reader. Salinger has become quite popular in the Soviet Union; and most of the more than twenty reviews, articles and prefaces written on Salinger have been done not by specialists in American literature but by other critics who were attracted to the new voice.

Vera Panova

ON J. D. SALINGER'S NOVEL

The Catcher in the Rye reaches the reader's heart in extremely subtle, secret ways. Why should the confused wanderings of ill-fated, infantile Holden Caulfield so concern us. No extreme David Copperfield calamities have befallen him. He does not wander on the highways of the American West like John Steinbeck's heroes, but in New York where his parents, sister, aunt, "and all my crummy relatives" and his numerous friends live. He does not ride the rails—he hires taxis. Holden Caulfield has never had to worry about a piece of bread. He is from a solid intelligentsi family, he studies in the most respectable educational institutions in the United States. Four times a year his ancient grandmother sends him money "for his birthday." And by a number of signs we gather that Holden is handsome, which of course is not unimportant for happiness, especially at sixteen. In a word, he is a rich man's kid, a loafer, and it would not seem that the reader has any reason to worry about him.

Besides, Holden has so many traits and does so many things which the reader simply cannot approve of. Holden tells his own story—and what language, replete with slang expressions and swear words! Holden has no respect for anything—not his school, or the teachers, or his studies, or his nation's history. "This crazy cannon that was in the Revolutionary War and all," he notes casually telling where he is during the football game. His infantile behavior makes an unpleasant impression: the scene in the washroom where Holden does a tap dance in front of the shaving Stradlater is so repulsive—we are used to sixteen-year-olds conducting themselves decently, and not making faces. Readers also become indignant because Holden is so stubborn about not wanting to study. Literature interests him; he reads a lot and writes excellent papers on literature. But when he has to write a paper on history, about ancient Egypt, he writes a few disdainful, parodistic lines. He does not know anything about ancient Egypt and does not want to. That does not interest him. Holden has been expelled from four schools for his failures. "What are you doing to yourself, boy," they ask, and he sits with a red hunting cap on, bill backwards, and reads Isak Dinesen's *Out of Africa*. And when a kind old teacher tries to persuade him he should think about his future, Holden answers patiently, "Yes, sir. I know. I know all that,"—but he is wondering where the ducks in New York's Central Park go in the winter. "I couldn't figure out where the ducks went when the lagoon got all icy and frozen over."

That's the kind of impossible, unreasonable, person this Holden is.

He makes the rounds of New York bars (very worried about getting alcoholic beverages which they do not want to serve him since he is a minor), dances with a woman of some sort, proposes to a girl he knows that she go away with him to "live somewhere by a river," and when the hotel elevator operator asks him, "Do you want a girl for the night?" Holden answers, after the initial embarrassment, "Okay."

And, in addition to all this, he is a liar! He himself says, "I'm the most terrific liar you ever saw in your life." How adroitly he lies to the poor sympathetic Mrs. Morrow on the train...

But this novel about a loafer, a petty liar, a swaggering dandy, a strange, unlucky young creature, a novel outwardly so simple, but so complex in its inner structure, creates a whirlwind of feelings and thoughts... This is the hallmark of a really important book.

It develops before us gradually; line by line each page of the novel strikes us by revealing new aspects, new secrets of a young human soul. Salinger strives to unveil all of these secrets. It is important to him that he tell everything about his hero, including that which literature often passes over in hypocritical silence. However, in baring the sores of contemporary American life, Salinger frequently resorts to the devices of decadence. We have in mind the selection of facts, details, the choice of situations, and finally, the misuse of slang.

This tribute to a fashion which is widespread in the West somewhat weakens the impact of the novel on the reader. However, on the whole the novel is truthful and realistic.

Holden is taken at a time in his life when he is surrounded by minor and major unpleasantnesses, when nothing is going right for him: his coat has been stolen, he forgot the fencing foils in the subway, and he has been expelled from school for the fourth time—he is afraid to go home—and the self-satisfied, experienced flirt Stradlater has started dating the girl who was once dear to him, and Holden comes out of a fight with Stradlater cut and bleeding... It is all disgusting; in his heart there is melancholy and depression. Is it not because of all this that Holden is deliberately rude on the first pages of the novel? It is characteristic of youth to hide its disillusionment and despair underneath rudeness. Yes, the reader becomes convinced as he learns more about Holden's pure and tender soul. This is all superficial, and affectation.

In a soulless barracks—the dormitory of a respectable school called Pencey—there are only two things left which console Holden: *Out of Africa* and the red hat which Holden bought for a dollar. But in these circumstances this is too little consolation, and Holden runs away from school. Driven by a number of annoyances, large and small, especially poisonous because they are insignificant, he "simply flies away" like a duck from a frozen pond where it is no longer possible to live. He plans to spend a few days in New York without showing up at home until Wednesday—to "live quietly" in an inexpensive hotel until that fateful Wednesday about which he speaks as if casually, but in reality he tries not to think about it.

We, the readers, cannot wait for this Wednesday either. But the narration stops at its threshold. We can only guess what happened that Wednesday in the Caulfield intelligentsi family. "My mother gets very hysterical," says Holden, in the main commenting on his parents correctly and with restraint ("of course, they're good people"), and on his mother with sad, tender pity... "Daddy will kill you, he'll kill you" Phoebe keeps saying. "I could probably tell you what I did after I went home, and how I got sick and all, and what school I'm supposed to go to next fall...but I don't feel like it. I really don't. That stuff doesn't interest me too much right now."

But however condescendingly tender Holden is to his mother, or proper to his father, they are aprt of the world which does not suit him, in which it is bad to live, where a person has no place to shelter his soul. And it is not by chance that Salinger's novel, along with Hemingway's *Fiesta* and Saroyan's *The Human Comedy,* was banned from the high school library in the California city of San Jose.

However, with his skepticism, and unconscious cynicism Holden is an intrinsic part of this world. He would probably be indignant if he were told this. But it is unquestionably so. Whether Holden likes it or not he is a prisoner of this world, its tastes, its customs; and basically his "revolt" leads to nothing.

Holden does not stop to think that this world can and should be changed, that he, Holden, should overcome much in himself, that his own passivity and lack of will hang on his legs like chains. Holden just rejects with repugnance a reality which maintains itself through force, "phoniness," and hypocrisy.

Six curs, six young Fascists torture the schoolboy James Castle, and "all they did with the guys...was expel them." Sated boa constrictors like Ossenburger get rich on poor people who die. "Pencey was full of crooks. Quite a few guys came from these very wealthy families, but it was full of crooks anyway. The more expensive a school is, the more crooks it has." The art with which they stuff people in America is vulgar, phoney, poison, not food for the spirit. With scorn and hate Holden summarizes the content of these phoney plays and films. He talks about the war with even more hate, and not he alone: "My brother D.B. was in the Army for four goddam years... All he had to do was drive some cowboy general around all day in a command car. He once told Allie and I that if he'd had to shoot anybody, he wouldn't've known which direction to shoot in. He said the Army was practically as full of bastards as the Nazis were."

Holden loiters in this world sadly and senselessly, alone and helpless before a life which is no good for him, trying to conceal his helplessness by being compulsively talkative and reckless.

They accuse him (and we have accused him) of behaving like a twelve-year-old boy. However, "sometimes I act a lot older than I am—I really do—but people never notice it. People never notice anything," says Holden tiredly. He knows disappointingly much about people; he knows, for example, that a grown-up looks at a sixteen-year-old from his grown-up tower and completely refuses even to attempt to comprehend what is happening in a sixteen-year-old's infinitely wounded soul, which is so full of ferment and confusion.

To whom can he go with this confusion? "I don't even like...cars. I mean they don't even interest me. I'd rather have a goddam horse. A horse is at least *human,* for God's sake. A horse you can at least—"

When Holden lies, people listen to him. But who listens to him when he tells the truth? When he talks about what interests him? "You ought to go to a boy's school sometime. Try it sometime... It's full of phonies, and all you do is study so that you can learn enough to be smart enough to be able to buy a goddam Cadillac someday... And I'd be working in some office, making a lot of dough,...Reading newspapers, and playing bridge all the time, and going to movies... Well, I hate it. Boy, do I hate it. But it isn't just that. It's every-thing."

Thus he speaks to Sally, asking her to "live somewhere with a brook and all." But what does Sally answer? "Stop screaming at me, please."

"Stop hollering like that, for God's sake," Louis says to him too.

And poor Holden searches for someone with whom he can speak! The three days during which the novel takes place are filled with these muddled, clumsy, unsuccessful efforts. Feverishly he telephones everyone in whom there is even the slightest hope in this regard. In the middle of the night he wakes up a woman with whom he is totally unacquainted, the friend of a friend. For a moment Mrs. Morrow's maternal affectionateness breathes on him. Two grey nuns pass by before him fleetingly, and their humble, quiet existence, their desire to do all the good in their power touch Holden, and he remembers them with respect and warmth. Warmth is essential to him. Oc-casionally, he has to warm himself a little somewhere. Even ducks retreat somewhere away from the frozen pond...

Some people who have temporarily lost all hope disappear in the bustling city without a trace. Others cause nothing but disillusionment.

During his wanderings and searchings Holden hears a song sung by a little boy on the street: "If a body catch a body coming through the rye." [In Russian translation: "If a body call a body..." C.P.]

This line could stand as the epigraph to the novel. To the story of how someone has gone astray, who feels lost calls for someone...and there is no reply.

It is considered that at sixteen it is obligatory for a person to be in love. Holden is not in love with anyone, even though many people think of love in the hardest days of their life. He is not in love with Sally—he simply tries to hold on sincerely to this life-loving creature who is satisfied with everything. His relation to "old Jane" is unclear to Holden himself. Something in her at-tracts and touches him; maybe their unhappy childhoods bring them together. But this is not all-consuming youthful amoruosness. Is Jane the reason for his fight with Stradlater? Or was it really Stradlater calling the sacred baseball mit of the late little Allie "a goddam baseball mit" ["some stupid baseball mit" in the Russian version, C.P.] which made Holden lose his temper. Or had he simply gotten tired, in his mood, of watching the brazen successes of the lucky Stradlater? For Holden love is still in the future, and he is not a profligate—"if you want to know the truth, I'm a virgin."

We know how the incident with the prostitute ended and how Holden had to pay for his virginity not only with extra dollars but also with blood. Yes, that is the way things are in the world in which Holden lives—they make you bleed for purity and virtue! The girl for whom he feels sorry for goes away with her protector, the elevator operator. Holden is alone in the room again, cursed and beat up. One more insult has been added to the long series. And it seems to Holden that there will never be anything else—nothing good. And a strange delirium begins in his feverish mind: "I started that stupid business with the bullet in my guts again. I was the only guy at the bar with a bullet in their guts. I kept putting my hand under my jacket, on my stomach and all, to keep the blood from dripping all over the place. I didn't want anybody to know I was even wounded. I was con*cealing* the fact that I was a wounded sonuvabitch." Here the essence of Holden's tragedy is concentrated in a few words.

The symbolic bullet, symbolic blood dripping onto the floor... The father's house where there is no place for his own son is symbolic too. But the symbolism is done extremely cautiously, so that it does not ruin the whole fabric of the novel. Take just the multiple significant line from the song: "If a body call a body..." Initially Holden hears it incorrectly, he hears: "If a body catch a body..." Only many pages later does Phoebe correct him, and he agrees, "She was right... I didn't know it then, though." And only by the extensiveness and detail of the conversation in which the words of the song are made precise does the author give the reader to understand that these words are important for his idea.

If people exist who reconcile Holden to life, whom he accepts without reservation, for whom he is ready to go through fire and water, they are children. And not only his warmly loved ten-year-old sister Phoebe, not only his deceased brother Allie, but all the children: the boy who sings the song, the kid in the movie, and two little ones in the museum, and the boys and girls studying in Phoebe's school. When he gets to the school, Holden notices that someone has written an obscenity on the wall: "It drove me damn near crazy. I thought how Phoebe and all the other little kids would see it, and how they'd wonder what the hell it meant,..I kept wanting to kill whoever'd written it." And Holden wipes out the graffito. But then he sees an obscenity on another wall too. "I tried to rub it off with my hand again, but this one was *scratched* on, with a knife...It wouldn't come off."

"You know what I'd like to be?" says Holden to his sister Phoebe. "I keep picturing all these little kids playing some game in this big field of rye and all. Thousands of little kids, and nobody's around—nobody big, I mean—except me. And I'm standing on the edge of some crazy cliff. What I have to do, I have to catch everybody if they start to go over the cliff—I mean if they're running and they don't look where they're going I have to come out from somewhere and *catch* them. That's all I'd do all day. I'd just be the catcher in the rye and all. I know it's crazy, but that's the only thing I'd really like to be."

He wants to save the children from falling off the cliff, but is he himself being saved? "You're riding for some kind of terrible, terrible fall," Mr. Antolini says to him, "It may be the kind where...you sit in some bar...Or you may end up in some office business, throwing paper clips at the nearest stenographer..."

Antolini doesn't know what will happen to his pupil. And Holden does not know what is ahead for him. But even the author does not see anything good for his hero in the future. The novel is tragically hopeless; everything is as if enclosed in a small space which is suffocating, gloomy, and without exit. But still we are sorry to think that Holden could start heading in the same direction as the vile Ossenburger or the murderers of James Castle, that he will accept life as a game which must be played according to the rules of Ossenburger and James' murderers.

The novel is not long—anything bulky which might hinder the clear expression of central matters has been omitted. Very great precision. Very great sincerity. The maturity of a strong and witty talent is felt in every scene. Everything seems to be written almost casually, but examine it carefully and you will see the subtlest, most masterful fine-finishing. It is as if nothing is described, "drawn;" everything is conveyed as if casually—but you see Pencey, and Phoebe's school, and the hotel, and the beautifully-done Museum of Natural History.

There are hardly any colors or painted tones, therefore those few objects which are colored cut into the memory like bright spots: the green dress of the prostitute, her pink dress on "narrow narrow" shoulders, Phoebe's blue coat, and especially, the bright red cap with the long bill which is mentioned repeatedly throughout the novel.

One could enumerate many felicitous discoveries, magnificent details, and brilliant dialogue.

Its best pages are the meeting of Holden and Phoebe in front of the Museum, their wanderings around the city, the walk around the zoo, and Phoebe's ride on the carousel during the rainstorm... "...I stuck around on the bench for quite a while. I got pretty soaking wet...I didn't care, though. I felt so damn happy all of a sudden, the way old Phoebe kept going around and around. I was damn near bawling, I felt so damn happy...It was just that she looked so damn *nice,* the way she kept going around and around, in her blue coat and all. God, I wish you could've been there."

When Holden's heart matures and the chaos of confusion abates in him, may he find that elevated goal, the one in the name of which one wants to live and for the sake of which it is not frightening to die.

AKSYONOV ON SALINGER

Vasily Aksyonov (1932-   ) is widely regarded as the best of the "younger generation" of Soviet fiction writers. His first stories were published in 1959, followed by the novel *Colleagues* (about medical students) in 1960, the year *The Catcher in the Rye* was translated. With their teenage heroes and idiom, his lively short works such as "Halfway to the Moon" (1961) are often said to have been written under the influence of Salinger. For some years Aksyonov was associated with the magazine *Youth,* which published much interesting prose and poetry during the sixties. Aksyonov's more recent story "Victory" is rated as one of the best works of short fiction since the war.

This brief review of the 1965 edition of Salinger's stories (including *The Catcher in the Rye* and "Raise High the Roof Beam, Carpenters") was published in *Foreign Literature* (No. 3, 1966). The informal manner is characteristic of many "non-professional" critics in the USSR.

V. Aksyonov

AN UNUSUAL AMERICAN

Here before me lies a book written by J. D. Salinger, a mysterious person from the United States, and translated by Rita Rait-Kovaleva. The talent of a successful writer and the talent of the translator, people so far apart from each other, have endowed the small book with a new life, a Russian life.

The novellas and stories which comprise this volume have appeared in the pages of our periodicals during the last few years and led to a quite lively, indeed almost intense, interest on the part of our readers. This seems to be a matter of our discovering a new American hero in the works of the American called J. D. Salinger.

Peoples far away from each other, and often even those not so far away, live in the grip of habitual, stereotyped notions about each other. This fall in Yugoslavia one young fellow asked me over a cup of coffee, "Do you have coffee in Russia?"

I looked at him with surprise, but then I figured it out—aha, I see, Russia—the samovar, therefore tea—no coffee. My subsequent conversation with this educated man fully confirmed my hypothesis.

The example is anecdotal, but still, admit it—at the word "American" something about cowboys, gangsters, and sports flashes somewhere on the periphery of one's mind.

Let's forget these banalities; I have something quite different in mind · here, to be specific, that image of America which appears to the intelligentsia reader (even if we suppose he is an expert on twentieth century American literature and an admirer of the famous "Big Five"), the image of the hero of that literature, the image of one writer—Ernest Hemingway—that's the usual image.

Hemingway—the living myth, the legendary "Hem," "Papa," whose every step fascinated newspapermen and their readers and became known to the whole world.

Of Salinger we know only that he "lives in Westport and has a dog."

Francis MacComber asserts himself by shooting buffalo, Seymour Glass by shooting himself in the temple.

We will not speak of Hemingway's last shot, but if we believe the posthumous legend, this was a shot at a buffalo too.

Lieutenant Henry, Jake Barnes, the writer Harry, Robert Jordan, these symbols of Hemingway's personality all combined to form the image of this modern Childe-Harold, and this was the image of a Man. Never admit defeat, defend oneself, honor, honor, and more masculine honor. A devoted woman, a carbine, hunting, quiet irony, honor... Lord, if only one could live that way!

Holden Caulfield, Buddy and Seymour Glass, the foggy Walt of Eloise's reminiscences—of the (possible) symbols of Salinger's personality (I can't imagine any other), these have formed an image which has eyes brimming with Jewish melancholy. And this is the image of a Boy. Here we see defenselessness, almost total vulnerability, melancholy, and fear.

The obscenities which elicit anger or quiet contempt from Hemingway's heroes elicit almost mystical horror from Salinger.

Robert Jordan saw blowing up a bridge as his goal. Holden Caulfield is a catcher in the rye. Imagine the strong figure of Jordan on a completely real Spanish mountain before actually approaching Fascists—and then the absurd figure of Holden running through some rye somewhere, saving some sort of children from falling into some sort of abyss.

I recall Fellini's films, or rather, their endings. The swarthy faces of happy youths circling around Giuletta Massina on motorcycles, their accordion *(Nights of Cabiria);* the tiny schoolboy in a white cape blowing his sad, soothing horn at the end of the clownish parade of humanity *(8½);* two little girls (again, wearing white) comically dancing a naive Charleston which interrupts Lesbian-pederastic delirium *(Juliet of the Spirits).*

Let us conclude the parallel with a reference to the imaginary Jimmy Jimmerino in the story "Uncle Wiggly in Connecticut" and make so bold as to add that the parallel is symptomatic. Symptomatic especially in our time when Fascism does not wear arm-bands with swastikas on them, or call itself Fascism, when at times it has almost irrational features.

The salvation of children, Salinger says. Salvation is in children, Fellini says. Salvation is in salvation, says Salinger.

Since it has come out this way, since the involuntary comparison of Hemingway and Salinger has come up, one should note that the latter has no particular reverence for the former. Holden Caulfield calls Lieutenant Henry a phony! How about that: our hero, our Lieutenant Henry—a phony!

Holden's categoricalness somewhat jars us old friends of Lieutenant Henry, but after considering it we realize that it would be absurd to defend the Lieutenant from the Boy, just as the Boy is not worth a brass farthing compared to the Man—different times and different wars.

Perhaps we can understand the irritability of the sixteen-year-old writer Holden Caulfield (and of course he is a writer—otherwise what are his discussions about "digressions from the theme") and the categoricalness of his opinions, because he is a new kind of American writer who "lives in Westport and has a dog." We can even conjecture that the duty of every writer to display his work for public evaluation is a sad duty for this writer.

"If I were a pianist I'd lock myself in a closet and play there," he thinks, watching the famous Ernie play and the public's clamorous rapture.

And then our Boy-writer, casting off all disguises, assumes a belligerent pose before the Man-writer and boldly announces: "The sign of immaturity in a man is when he wants to die nobly for a right cause, and the sign of maturity is that he wants to die humbly for a right cause."

These words are not Holden's; they belong to Mr. Antolini—but also to J. D. Salinger—that's the way it is.

We will not attempt to find the right side in their perhaps somewhat strange polemic; as the curtain falls we will say only that it would be a mistake to imagine Salinger a sage who has taken the "lighted candles into the catacombs, deserts, and caves," as he goes away from the world.

It is generally a generally accepted fact that a base his work only on a presupposition of the vastness of human society and the cosmic greatness of his passions. Thinking about the insignificance of man destroys a writer even if the dimension of his personal tragedy is increased to infinity.

Salinger has taken a lantern and is making a journey around the cosmos of American life. He is a real American writer of our time, an unusual American.

TUGUSHEVA ON McCARTHY

M. Tugusheva has written rather widely on American literature, most often reviews, including ones on Mailer, Capote, Herman Wouk and Leslie Fiedler. She has also written on Negro writers, especially Baldwin *(Foreign Literature,* No. 6, 1965). Among the article-length studies is her preface to the 1967 edition of Salinger. Like many other Soviet critics she began the sixties with an optimistic appraisal of recent American literature; in her review article in *Questions of Literature* (No. 6, 1961) she praised *Rabbit, Run; Set This House on Fire;* and *The Child Buyer* as novels striving to show the spiritual tragedy of man in a capitalist society.

Mary McCarthy has not been translated into Russian except for one of her short pieces on Vietnam (1967). There is a brief note on her opposition to Steinbeck's view of Vietnam in *Questions of Literature* (No. 8, 1967). Tugusheva's review of *The Group* (published in *Questions of Literature,* No. 10, 1964 and in *Contemporary Literature Abroad,* No. 4, 1964) seems to be the only critical article on her fiction. G. Zlobin wrote a critique of her articles in *Harper's* and *Encounter* on realism in the American theater, calling her ideas puerile and banal *(Questions of Literature,* No. 3, 1962). At present there seems to be no move toward translating her, but given the subject matter it would not be impossible for some of her more recent works to be published.

M. Tugusheva

THE EMPRESS'S NEW CLOTHES

Mary McCarthy has the reputation of being America's most "intellectual" and militant literary lady. She is a severe critic as well. Never missing,
as befits Pallas Athena, she hits her targets with the lance of merciless wit,
and she destroys reputations in an almost off-hand manner, sometimes reputations won by long and persistent work. She has zealous admirers, the sub-
scribers to the *Partisan Review,* "wisemen who haven't finished school" in the
words of the American magazine *Newsweek.* Along with a multitude of "highbrow" critics, they greeted her new novel *The Group* with acclaim. *The
Group* was number one on the best-seller charts. It's also well known that
Otto Preminger, the director, offered the author $250,000 for the film ver-
sion of the novel. It is said that Mary McCarthy herself is somewhat disturbed
by such fame; from the point of view of the *Partisan Review* such success
en masse is vulgar.

However, McCarthy's work did not elicit boundless rapture from all the
critics in America and England. Several serious articles appeared which treated
her latest child with asperity worthy of "mad Mary" herself.

Mary McCarthy's work belongs to the so-called "intellectual" genre of
contemporary American literature. The main problem posed on the pages of
"intellectual" prose is the "battle between past and present," i.e. above all a
discussion of the idea of progress, the possibility of stage by stage development of humanity in general and development in the sphere of spiritual life
in particular. It cannot be said that the authors of such works really have a
good knowledge of what things were like in the past, but nevertheless the
present and future inspire disgust, and sometimes fear, in them.

"Faith in progress," the American critic Richard Hofstadter wrote not
long ago, "is not simply lost, it is overlooked. Woe to the intellectual who
cannot prove quite simply and with unbearable lucidity how much worse
spiritually and culturally things are in the world today than they were in the
misty but unquestionably more perfect past."†

In a recent interview Mary McCarthy stated that "since the War America
has been getting more repulsive with terrifying speed."† Such a sharp rejection
of America forces one to suppose that she has in mind such negative aspects
of American reality as race prejudice and hard-core poverty. But not so. Such
"mundane" problems are not much a part of the elevated spheres of her
higher wisdom. Her novel *The Group* bears witness to this—it covers the
events of seven years, 1933-40, from the beginning of Roosevelt's "New Deal"
to World War Two.

The novel tells about eight graduates of a privileged womens' college,
the well-known Vassar School. All of them belong to the middle bourgeoisie
and intelligentsia. The writer looks at American reality of the Thirties through
their eyes. The girls try to be "contemporary," particularly in the sphere of

romantic relations. They dream of doing something for "developing" America; their ideas are liberal enough to relate sympathetically to Roosevelt's New Deal and "in general to be radicals." The author says that more than anything else on earth they fear being "like mama and papa." By the end of the novel the majority of them have basically accepted the conditions of the society which they earlier rejected. Kay Strong Peterson is the most complex and contradictory individual. The novel begins with her marriage and ends with a description of her funeral. In her marriage to Harold, an unsuccessful dramatist, a neurotic and hypocrite, she strives to be "up-to-date." Kay, who secretly has no special love for the poor, "flirts" with socialist ideas and even participates in a strike movement.

In contrast to Kay, the remaining members of the group are as "alike as Disney characters" (in the words of the English weekly *New Statesman).* Polly Andrews is the only sympathetic character of the eight. After an unhappy liaison with a "communist," she marries her "ideal" man, the totally apolitical doctor Jim Ridgely. Priss, another representative of the group, supports the politics of the New Deal more actively than the rest, but the reader doesn't learn anything about this side of her activity. The time the author devotes to her goes totally on endless arguments with her husband who insists she breast-feed their baby, while Priss, who is exhausted by the baby's wailing (she has absolutely no milk), dreams of bottle-feeding. The reviewer for the *New Statesman* notes, however, that still "the novel is written about the thirties and one of its main ideas is that it would be better if each of us stayed away from politics and remained in Dr. Ridgely's blissful state of ignorance."[†]

McCarthy has especial hostility to people who take part in the social struggle. Her political antipathies are revealed in the caricaturistic figures of Putnam Blake and his wife Noreen, whom she passes off as Marxists. Quite in the spirit of Jane Austen (where is all the striving to be "up-to-date" here?) one of the Vassar graduates gives Noreen a lecture on personal—physical and moral—hygiene.

Even more degrading and disgusting are the grossly naturalistic details which the writer "informs us" about Putnam, giving him not only a bad character but secret physical defects.

Mary McCarthy describes anything that debases man, anything that shows him in an unattractive light with special care. She devotes great attention to detailed description of the "external" world surrounding her heroes, and she has far more sympathy for things than people. Kay's death (she throws herself from the twentieth floor) hardly touches the author; she is far more interested in Kay's white pleated dress as she lies in the coffin than in the tragic fact of a life cut off absurdly.

Though in McCarthy's own words she was striving to debunk "the idea of progress in a feminine environment,"[†] *The Group* is an attempt to "reconsider" the idea of progress as a whole. Or, as McCarthy herself says about this, to show how "the mirage of political and social progress got the youth of the thirties off on the wrong track."[†]

Fascism and the horrors which it brought into the world, death camps, the ruin of democracy, destructive wars, the shadow of nuclear death hanging over the world after the War—all this makes many artists in the United States have a negative attitude toward contemporary society—in some this hostility leads to defeatism and despair; in others, however strange it may seem, to a call (in the final analysis) for people to be satisfied with what is and not to seek changes along the path to the future. As a rule, in such cases the writer comes out against the idea of progress in general; he reconsiders and rejects the idea of democracy and faith in the future, and tries to debunk all this as just another myth which "befogs" the consciousness of humanity. Faith in progress is a dangerous deception, say these writers. It is like a blindfold over the eyes of a man who is moving steadily toward an abyss. Perhaps they are trying to tear off this "blindfold" so that humanity can see some other "eternal light" and stop somewhere at the edge of the abyss called hopelessness? No, they offer nothing as a substitute, except perhaps another myth— about irretrievably lost harmony. So accept everything as it is.

It is this mission of cutting humanity off from hope that Mary McCarthy undertook when choosing as the target of her attacks the thirties—a period of intensified ideological and political struggle in America, of widespread Marxism and a new consciousness among American workers, the time when proletarian literature was born in the United States. While doing this she does not hide her intentions. However, the "new clothes" of this queen do not allow her to do that. They are too transparent and cannot be used to conceal such ugly features of the contemporary reactionary, "intellectual" genre as anti-democratism, naturalism, and impenetrable pessimism.

TUGUSHEVA ON HENRY MILLER

Tugusheva's review of Miller's books is the only thing that has ever been written on him in the Soviet Union. His *Tropics* have been translated into Russian—but only abroad, not in the Soviet Union. He is not even listed in the recent seven-volume *Shorter Literary Encyclopedia.* This review was published in *Foreign Literature* (No. 2, 1967). It is an example of Soviet writing about a totally unacceptable modern writer.

M. Tugusheva

THE CONFESSION OF AN AMORALIST

In the last few years great changes have taken place in the fate of the American writer Henry Miller. It wasn't long ago that his works were printed outside the borders of the United States and carefully hidden from the sharp eyes of customs inspectors.

A few years ago the American censorship removed the ban on the publication of some pornographic works including Miller's. And now the Grove Press is publishing Miller's early works, which caused a scandal, such as *Tropic of Cancer* and *Tropic of Capricorn,* and then the trilogy *The Rosy Crucifixion.*

Everything Miller has written is a kind of novelized autobiography. *The Rosy Crucifixion* is the story of those years of his life when "the ordinary mortal in him died so that he could be resurrected as a writer."[†] Foreign critics have warmly hailed Miller as "the master of pornographic literature."

But he is not one of those adepts of "porn" who is interested only in the narrow sphere of man's sexual life. The erotic scenes in his novels are interspersed with "arcs" of "surrealistic," "hallucinatory" prose, "transcendental" effusions on the inscrutability of good and evil, the relativity of all principles—and this goes on for almost 1600 pages.

However, *Sexus,* the first part of the trilogy, is tiring in quite a different way than "philosophically." The reader is offered a thorough "study" of Lesbian love. Henry, the second "I" of the author, shares his beloved Mona with her girl-friend. The hero's life is a constant watching, surveillance through a key-hole, which has a very fruitful "literary" aspect. Everything Henry sees gets blasphemously fixed on paper.

The trilogy's second part, *Plexus (Network),* tells how Henry and Mona enjoy the luxurious life for which Mona's jaded friends pay. At a table covered with "good wine and good food" Henry sometimes recalls the daughter he abandoned. But why upset himself with unpleasant thoughts? And later it is so much in his character: "to respect the past and spit on it. I do the same with friends and writers. I accept and cherish in the past only that which can be made of account in my works."[†] And there is much that is turned "to account"—indifference, shamelessness, elementary meanness (Henry never pays off his debts), ingratitude and baseness of every type from "petty" vandalism in revenge on his landlady to mocking an unhappy old man.

Man's nature is base and unchanging, Henry asserts, so is it worthwhile regretting treachery (in giving a friend false hope), is it worth agonizing over a total lack of honor?

Family harmony is destroyed by the appearance of a new friend of Mona (a woman again). *Nexus* (the joining link), the last part of the trilogy, is

devoted to their unhappy *menage à trois.* The third novel is somewhat different from the others. It is here essentially that Henry's "resurrection" occurs
—from the dust of his former existence to the life of a writer. The epigraph to
the book is Gogol's celebrated lyrical digression of the "bird-troika" —which
Miller uses in an extremely strange way. He frequently employs the troika as
a parabola for the writer's (i.e., his, "Henry Miller's") existence. The writer's
life is a "swift, uncatchable troika." If one asks the question "whither art thou
headed?" you will get no answer. Beliefs, hopes, and principles are dust under
the horses' hooves. Reaching this conclusion, Henry suddenly realizes how to
"save" himself. One must go one's own individual way, go—or better, fly, on
the "troika" past "everything on earth"—wars, revolution, human misery, and
cares.

Henry lives in a country which he hates with all his soul. For him
America of the twenties and thirties is the kingdom of military technology in
which a place is prepared for him as "hooligan democrat, doomed to progress,
racism, and success."[†] It's always like this for Miller. A perfectly clear concept
of the concrete socio-political shortcomings is ruined by total nihilism, from
which it is only one step to total acceptance of anything. We are present at the
transformation of a bourgeois individualist into a total amoralist.

Rarely does one encounter anyone so completely consumed by the
need to convince people that "a world built on the laws of humanity, a world
sensitively attuned to the ideas of man, his dreams and desires, is impossible."[†]

But what is the significance of literature then?

Perhaps in "helping man learn about himself, strengthening his faith in
himself, and supporting himself in his struggle for truth,"[†] Henry concludes,
pointing to Dostoevsky.

No, Henry—Miller shrinks from the truth and from the desire to help
his neighbor and from any struggle. What is the aim of truth in literature? After all, when all the works "have been read and rehashed people will still do
rotten things to each other... Who needs to change the world? Let us all rot,
die, and vanish."[†]

Certain pages of Miller's trilogy lead one to suppose that Henry truly
loves Mona. But literally before our eyes the disintegration comes, the de-
thronement of love. Henry carefully destroys the intimate world of feelings;
he undervalues and standardizes that which is not subject to be seen as a cli-
che, tramples tenderness for the woman he loves into the dirt. He considers
that for him all is allowed; he dreams of moving to Europe—there, he is sure,
"complete freedom" awaits him. For him Europe is a kind of personal haven
on the gates of which is written, "Do what you want, Henry."

Miller's "pornutopia" is reactionary. Of course, Miller does not dream
of a beautiful life for all humanity. The indifferent loner is not touched by
any social calamities. Miller's utopia is devoid of movement and development.
It is a mechanistic "given" of pleasure which, without changing, migrates from
novel to novel. The mechanicalness here is a direct result of the dehumaniza-
tion of the relations between two people who come together.

Miller's individualism is an extreme expression of bourgeois egotism in the modern age; egotism which has shrunk the utopia to the size of a personal atomic bomb shelter in which one can watch the collapse of the world in complete comfort. In that small space of eternity which is human life one should, in Miller's view, "work" only for oneself. If at the same time this eternity is "cut down" to the size of the present minute, if the past and future are discarded, it turns out that human progress, morality, and courage are no more than fine words. Henry is an individualist and amoralist who wants to be free and happy at the expense of the freedom and happiness of others.

Other people can live on "this side" or "the far side of paradise," suffer, strive for ideals—Miller's heroes have chosen a "softer" way. He already lives (others take care of him) in an earthly paradise, having freed himself from work, responsibilities, conscience. This philosophy of irresponsible, free "bliss" rests on hypocrisy which has reached the most extreme degree, which has "resurrected" the hero with a new understanding of things. Not long before Henry had been a desperate nihilist. Now he accepts everything. You say the world is terrible? Well, I tell you it is beautiful. Proof? "Credo quia absurdum"—I believe because it's absurd. This cannot be understood by reason. Men have always striven to explain the world. The infinite pain and torment of realization and struggle are the results.

"I can reconcile beauty with evil, the divine impulse with repulsive ugliness, immortal substance with absolute fruitlessness. Lightning destruction or eternal life—all are one for me. I maintain my spiritual imperturbability."[†]

Thus, Henry Miller has achieved complete harmony and "freedom" of personality for which all is allowed, including, incidentally, "porn."

When in Norway in 1957 the first part of *The Rosy Curcifixion* was banned by a court as indecent and amoral, the American magazine *Evergreen* printed Miller's letter to the judges. Defending the right to publish pornographic literature, Miller appeals to the right of free expression of thought, freedom of speech which is dear to everyone. And he was not alone. Thus, Maurice Girodias, editor of the Olympia Press does not hesitate to call "absolutely free erotic self-expression" true freedom for writers' creativity. "The contemporary Frenchman," Girodias wrote not long ago, "has completely forgotten his liberal, socialistic, and revolutionary past. The very word 'freedom' is an abstract and even somewhat indecent concept for him... The sex instinct governs the world, and it is precisely in the sexual sphere that the concept of 'freedom' reveals itself in its most candid and concrete form."

Polemicizing with Girodias, the American scholar George Steiner correctly spoke of the profanation of moral feeling and the corrupting influence of "porn" on human culture.

In Miller's works the antihuman element of "porn" has found that expression which is adequate to it. Precisely for this reason they stand outside of true literature; precisely for this reason we can call the American writer Henry Miller an enemy of man and of civilization itself.

LITVINOVA ON CHEEVER

Tatyana Litvinova (daughter of writer Ivy Litvinova) is one of the Soviet Union's finest translators of prose fiction. She is responsible for introducing the Soviet public to Cheever's works, beginning with three stories in 1961. This was followed by a collection of stories in 1962 (foreword by Kornei Chukovsky). A small book called *The Angel on the Bridge* was published in 1965 in V. Kotkin's translation—but a larger collection including "The Brigadier and the Gold Widow" and "The Angel on the Bridge" was translated by Tatyana Litvinova in 1966 (Moscow, "Progress" Publishers, 265 pp., 100,000 copies), and it contained her own introduction. Apart from a half-dozen other Cheever stories his *The Wapshot Chronicle* (translated by T. Rovenskaya) was published in 1968. His stories appear in a variety of anthologies. No single critical articles on him have appeared, but a major part of M. O. Mendelson's essay "Social Criticism in the Works of Bellow, Updike, and Cheever" (see below) is devoted to him.

This review by Litvinova was published in *Questions of Literature* (No. 2, 1965).

T. Litvinova

JOHN CHEEVER'S THE BRIGADIER AND THE GOLF WIDOW

We enter the world which John Cheever opens to us in his new collection of stories with both sadness and gaiety. Sadness because it is a world of catastrophes, desolation, growing old, humiliation of human value, devaluation of human feelings, a world of animal egotism and indifference. Gaiety because the artist who draws the picture of this world is gay, merciless, and unsentimental. He has not been infected by his heroes' melancholy, aimlessness, or feeling of hopelessness. For him human values do not cease to exist because they have been trampled. These values are unshakable: he is sensitive to the slightest ugliness and sees it where the superficial observer would see only an everyday norm; he is not deceived by an external gloss of well-being, and he sees the modern world with all its catastrophes.

There are sixteen stories in the collection. What are they about? About life and the instability of life. Cheever's hero is the well-to-do American of the end of the fifties and beginning of the sixties. Oh, he lives very well! He has his own swimming pool, several cars, a house in the suburbs with two bathrooms and two televisions. He is served by a maid, cook, and gardener. And if he is a little poorer he has only one car in the garage, and maybe not the latest model, and a baby-sitter instead of a cook and maid. Everyday life is not burdensome: vacuum cleaners, washing machines, dishwashers, refrigerators which hold enough food for a week or more, and stores with a varied assortment of products. But why is it his wives burn dinner day after day. Why is it he and his wife—and even the minister—drink so many martinis, so much gin and whiskey? Why do these well-to-do people wander through Europe by the hundreds and thousands like people without a country? Why is it they think that misfortune, difficulty, and unhappiness dog their every step? Why are they so exhausted, why do they despair, why do their lives seem void of meaning to them? Why does an absurd dreamed sentence composed of nonexistent words become the only reality in a life which seems more and more illusory and mirage-like each year?

These rhetorical questions, which require no answers, are reiterated through the whole book like a kind of leitmotif.

Cheever is a musical writer, and this collection of his stories is not a chance selection, but a kind of musical suite. The main theme of one story comes up again in another as a secondary theme; and though every story has its completely independent right to existence, they all gain by their proximity to each other.

The theme of the opening story is fear of atomic war. The Pasterns are the owners of a well-equipped bomb-shelter that cost them 32,000 dollars. Mr. and Mrs. Pastern decide in advance not to take in their relatives—young nephews and an aged mother. But it turns out that these callous people have their own illusions: Pastern finds relief from the burdens of modern life in the arms of a neighbor, the wife of a travelling salesman who sells plastic tongue depressors, and Mrs. Pastern quenches her spiritual thirst with "social work" (she collects funds to combat infectious hepatitis); and she believes in the righteousness of her spiritual pastor, a bishop with the tortured eyes of someone drugged who decides to please her with an unexpected visit.

Both Mr. Pastern's love and Mrs. Pastern's tall guest have the same goal—getting into the bomb shelter. The lover gets the key to the bomb shelter from Mr. Pastern and his wife finds out. The family falls apart. Pastern is ruined, takes to theft, and lands in jail. Pastern's lover is also forced to get divorced from her travelling salesman, and at the end of the story she appears like a ghost, as a symbol of the madness of a catastrophic world—wearing a thin dress and high heels she wanders through the snow around the well-equipped bomb shelter which has long since passed to the next "Pasterns" who have bought the property.

"The Angel of the Bridge," the second story in the collection, is also devoted to fear—fear of life. The narrator's mother is afraid of flying, his brother of elevators (he has even lost his job because of this, since the firm for which he worked was on the 52nd floor), and the narrator himself is gripped by panic every time he crosses a bridge in a car. But then one day a girl carrying a small harp under her arm asked him for a ride, and she sang him old folk songs the whole way and he forgot his fear. Who was this "angel?" Poetry? Art? The Muse? The commonfolk? Cheever does not say; although his stories are full of symbolic significance, they are by no means allegories. Whatever the case, true to his sense of the instability of the world, the narrator admits that he does not want to tempt fate; and as before he avoids the Washington Bridge on which this inexplicable fear first struck him—"this fear of the future of the world which he clumsily hides from himself."

The theme of "expatriation"—homesickness both away and at home—runs through the entire book like a cold wave. The crest of this wave is the story "A Woman Without a Country."

A heartless and barbaric law deprives Anne Marchand of her baby. And as if to finish her completely, all America starts singing a vulgar and insulting song written by some wit about the same celebrated custody trial in which she was the victim. Anne wanders across Europe, she wants to forget her past and everything. She even conceals America and the fact that it is her true nationality from the clerks at hotels. However, she is unable to hide her growing homesickness from herself. Finally she can bear it no longer; she gets on a plane and flies home, home, to her homeland! Alas, it turns out that America has not changed a bit. The first thing that the repatriate hears is the same heartless song which doomed her to wandering. Without leaving the airport, Anne gets on another plane and again goes to suffer her homesickness in an alien land.

In Cheever's stories capricious fantasy intertwines with reality, for as the author says, "In comparison with reality the wildest flights of imagination seem as dull as the entries in an accountant's book."[†] Occasionally in Cheever time bears a double load. Thus in "The Swimmer" (perhaps the most important of the sixteen stories) the hero "swims" through his entire life in some two or three hours on a midsummer day. In the beginning of the story we see him young and strong, passing under the branches of a blossoming apple tree, and in the end, he is a worn-out, bent old man, red and yellow leaves are falling around him, he is homeless, he has lost his family, he has nothing left except the pair of swimming trunks in which he set off swimming.

The story with which Cheever concludes this book is entitled "The Ocean," and like an ocean it contains all the book's elements: family discomfort, the senselessness of life, whiskey, and a solitary protest in which one can hear the voice of the author himself: "I didn't want to study sadness, madness, melancholy, and despair. I wanted to study triumphs, the rediscoveries of love, all that I know in the world to be decent, radiant, and clean." In spite of this desire the story (and the book) ends with the hero's insanity and his falling into an absurd, fantastic dream which turns into the sweet sleep of oblivion.

And nevertheless—for such is the dialectic of art—we close the book with a feeling rather happy than painful: on every page, like an underground spring, there is acknowledgement of the fact that life has its "decent, radiant, and clean" side. And if it has it, as the author seems to suggest, we must seek it, and it can be found.

Cheever is not a muckraker; he is rather a "lyrical satirist." Like the heroine of one of his earlier stories, he does not complain, but "sings his sadness." Like every real prose writer, he is a poet.

And like the girl with the harp, his muse helps the reader go fearlessly over the bridge built across the abyss of despair which John Cheever shows us so mercilessly.

LANDOR ON BELLOW, UPDIKE, STYRON AND TRILLING

Mikhail Landor is another younger critic who began writing at the beginning of the sixties. One of his first publications was a long review of Arthur Mizener's biography of Fitzgerald. This review was the Soviet reader's introduction to Fitzgerald, who was known only from a story published in 1958. *The Great Gatsby* followed in 1965 (Landor's review is translated below). Landor has written other things on Fitzgerald and presented samples of his letters to the Soviet public. Generally Landor is a careful rather than a prolific critic; but he has done a few other articles on post-war American literature. In the Soviet Union the essay translated here is regarded as one of the major pieces of writing on American letters during the last decade.

"Centaur-Novels" opened up new areas for Russian criticism. Trilling, of course, has not been translated and is almost totally unknown in the Soviet Union. Except for a few short reviews, generally very negative ones, Bellow had not been discussed in Soviet literary periodicals—and he has not yet been translated. Except for two pages in Inna Levidova's bibliographical survey *(Artistic Literature in the USA 1964-67,* Moscow, 1968), little was written on Bellow during the rest of the sixties. Only with Mendelson's essay on "social criticism" (see below) and Alexei Zverev's major article in *Foreign Literature* (No. 2, 1971) was Bellow's work really introduced to the general reader.

Styron's fate is similar. Tugusheva had reviewed *Set This House on Fire* in 1961 and seen good in it, but until 1967 *(The Long March)* Styron was not translated. Very little has been written since Landor's essay appeared.

Updike fared better for a while. Andrei Sergeev translated a few of his poems in 1964, and several stories followed. *The Centaur,* translated by Victor Hinkis and with an introduction by Simon Markish, appeared in 1965 and created a great sensation. Updike visited the USSR (see *Bech: A Book)* and *Foreign Literature* published a brief interview with him. A translation of *Of the Farm* followed in 1967. *Rabbit, Run* cannot be translated because of its "naturalism"—also true of his later works (see Mendelson's critique of *Couples* below). Since 1967 the Soviet attitude to Updike seems to have become rather cool.

M. Landor

CENTAUR-NOVELS
1.

Like books, literary schools have their fates. After the war American prose had very high prestige in Europe, and many writers of the new generation studied Faulkner and Hemingway. But when Nobel prizes were awarded to Americans in Stockholm the United States literary world underwent a stringent "re-evaluation of values." It was headed by Lionel Trilling, one of the most authoritative liberal critics. He vehemently maintained that America had never had and did not yet have its own novelistic tradition.

Pointed independent critical thought has accompanied progressive American prose all during our century. At the start of the fifties interest in it grew to extraordinary proportions; it was felt that a turning point in the development of literature was at hand, everyone kept waiting for programmatic statements containing analyses and prognoses. Publishers sensed this demand and began mass printings (hundreds of thousands of copies) of critical essays which not long before could appear only in small journals for the cultural elite. A paradoxical thing happened; Trilling's collection of essays *The Liberal Imagination* surpassed some best-selling novels in popularity.

The critic complained that the texture of the American novel was too thin. Trying to explain this, he recalled Henry James' old complaint: in the New World there were no castles and palaces, no aristocracy or ivied ruins, ancient universities or cathedrals, or many other things which fed the imaginations of European novelists.* In other words there wasn't the variety of manners and morals customary in those societies which had gaudy feudal pasts.

Trilling summarized his point of view in one sentence. "In this country," he observed, "the real basis of the novel has never existed—that is, the tension between a middle class and an aristocracy which brings manners into observable relief as the living representation of ideals and the living comment on ideas."**

This taut formulation is doubly striking. Trilling had long been close to the *Partisan Review;* this was once the organ of the radical intelligentsia and it valued highly the originality of American culture. But now its eminent contributor plainly preferred English stability to the American spirit of revolt. And he went so far in his European dogmatism that he puzzled many readers in Europe. They were unaware that *Moby Dick* was written on a dubious foundation; they loved the American novel and did not reject those things in it which were unlike customary images.

---

*Landor paraphrases Trilling's essay "Manners, Morals and the Novel." *[Editor's note.]*

**Quoted from Trilling's "Art and Fortune." *[Editor's note.]*

But it would be rash to think that with his panegyric to the "thick social texture of the English novel" the critic did not feel the urgent demands of the American novel. The most influential writers in American literature between the wars were prose writers with a lyrical bent—Anderson and Hemingway. Following the old romantics, dissenters and loners, they are more concerned with the internal world of personality than the environment, their surroundings and social nuances. A tendency to embrace reality more fully arose after the war. The American novel turned to the possibilities of the genre which the Old World adopted long before. And eve if it be exaggerated and extreme, a disturbing depiction of the manners and morals of various layers of society would be appropriate if...

If Trilling's reproaches and exhortations did not have such a heavy conservative coloration. It is obvious that the attachment of Americans to the lyrical novel was tied to their defense of free personality, their critical and dissenting stance. In itself this stance certainly does not prevent careful study of manners; the texture of such novels as *Babbitt* or *Sister Carrie* is certainly not thin. But for Trilling dissent and weakness are virtually synonyms. It is hardly worthwhile for him to mention the accomplishments of American prose, since under his pen they turn out to be as illusory as they are respectable. The critic is willing to praise the social feeling of Dreiser and Dos Passos, Lewis and Faulkner. But this does not prevent him from concluding in despair: "We do not have a novel which embraces what is essential in society and its manners."[†]

Besides its ignoring of manners, Trilling criticizes the American novel for its spiritual weakness. Too often the severity of the judge seems unfounded: one self-educated writer is blamed for not being a profound philosopher, another for not having the erudition of Stendhal. But in Trilling's case this negative criticism of bright talents (which makes one recall the "despicable" Tertius) is combined with a sensible and precise prognosis. *The Liberal Imagination* predicts that soon the American novel will be drawn directly into the ideological life of society, a life which concerns masses of readers.

Unlike other American journals of the arts, the *Partisan Review* emphasized the life of ideas. And in the latest speeches of its contributor the old "enlightenment" notes are heard. Trilling made a beautiful reply to those who asserted that the novel form was dead:

> Nowadays the criticism which descends from Eliot puts explicit ideas in literature at a discount, which is one reason why it is exactly this criticism that is most certain of the death of the novel, and it has led many of us to forget how in the novel ideas may be as important as character and as essential to the given dramatic situation.[*]

But Trilling has moved very sharply away from the original direction of

---

*Quoted from Trilling's "Art and Fortune." *[Editor's note.]*

the journal—that is what made him the liberal idol. The earlier *Partisan Review,* following Parrington, had no pity for the dry university intellects who preferred the legends of the Old World to the full-blooded life and traditions of the pioneers. Now, marching under the banner of freedom of intellect and imagination, Trilling is tuned to the same conservative key as the anemic university dreamers. American history seems too simple to him: he is not touched by the first settlers with their spirit of independence—but by ancient castles and ivied ruins.

In the thirties the intelligentsia was disturbed by the cruel and dark pictures of reality which Dreiser and his successors drew. The new liberal idol is no more interested in the cruelty in American life than he is in the simple manners of the pioneers. But quite another matter are changes for the good in the course of which the life of America grows more complex and broad new possibilities for the novel arise. In a striking way Trilling's free imagination draws inexorably toward conformism.

He apparently reached the farthest extreme when answering the 1952 *Partisan Review* questionnaire on the state of the American intellectual.

Trilling did not dispute that the old and slumbering prejudice against men of books existed. But he maintained that the intelligentsia had won itself a place under the American sun; its influence in political circles and corporations is great, mass culture cannot do without it (the editorials of *Time* are not written by dull people. Nowadays even the grumblers among the intellectuals don't cut themselves off from their country, which is more and more isolated in the modern world. And even these ingrateful loners have now started to value "not the least important things—they don't fear for their own skins, they don't worry about what they're going to eat next, and they have the right to say whatever occurs to them."* This was written when Senator McCarthy was conducting his lively witch hunt!

Nostalgia for the past, for Tradition with a capital letter, and an obvious tendency towards conformity—this was a strange mixture, but it was remarkably popular in the circle of former "left" liberals. This new way of thinking was distinguished not by clear-cut definition, but by ambiguity and eternal vacillation. When it was suggested that Trilling wanted to resurrect "tender realism," he was offended. Does that mean he does not totally reject the revolt of the twenties? But in the same answer in the questionnaire, he says that transferring the conflict between French artists and the French bourgeoisie onto American soil was artificial. It would seem that the rather general and not particularly bold words at the end of this answer, that art is "criticisim of life," are also in force.

It is no accident that Trilling did not find a single novel which met his new credo. But with even greater enthusiasm he responded to David Riesman's book *The Lonely Crowd*—a work on social psychology that is very well-known

*Retranslated. From Trilling's *A Gathering of Fugitives.* [Editor's note.]

in the West. The critic found in it a fresh analysis of manners and an intellectual trend close to his own.

He praised the book to the skies: "Mr. Riesman writes with a feeling of social reality which Scott Fitzgerald could envy. He is doing a service to literature in showing novelists that there are magnificent new, untilled social fields which they can work."[†] In other words, Riesman is laying down a path for the American novel.

His book was one of the first responses to the postwar boom. It describes an amorphous and colorless world of "white collar" workers in corporations and offices, advertising agencies and commerce. They are people who are as alike their neighbors and co-workers as two drops of water. The "Era of Consumption" had begun, and everything in their lives is determined by a stereotyped and insatiable consumption of cars and kitchen appliances, political news and Hollywood movies.

The expansion of this faceless and satiated world, says Riesman, has been accompanied by a change in the American character. Two psychological types are at the center of the book: the independent (the author calls them "inner-directed") and the dependent (in his terminology, "other-directed"). The industrial revolutions have inspired people with initiative and persistence. And the tradition from the "Era of Production to the Era of Consumption" generated many cautious and inert clerks—their name is legion. The definitive type of our time is not the captain of industry, but the conformist office-worker.

Many received this book as an elegy: to replace the pioneers and independent farmers came shadow-people, leading spectral lives. This gloomy antithesis in itself is not new—it runs through all the dissenting prose of the twenties. It is enough to recall Lewis who gave a bitter picture of a descendant of the pioneers in Babbitt. But *The Lonely Crowd* would never have gotten such praise from Trilling if it had followed this line. And the point is that the trend of thought and approach to American life here are quite different than in Lewis' best work.

Riesman tirelessly polemicizes with those who do not see the virtues of a flourishing America. It opens up extraordinary possibilities to people, and even consumers who are "other-directed" can use them. The radicals, Riesman asserts, are too narrow-minded and hasty in their conclusions. And he changes around the accents, moves the lighting, trying to find something cheerful in what is ugly.

Here is a reversal of thought that is typical of him. The subject of corporation office workers comes up: they live cosily, but in eternal anxiety—their fate depends on external forces. It would seem there is little good in this, but Riesman observes: "We should ask anyone who opposes the manipulation of people in modern industry if he would prefer to return to the cruel oppression of the early days of the Industrial Revolution."[*] Skeptical people could

---

*Retranslated. From *The Lonely Crowd*. [Editor's note.]

ask: can it be that humanity has no other choice? And unskeptical ones make the conformist conclusion: in the comfortable world of corporations there is no longer any place for brute force, and manipulating people is not as bad as people say.

There is a striking and challenging switching of accents in this author's judgments of mass culture too.

Riesman speaks in the name of the new American reality, which all those who criticize comic books and cowboy movies customarily oversimplify. He wants to show that mass culture is moving close to serious culture; even the Hollywood movie can teach a great deal, and on the other hand, first class books are now coming out in editions of millions.

Much really has changed in the cultural life of America, and its best artists after the war had an audience such as they had never had before. But in no way does this erase the boundary between serious and commercial art. On the contrary, it is even more obvious when the same bookstall sells both Faulkner's novels and Mickey Spillane, when on Broadway a play by Arthur Miller has to compete with box office hits. The proximity of the two certainly cannot be considered idyllic.

The author of the book keeps confusing the possibilities opened up by gigantic development of production with what he has before his eyes at the present moment. But he does not conceal his sadness, reminiscent of his spectral heroes, because their lives are "alienated." While accepting current practices, Riesman dreams of autonomy for the inert clerks. The incomprehensible thing is how people who are being manipulated can have autonomy.

Criticism and apology intertwine in Riesman's book, and this duality explains its unusual fate. The praises of the "Era of Consumption" were taken up by mass culture: the unusual terminology and the rather heavy style of the book made it seem scholarly. And among the liberal intelligentsia *The Lonely Crowd* was taken as a critical analysis of modern America; but they made no distinction between precision of observation and novelty of material on the one hand, and the switching around of emphasis and the conformist tendencies of the author on the other.

Now it seems a paradox that the critic John Aldridge, while praising heretics and rebels, put the name of Riesman and Wright Mills together: both sociologists were ahead of the novelists in showing the new America. After all, the trend of their thought was quite different; the author of *The Ruling Elite,* a nonconformist of the old stamp, never worshipped the changes in American life.

Another thing is even more paradoxical. Trilling praised Riesman for not having a predilection for the "narcotic of pessimism." Pure negativism is not for for author of *The Lonely Crowd.* But if literature accepted one of his basic conclusions—the fate of America is conformity—this cheerful deduction would be more disastrous for it than the blackest despair. The postwar novelists were perfectly aware that the morality of accomodation and standardization of personality led to death for art.

In the forties and fifties, the rebels expressed their sharp hostility to the "era of consumption" for the most part obliquely: they did not find their heroes among the dull and zealous members of "respectable" society, those quick to observe formalities and rules, but among those who broke all of society's commandments—among the disobedient soldiers and in the "underground" world of crime. There individuality is still strikingly alive; there people don't worry about established taboos.

In James Jones' novel *From Here to Eternity* (1951), when the hero lands in the brig, in solitary confinement, the author writes tenderly about the tanned faces of his comrades who are used to deprivation and misfortune. "There was not a single fatfaced insurance salesman from the new America here."[†] This is a direct response to the changes in American life.

It took great bravery to throw down the gauntlet to prosperity. The reactionary writers, as a rule not of high quality, but just as indefatigable as the vigilantes in California, rushed to attack the disturbers of the peace. One of them, the critic Edmund Fuller, saw Jones as the head of a new anti-social trend and resorted to the not quite parliamentary expression, saying they were "paranoiac novelists."

Fuller spoke for the offended insurance salesmen and other respectable citizens. Jones, he says, is glorifying troublemakers and doesn't recongize the powers that be. "If you listen to this long enough you get ashamed that you're sober and not in jail. It's not compassion, it's paranoia."[†] He tries to be refined in his use of this kind of abuse, as the critic pretends that he is interested only in the health of American literature. He even pompously cites Rolland's *Fair on the Square.*

In this work, which is now bombastic, now crude, one feels a persistent attempt to turn American prose off the path of criticism.

For Fuller, almost all the important writers of America are goats. He sees the beginning of their current misfortunes in Steinbeck and Saroyan singing the glories of likable tramps, not finding a kind word for the world of business, or as this fighter of depression says "the world of respectable people with solid economic positions." It's only a stone's throw from here to disrespect for power and the authorities. And Herman Wouk is the lamb in contemporary literature (certainly!). After all, Wouk has "healthy" American views, no extremes; he can show life inside out, but he stands like a pillar for the existing order.

Fuller's book, which bristles with citations from the classics, is written quite professionally. But it is surprising to what a degree his ideas are close to the literary program of the magazines *Life* and *Time.* It was these champions of mass culture who raised Wouk's novel as the banner of conformity in contemporary literature without fearing being laughed at. But they compared the writer who, as formerly, was dissatisfied in a time of "unprecedented" prosperity, with an unemployed homosexual at the city dump.

This choice abuse lets one see just how strong the pressure of the conformists on the critical trend was. But even more often, *Time* and *Life* sang like sirens, trying to get yesterday's rebels on their side. With their sharp pens (we must give them their due!), these luxurious weeklies attempted to construct a bridge between the intelligentsia and business.

Their editorials were full of lofty words about responsibility to the nation. It was the goal of this pedagogy to win the intelligentsia over to the side of the foreign policy which the ruling "elite" cursed by Mills was conducting. The humane and enlightened manners characteristic of America during the boom were listed along with a mass of historical parallels (in our time it's even gotten to the point where the current president was called "a modern Medici"). The hero of the most advanced essays was an intelligent and well-schooled businessman who was accustomed to working with others and stood on the highest level of the age.

By promulgating these "fairytales for adults" *Life* was repeating (and exaggerating Riesman's conformist arguments. That is why Norman Mailer's attack on these liberal "controllers of thought" was of such great import.

Mailer wrote an excellent lampoon in the name of the radicals.* He showed that *The Lonely Crowd* did not give a complete picture of the new reality. It is a professorial book; it describes a complacent though uneasy world of clerks and administrators which a university professor has encountered. It is naive to consider Riesman's conclusion rigidly scientific. By simply turning cliches inside out he is able to create myths about altruistic businessmen and social harmony in the world of corporations.

So the "untilled" social field discovered by Riesman and advertized by Trilling did not attract the leading prose writers. But forceful new novels about a new American unlike the one turned upside down by crisis did appear: this happened at the beginning of the sixties. It is to three quite different kinds of book which evoked response all over the world that this article is devoted.

They led to polemics in American criticism. It was said that they were not social novels in the spirit of the thirties; it was even observed that they were in large measure "asocial." One could only be confused by using such opinions as starting points. At the same time, there was as little taking into account of the American tradition of the lyrical novel and the logic of its development as there had been in Trilling's *The Liberal Imagination*.

Here we can only briefly discuss this logic so as to put things in perspective.

As is well known, in Anderson's and Hemingway's lyrical prose the larger world is put into parenthesis. But criticism of civilization defined the entire artistic systems of these two writers, both natives of the Midwest. The abnormalities of everyday life with the constant cruelty and quest for the dollar were reflected in their grotesque characters; the dominance of auto-

---

*N. Mailer, "David Riesman Reconsidered," *Advertisements for Myself* (London, 1961).

matism and standardization intensified their drive toward the primordial elements of life, untainted colors, whole people. For them the novel was unexpectedly simple—both in style and in structure; it bordered now on a series of novellas, now on reportage. But a complicated and critical perception of modern life underlay all this prose (which avoided "literariness"); beyond the provincial sticks stood the entire West. This was the source of American prose of the thirties and the sixties.

The Great Depression forced writers to come to grips with social problems; the surrounding world lost its former stability and attracted extraordinary interest from novelists. They tended toward the epic, but the momentum came from the direction of lyrical prose, not any other way.

Apparently the highest models of the American epic were given by Steinbeck in *The Grapes of Wrath,* and Faulkner in *The Hamlet.* These books, and the paths of their authors are rather different. But they both felt a very strong influence from the novella-type novel of Anderson. And in books which are striking for their epic power they preserve many things from his lyrical prose; grotesque characters certainly did not disappear (like One-eye in *The Grapes of Wrath),* the setting remained the same—life in the provinces.

The writers of the sixties expand the frame of the lyrical novel in a new way. They strive to immanently introduce into the novel the *spiritual life* and conflicts of the modern world. Political and philosophical arguments, religious and moral quests—all this allows one to examine American life in its more complicated form, from a good vantage point. The style changes correspondingly; the former precision and laconism are combined with intricate and extremely "literary" devices.

These new novels can be called centaurs, to use the title of Updike's book (which we have translated into Russian). Not in the sense that in each of them the realistic level is so experimentally combined with the mythological. The point lies elsewhere—these novels are both close to the native tradition of lyrical prose and beyond its limits. Full-blooded, fresh, opening up new worlds, they immanently contain the spiritual element; in them the role of ideas grows in importance as Trilling foresaw (though the ideas are far from what Trilling had in mind). They are also earthly, as before they strive toward the bases of life with renewed inspiration. There is something transitional in their entire structure, a certain heterogeniety and disunity of sources. This is also reflected in their relation to the European novel.

Compared to the lyrical prose of the twenties the new books are closer to the nineteenth-century classical novel; characters are developed graphically and gradually, a lyric tone is combined with analysis of the environment.

And simultaneously they tend toward the most modern European prose with its excessively refined psychological analysis. One senses behind this a striving to defend individuality in a standardized society. And, however paradoxical it may sound, they have a trend toward expanding the bounds of the novel: the contemporary life of the world is reflected in the most highly subjective forms of internal discourse, with capricious associations and chronological shifts. What formerly was conveyed directly by the author, or not captured at all, is now revealed to us in a direct presentation of the spiritual life of the personality.

It was not on barren ground that these centaur-novels, combining the incompatible, appeared. The contemporary writers had direct precursors who strove to transfer the discovery of the rural writers from "minor" lyric prose to big novels.

In the huge volumes of Thomas Wolfe (which are written in a dissenting spirit) all of American life is refracted through the authorial "I." Experiments with interior monologue in the spirit of Joyce and various chronological planes did not prevent Wolfe from idolizing *War and Peace,* and he wanted to raise the autobiographical to the universal level as Tolstoy had.

Scott Fitzgerald is very close to the new generation. In his lifetime he was often taken as a writer of manners, or else as the singer of the "sad young people," the heroes of the "Jazz Age." After his death critics came to value this novelist's original thought, which he showed magnificently in his lyrical books about the inside workings of the boom.

And finally Faulkner. Extreme subjectivity combined with the insatiability and scope of an epic writer; stubborn "provinciality" which does not preclude the intellectual force and general significance of his art. Faulkner carefully followed the development of the novel after the war, he encouraged talented newcomers. And he himself, more decisively than they, included the spiritual in the novel; the purely Faulknerian stories told with such virtuosity in *The Mansion* and *Intruder in the Dust* become commentaries on contemporary events and problems. Thus the boundaries of Yoknapatawpha expanded, and its creator took part in the search for the new synthesis toward which the American novel was moving.

2.

In the very beginning of a long book of great scope, William Styron's *Set This House on Fire* (1960), there is a direct response to the postwar boom—or, as Reisman puts it, the period which opens "new possibilities for leisure, human good-will, and abundance."[†]

The narrator, a young lawyer, returns to his home town in Virginia and does not recognize it. The old magnolias have been cut down, a highway has been built right beside the ocean. There are no longer any oaks or elms; the former shady town has become a noisy business center. There is plastic, neon, and chrome everywhere. About the only thing the same is the children digging clams on the beach—the "marauding clutch of progress" has not reached this far.

These changes make the narrator sad; nothing is left of the poetic world of his childhood. And his father, a Democrat of the old stamp, talks about the new times beside himself with anger. What has become of people in this "era of satiety and silence?" The old man, brought up on the Old Testament, scolds his brainless fellow citizens with the fury of a prophet.

Sorry and unhappy times have come. The country needs a good shake-up for people to recover human form, but the way it is they are "a bunch of smug contented hogs rooting at the trough." They are crazy about comforts, and with their chewing gum and modern kitchen appliances they have forgotten the meaning of life. "We've sold our birthright and old Tom Jefferson is spinning in his grave."

The honorable Southerner is close to despair as he castigates his blind countrymen. Everything seems to have gone according to the behest of the founding fathers; the mass of people has been able to satisfy its "pursuit of happiness." But physical well-being gave them neither wisdom nor dignity. And modern America reminds the old Virginian not of the ideal democracy, but of the Roman Empire at its lowest ebb.

This scene is an original introduction to the drama which lies at the center of the book. In a distant town in Southern Italy, an American who is no less perverted than a Roman patrician rapes a peasant girl. And he perishes at the hands of another American who avenges defiled beauty.

Set This House on Fire is structured as a novel-memoir and a novel of personal research. The narrator was a childhood friend of the brilliant millionaire Mason Flagg; he was in Italy when Flagg committed the crime and suffered his punishment. But much remained unclear to him. And the young lawyer's goal is to reconstruct a true picture of the events.

In his fury and independence the narrator's father recalls the lonely Southerners who defend justice in Faulkner's Yoknapatawpha. But his son Peter makes one recall another writer—Fitzgerald. Somewhat insipid in his punctiliousness, without creative fiber, without a bold imagination, he is akin to the narrator of *The Great Gatsby.* Thus from the very first pages Styron leans toward two different masters who are extremely close to him in his reflections on America and in the art of the novel.

The same orientation on Faulkner and Fitzgerald is obvious in the portrait of the book's amoral hero. Mason's chilhood on a luxurious estate stylized as a castle, amid glitter and boredom, surrounded by film stars, is shown in the spirit of Fitzgerald and his stories and novel *The Last Tycoon* devoted to Hollywood (we mean not just the material, but a special lyric tone: the magnificence of the milieu allows one to feel the ease and mobility of the life of those who do not have to worry about their daily bread—and to feel the emptiness of this sweet life paid for by other people's misery and work).

And Mason himself, an unbridled character who despises all human norms, who is ready to overstep any limit, a monster of vice, a poet of evil—is akin to the "blackest" heroes of Faulkner, those like Popeye in *Sanctuary*. True, Mason is not just a villain by profession, he is also a philosopher of evil. Through traditional American prose we approach a new type which Styron has discovered.

Mason and Peter establish jocularly friendly relations. The colorless narrator is enchanted by the bold sallies of Mason. However wild his behavior may be at times, still one can see that he shows imagination, fantasy, contempt for philistine conventions. Beside him Peter now feels his own ordinariness, now feels proud of his decency. And Mason tells him amiably and jokingly, "I like you because you're such a square."

Breadth, brilliant imagination—and the humblest of endings. But Styron develops his character in such a way that his end does not strike us as an accident.

Mason despises mass culture. Only in the movies, he says ironically, are spies supermen who creep along with knives in their teeth. And he tells how he was parachuted into the Yugoslav partisans, how they betrayed him and he was forced to run, how his comrade was wounded and a fountain of blood spurted out of the wound... The story of a "man who has been around" is no less full of effects than the sensational films. And all of this, which is full of fantasy quite on the level of mass culture, turns out to be pure sham—Mason avoided the draft and never saw the war. This doesn't prevent him from repeating Nietzsche's advice: "Live dangerously."

He comes across as a pure intellectual, almost an encyclopedist—so frequently does he spout names, facts, and quotations. Brecht and the Marquis de Sade—who, he says, was the first psychoanalyst who understood that one must not represss the most destructive sexual urges, drive them into the world of fantasy—but freely act on them. It seems that Mason stands on the level of the Parisian salon; incidentally, after the war it was fashionable to discuss the misfortunate de Sade as not so much a villain as a defender of free personality, and Brecht, who did not acknowledge Aristotelian rules, also became fashionable. But this fondness for the latest European novelties does not prevent the young millionaire from despising both art and Europe. Mason likes to discourse on how the muses are at death's door and the "uncreative age" has begun. And he puts a cross on Europe. "We are *in fact* the nation of the future."[†]

Behind this self-confidence of the aristocrat of the spirit who possesses inherited millions Styron sees yankee immaturity and the falsity of all commercial civilization. Around Mason there are witty writers and talented actors. But they waste themselves on childishly absurd escapades or gloomy and superprofound pornography. Talent chokes in this atmosphere of the sweet life and gilded Bohemia. And this philosopher of vice who grasps at the tinsel of European culture is no better than his countrymen who constantly buy up the paintings of the latest extreme trends, unshakably convinced that the center of the Universe is some sort of Babbit's Zenith.

If it warmed the cockles of Riesman's heart that the boundary between high culture and mass culture was being erased, Styron continues to despise mass culture where it is disguised as the most "highbrow."

This disguise is ridiculed in the second part of the novel. Here Cass becomes the narrator—an American artist who even in Europe tries to stay as far as possible away from his art-blind countrymen. Mason takes him for a celebrated beatnik—the scene where they meet is very comical. The millionaire fawns before the beatnik; the man who knows how to value the beautiful wants to show that he is not behind the times. "In general," Cass observes, "there was about as much of the avant-garde in Mason as in J. P. Morgan." The enlightened patron of the arts reminded him of a beauty smiling from an automobile ad.

He likes to say, *"Epater le bourgeois!"* It would be funny if it hadn't turned out sadly for the penniless Cass. Mason gets a death grip on him. Even if it is an "uncreative age," let him paint indecent things for dollars. Decency aside, let him, an artist, fawn before guests—it is a wild spectacle in the taste of the contemporary patrician. And when Cass falls in love with an Italian girl, behaves rebelliously and is ready to escape submission, Mason does not want to stand for that. Humiliate them both, let them know their places.

But retribution awaits the all-powerful millionaire. Naked and amoral lack of spirituality does not go unpunished. Cass pushes Mason off a cliff. And without a shadow of condecension Peter thinks about his friend: "There was no history for him, or if there was it only began with his appearance on earth."[†] The wise Italian keeps telling him that he is a strange breed of man. "The American with an empty face, like a cute child."[†] Likening the self-confident philosopher of vice to the pretty girl in the advertisement as Styron did meant digging not just at millionaires. He discovered a type in Mason, a national type: a man with no spiritual life and no history, seemingly an enlightened rebel, but in essence a child of commercial civilization. The writer told the reporter for the paper *Lettres francaises* that many Americans could not forgive him this character.

If in the first part of the novel a chance witness relates the tragedy, in the second one of its main heroes takes the floor. Here the events are filtered through the lyrical perception of the artist, they correspond to his moral searchings. The character of Cass is no less new and profound in conception than that of his debaucher and tormentor.

Cass is a native Southerner with a keen sense of guilt. A giant in glasses, he went through World War II in the navy and returned from the Pacific front with a disturbed mind. Much about the United States bothers him, especially the triumph of commerce over the spirit, the crudity and immaturity of mass culture. Cass wants to save himself from the yankees in Europe; he is inspired by pure landscapes full of light, such as Cezanne's (he wants to paint gulls flying through an aquamarine sky). The Italian town seems to him a model of classical antiquity: a green-blue paradise out of which a faun could emerge and shepherd girls start talking the language of Virgil. No dishonorable though quite "normal" games with money (one of these left the Cass family penniless), no unbearable self-confident, insistent, over-familiar countrymen.

But the feeling of guilt pursues Cass even in Europe. On the idyllic green slopes he sees emaciated old women bent beneath huge loads—they recall mules, beasts of burden, the same poverty as before—and in our time. This sight gives Cass no peace; this image is refracted in his nightmarish dreams and thoughts about a world without a god or morality. And it makes him feel tormenting shame for America, rich and indifferent to the pain of others.

As he sees it in Europe, the image of America is quite unlike Trilling's conformist fantasies. Both Cass and Peter (who, incidentally, had been a clerk in the "American aid" program) are ashamed of this overstuffed philanthropy when they land in the poor and smelly cottage of the peasant. Cass blushes for his country and frequently calls it "cellophane-wrapped" and "inimical to beauty." All these unflattering epithets apply to the America which has undertaken the Americanization of Europe.

A Southerner who has been brought up on the French masters, he is by no means a rolling stone. He remembers sunset in North Carolina, the Negro church in a grove of trees, the Negroes walking through the town. His feeling for his country is tied to them, their simplicity and closeness to the soil. But also tied to them is the original sin of American history—slavery. The old women with the huge loads make Cass remember what he is most ashamed of—as a boy he wrecked a Negro shack, he was dragged along in a raid. And the feeling of guilt will not leave the conscience-stricken artist: he experiences the guilt both for the current boastful richness and for the slavery of old (which has not yet become a thing of the past).

Cass's spiritual life is recreated by means of fine psychological analysis. The dreams in which the things the hero fights (sometimes unawares) in waking life are strikingly graphic and full of bitter perceptions. Diary entries, first-person narration, interior monologe—under Styron's pen all these forms are capacious and interconnected: the repeated images of the book clash and intertwine in them. The lyrical novel is made denser by moral problematics. The source of Cass's drama, which is unusual in contemporary prose, was well defined by the title of one French review of the novel—"The Sin of American Life."

Cass cannot bear the terrible oppression of evil. For the most part we see this big American humbled, lost, devoid of taste for life or art; drunk almost to the point of irresponsibility, he easily becomes Mason's victim. As early as the war he turns up visitng a psychoanalyst; one could guess that Cass's mental instability and nightmares will be given Freudian interpretations. But as he enters the outer spheres of psychoanalysis Styron argues against it.

Cass himself thinks the kind psychoanalyst cannot understand anything about his dreams and nightmares. After all, it is accepted that one must find traces of a sexual drama experienced in childhood, but Cass is pursued by scenes of injustice—with capricious (as in a dream) shifts and associations, so that his native South is combined with gas chambers. And if Cass is able to cheer up, the psychoanalyst friend's only service is in giving Cass a volume of Greek tragedies, and he finds support in the torment and fortitude of Oedipus.

Having found himself again, the hero throws Mason off the cliff. This is retribution for all the evil the millionaire sadist has committed, amorality itself protected by a checkbook. But there is no moral victory in this retribution.

There is an atmosphere of tragedy in the first half of the novel. The terrible silence in the streets strikes Peter, the town seems to have died out or the Saracens have beseiged it again. Only the measured peals of a bell like the sound of fate. Its inhabitants who only yesterday were taking off their hats to the brilliant Mason now talk of him with horror and contempt. Even though he is dead, the cold-blooded rapist makes no one feel pity.

But in the second half, when the sequence of events becomes clearer, it is reminiscent not so much of a tragedy as of a detective story. And with new revelations the stress changes—it turns out that Mason is less guilty than was thought; a local degenerate chanced to meet and disfigure the peasant girl in the hills, and now Cass has Mason's murder on his conscience.

This turn of events directs the reader's attention to the metaphysical aspect of the novel. Its title is taken from a sermon by the seventeenth-century English poet John Donne—the context is the terrible torment of a soul cut off from God. In the novel Cass's drama is illuminated as the drama of a man of our time when "God is dead" (in Nietzsche's famous words) and immorality is triumphant.

Cass himself, in contrast to the pure Cezanne landscapes toward which his soul strives, is presented in the existential mode: the torment of his spirit is reflected in a slavish dependence on physiology. And he is given an existentialist's world-perception; man is locked in a cell of loneliness for life and has before him the choice between Sartre's categories of Being and Nothingness. In the end the hero, who has often been on the verge of suicide and has often been humiliated by Mason, chooses Being; and after the tragedy he returns to America, to the land not only of sin and vice, but of hope—to the sweet landscapes of his native land, to creativity.

Thus there is a somewhat anemic French philosophical superstructure in an American "Southern" novel with its full-bloodedness, its marvelous and varied secondary and tertiary figures, and its dark humor. Conceiving the new American reality with great moral sensitivity, Styron has expanded the bounds of the novel; but the introduction of existentialism into the novel reveals all the more clearly artistic losses, not gain.

Its ending is frankly illustrative. The real Cass with his American experience and torment, turns into a philosophizing "everyman." It is not surprising that in almost every interview Styron was asked about the metaphysical meaning of the novel; the philosophical intrusions do not always fit the logic of the plot, and they are not very clear.

And there is something strange about Cass's evolution. Inasmuch as the words "God is dead" are taken as a starting point, the sharp criticism of bourgeois civilization is associated with lack of faith; Cass himself admits, he was as much an unbeliever as a strong character. But at home after the tragedy which has made him look into the face of Nothingness, the hero is pacified, he has acquired at least a modicum of faith, he can work. Thus criticism, after confronting Nothingness, leads to self-negation.

Set This House on Fire caused much comment both in Europe and America. The novel became an event in the postwar literature of the West.

In the States the reaction was contradictory. The book landed on the bestseller list, but its directness and pointedness (in Styron's own words) shocked many readers. The novel had its enthusiasts in literary circles, but probably the majority of reviews were rather sour. It was not difficult for the critics to find something transitional about the book. And often they gave Styron a quick esthetic trial without concealing their indifference or hostility to what interested him. In the *New York Times Book Review* (June 5, 1960) Arthur Mizener concluded that it was not a tragedy, but a melodrama, a contemporary variation on the Gothic novel of horrors; he also considered the critique of materialistic American civilization banal and denied the novel had any general significance (his review was called "A Few Men of Our Time"). D. Stevenson, the author of the essay "Styron and Prose in the Fifties"* complained that there was much in the book which was not "novelized"—he also considered the character of the old Southerner superfluous, not seeing that his speeches presage the future tragedy.

The tone of the French reviews is quite different. The review in *L'Express* is called "The Most Thoughtful and Optimistic of the Great American Tragedies." The French turned out to be very sensitive to Styron's national self-criticism, and they perceived the novel as a tragedy which had very broad meaning. True, they saw the shift of the Southern novel into an existentialist essay as an artistic weakness. They considered Styron an optimist—compared to Faulkner in the thirties or Sartre in the forties. Still, the optimistic resolution of Cass's spiritual drama did not please everyone. In *L'Esprit* it was noted

---

Recent American Fiction. Some Critical Views (Boston, 1963).

that this was perhaps homage to American illusions about the New World. Along with an ecstatic attitude towards Styron's literary craftsmanship, reproaches were made: the novel is too well-planned, in this one feels the engineer more than the poet, and it was unsuccessful in achieving a complete unity of descriptive and metaphysical aspects.

Some critics both in America and in France took the novel as an existential variant of *Crime and Punishment.* There were others who found this comparison unnatural. They correctly noted that the book lacks "moral power in the spirit of Raskolnikov." Switching the action onto existential lines prevents the novel from becoming high tragedy.

Apropos, Styron's talent is lighter than Faulkner's even in *Sanctuary,* the lawyer Benbow exclaims: "O tempore! O mores!" But here the pessimistic philosophy undercuts the protest against the motto "all is allowed" and forces one to go from amorality in the modern world to the solitary confinement in which everyone is locked.

In his thoughts on America Styron came out of the tradition of Faulkner who saw the source of modern tragedies in the curse of racism, and the tradition of Fitzgerald who felt so keenly the contrast between the historical promise of the New World and its bourgeois prose. In Styron as in Faulkner, the South turns out to be the ground of nonconformity—out of it develops his attack on bourgeois self-satisfaction in the "era of satiety and silence." Styron wanted—no matter how hard it was for a single writer in the postwar world—to protest directly against the dominant amorality. And if he did not succeed in everything, if his novel has transitional characteristics, we must value the moral impulse of the author. And his strong talent, refuting the pitiful sophisms about the "uncreative age."

3.

In 1960, the same year Styron's book appeared, John Updike's novel *Rabbit, Run* was published.

The plot is not at all new—the hero takes off running to escape a depressing family life and monotonous everyday existence. When Sherwood Anderson began his novel *Dark Laughter* (1925) with this situation it was still a novelty; but since then the motif of running away and his laconic and lyric manner of writing had become the property of epigones. It is curious that in one of his stories Updike presents a certain student with literary ambitions this way: "He was a student of Anderson and Hemingway and he himself wrote without adornment, like a newspaper."[†]

Though it is traditional in plot, two new features in *Rabbit, Run* do strike one. It is not lyrical prose in the spirit of the twenties—which was so close to the long novella. While preserving the lyrical tone, Updike wrote a full-bodied novel; every figure, whether it be the runner's parents, his basket-ball coach, his wife's parents, has his own character which is revealed tersely and precisely. But even earlier one notices that the "rabbit" himself, Harry Angstrom, has been given a devilish sensitivity, and all of his impressions, reactions, and chance associations are stated with Proustian completeness.

In such a style—itself the complete opposite of reportorial concision—one sometimes senses something exotic, excessive. But the hero's receptivity helps us to see a new reality behind this small town in Pennsylvania—the "society of mass consumption" in miniature.

At the beginning of the book Harry and his wife are watching television. She is attracted to its vacuous programs no less than to whiskey. And he main-tains he has a purely professional interest in the commercials. Harry demon-strates kitchen utensils in dime stores. The figures on the screen sing and dance; a clever commercial is already on, and this is a kind of popular course in American philosophy. Everyone has a talent, all that is necessary is to dis-cover it, to be oneself—and happiness awaits you. Harry explains to housewives that the new tool for peeling turnips is indispensible, it is simply wonderful—but can it be that this is his fate?

And when he suddenly and unexpectedly for himself runs away from town in his new 1959 Ford (his father-in-law gave it to him cheaply—what is a young family without a decent car), he wonders—has he become alien to all America? Everything around is familiar; identical cars run along identical highways—beside him go the same kinds of little towns, cafes selling coca cola, gas stations. The radio in his Ford broadcasts a commercial for napkins and woolen suits, or political news, food for the philistine ("Where is the Da-lai-Lama?"). Finally the road strikes the hero as a trap and the map a net. He returns to his own town.

Before us is a prisoner of things. For him advertised happiness has turned into a nightmare. His wife, who has grown flabby and run-down, who gulps down whiskey and TV programs, seems not to live life in "the best years of our lives." And with his exhortations to housewives Harry drags out a kind of phantom existence.

Only by breaking away to freedom does he come to life; it seems to him "freedom is poured through the air like acid."[†] And he grows even more alive when he remembers the past. How in childhood he took his little sister tobagganing. And when he starred on the basketball team in high school—it was then that he was nicknamed Rabbit—and now, now all he has to do is take a ball in his hand and his former elasticity and coordination return. Then everything was first-rate. But now life in the same town that had once held so many hopes has deceived him and become depressingly second-rate.

Updike reveals an unexpected contrast in a hero who seemed quite ordinary.

Rabbit exists "inside his skin"; crushed by things, he is afraid—all he has to do is come outside and people will manipulate him exactly as if he were a thing. But he is just as indifferent to other people as life was to him. Tender and soft by nature, Rabbit can be furiously cruel; he simply cannot put himself in the place of another person. And without losing the lyrical tone, Updike can be merciless to his immature hero.

Harry lacks maturity—that is what his beloved coach and everyone around says. This is true of course. But from Ruth, a former prostitute who is his age and with whom Rabbit finds shelter, he hears something rather different. Ruth tells him what she likes about the unsuccessful runaway: "The fact that you failed. The fact that in your stupid way you are still fighting."[†]

Of course, what kind of fighter is Rabbit—one could say rather that he is floundering. But from childhood he has taken in the Protestant concepts of good and evil and now he cannot believe that his mechanical life is illuminated by God's name. The book's religious theme arises: Harry's vague strivings and his arguments with the minister Eccles give his story a broader meaning.

But at this point we must digress—compared to his predecessors, Updike has something new in this respect.

When the writers of the twenties and thirties touched on the numerous American churches, they usually showered Rabelaisian jokes on the bigotry and hypocrisy of the preachers of various denominations. They revolted against the well-behaved prescriptions of Sunday school and the gloomy, joyless puritainism. In Updike too, sometimes (though, true, it is not so lighthearted) one finds jokes aimed at the bigots. Rabbit's girl-friend Ruth remembers one "client" who used to leave her and go directly to teach Sunday school. But in general Updike's approach to religion is different.

He has a story called "The Christian Roommates." The subject is college students. One is a straight and punctilious American, a medical student who has planned out his whole life in advance. The other is an eccentric, an odd fellow who gets carried away by Hindu beliefs, but when the war in Korea begins he flatly refuses to take part. For one Christian beliefs serve as a basis for revolt, for independent behavior; for the other they are simply unnecessary—something habitual and dead. The medical student has achieved everything he wants. And (this is the last sentence in the story), "He never prays."

This antithesis (in markedly different types of variations) comes up in Updike's other things too. Moral searching, doubt, spiritual independence—and commonplace faith combined with conformist behavior and purely worldly interests.

In *Rabbit* this antithesis turns into a paradox. Before us is not the minister from *The Centaur* who never loses sight of the beautiful Venus while Caldwell bores him with his doubts. No, here the minister is self-sacrificing—he does not begrudge time for any single lost soul; he is kind and humane—the weak seem more sympathetic to him than the self-confident; he even tells Rabbit with a smile, "I'm immature myself."

But Harry is petty, and at times banal. Not only his concept of sin is

tied to religion (for example, whiskey is the "sin of the bad breath"). It supports his higher impulses—to get away from this dull ordinariness.

The thoughtful pastor Eccles falls into an ambiguous position. He has
been sent by the parents of the abandoned wife to return the runaway to
the bosom of his family. But as he chats with this n'er-do-well lad, Eccles
feels sympathy for him and perplexes those who sent him—who think he
may have gone over to Rabbit's side. Then what is he trying to do? It turns
out that the thoughtful minister defends the purely priestly morality—every
marriage is at once holy and bad.

His talks on responsibility add up to only one thing—returning to the
old quotidian life. He is no more successful when he mentions Hell—the
maximum distance from God. Well so what, Harry replies, in that case we all
live in Hell. And when Rabbit starts talking about a different God, not the
one who sanctifies the status quo, the pastor waves his arm in fright—there is
no such God.

In all these arguments the intelligent minister turns out to be the defender of order, peace and quiet. And all of his victories over the disquieted,
rebellious Rabbit are transitory.

By no means does Updike glorify Harry's impulse toward the infinite.
"...you *are* religious aren't you," Ruth says to him with total contempt. That
is, you hobnob with the minister and in your elevated talks you forget about
other people. Here the blasphemous Ruth, the outcast one, becomes a merciless commentator.

She too was offered Sunday-school wisdom: everyone is born with his
own talent—this sounds depressing if one remembers her fate. And it echoes
the popular lesson of Americanism which Rabbit hears on TV. In general
the pastor's conclusions are not new—and he is ready to put on man the
responsibility for a life, "alienated from him by reality."[†]

But all the while one senses the author behind Rabbit—that he is just
as attached to his home town, beloved since childhood, to the land once
tamed by the first settlers. And that he too is striving to go beyond the
bounds of a mundane, oppressive everyday reality. At the end of the book,
it is said of Rabbit (but is it really relevant just to him?):

> Why was he set down here, why is this town, a dull suburb of a third-rate city,
> for him the center and index of a universe that contains immense prairies, moun-
> tains, deserts, forests, coastlines, cities, seas?

This combination of the author's thoughts and the n'er-do-well Rabbit's
strivings and impulses turns the novel into a book about freedom—the deepest
human instinct, which was not atrophied even during the years of the boom.

Rabbit, Run is probably Updike's most important and well integrated
novel; it caused the most reaction both in America and in Europe. But there
is also something transitional about the book. While striving to broaden the
limits of the novel, Updike sometimes overdoes it with Rabbit's transcendental

impulses; for all his masterful handling of narrated monologue, the author overwhelms the hero. The whole book, which in material is alive and throbbing, is excessively literary.

I do not have in mind the fact that Updike has virtuoso control over the techniques of modern European prose (above all Proust and Joyce). In some episodes technique distracts one from the basic concerns, becomes autonomous. In intonation Ruth's stream of consciousness is almost a copy of the interior monologue which concludes *Ulysses,* and after all, in character Rabbit's girl friend, who is embittered against church people, who is vivacious, who is not without her good points, is totally unlike Bloom's wife. Often the minute sensations and Proustian detail seem excessive, and at times they lend an odd tone to scenes of horror. For example, in the description of how Rabbit's drunken wife drowns their newborn baby he describes the grease jumping in the frying pan and compares it to silver splashes of a fountain (in general Updike likes bright, silvery colors). The elegant simile is hardly appropriate here.

But its literariness is a virtue of the novel more than a shortcoming. Updike does not repeat cliches, he tries to tell about ordinary things in a new way, to get inside them, to discover something new in them. This attempt to broaden horizons is even more noticeable in *The Centaur.*

To what has been written about the latter novel in our country I would like to add a few remarks.

Here too the hero is completely traditional, a provincial Don Quixote, a noble intellectual who seems grotesque against the background of a comfortable but dull everyday life. But Updike approached him using a very elevated standard of measurement which excludes the possibility of him being pitiful. He was not afraid to shift the story about a person dear to him into a sphere of high comedy; the Centaur orients himself into reality no better than the knight of La Mancha and at every step he gets taken in. And precisely this approach makes it posisble to glorify the heroism in his character—his recklessness, wholeness, kindness.

The author himself was precise about the reasons why he turned to the myth: "A thinking man who ponders the spiritual side of life in this materialistic world is already a demigod. The image of the centaur—half man, half horse—helps me to contrast to the world of dirt, money-grubbing twilight darkness a certain higher world of inspiration and good."[*]

Thus through the myth we approach Updike's basic orientation: to expand descriptive possibilities, to bring the "cursed" questions of the spirit directly into the novel.

Very important in the book is the juxtaposition of "then" (1947) to "now." As a schoolboy the dreamy Peter, an admirer of sunny Vermeer,

*Retranslated from an interview in the USSR, published in *Inostrannaia literatura [Foreign Literature]*, No. 1 (1965), 256.

drew himself a picture of noisy fame in New York, but he became a run-of-the-mill abstractionist, a banal inhabitant of Greenwich Village. But if in childhood as he himself says, Peter saw only his father's "legs," now the humble science teacher has grown to the proportions of a demigod in his eyes—and the son creates his myth of the wise and self-sacrificing centaur from a Pennsylvania town.

Pagan Greece, the nation of poetry and philosophy, is juxtaposed to the gloomily Protestant, rustic American small town loaded with the most modern comforts. "This is not the 'Golden Age', that's for sure,"[†] says the hero of the book in 1947. But the dream of the "Golden Age" lives on in this powerful and truthful book—no matter how different Caldwell's lesson at school is from the talks of the wise Chiron with his enlightened pupil in a shady grove.

Perhaps we can best understand what is new in Updike "by the opposite"—by turning to Norman Podhoretz's abrasive article, "A Dissent on Updike."

University circles sang hossanahs to the author of *The Centaur*. He was hailed as a virtuoso stylist and writer with an inclination toward the infinite (the fact that he puts the eternal questions as a contemporary and profound observer of American life interested them very little). These unqualified, sometimes cloying ecstasies are what angered Podhoretz; he apparently felt himself a rebel crushing an overblown reputation.

The critic approached Updike using the criteria of simplicity and precision. And without difficulty he noted that Updike's techniques do not always fit the emotions of his heroes, that some of the mythological parallels in *The Centaur* are forced. But Podhoretz did not stop there—he wanted to demonstrate that the intricate form was a concealment of intellectual poverty. And he interpreted Updike's complex ideas in a depressingly trivial way, making his critical victory easy for himself. Thus for example he takes it literally that Caldwell sacrifices his life for his son: as if the teacher, like Chiron, committed suicide. After this the admirer of bare simplicity can ask "ingenuous" questions such as "what is this mythological level for, what is the point of these stylistic intricacies," etc.

Not only Podhoretz, but even some liberal critics who were well-disposed twoards Updike did not see him as a man who was discovering a new reality. This is what Jacques Cabeau expressed aphoristically when he wrote in *L'Express* (15, III, 1962): "In place of Babbitt's blissful optimism which ruled in his world of things, came the horror of the sorcerer's apprentice oppressed by material comforts."

In this new world Updike also describes the drama of lack of spirituality and the tragedy of a solitary moral quest. His style makes it possible for him to capture the slightest impulses of the soul and urges to get away from the oppressive conformity and stereotyped mass culture in a standardized world of things.

4.

Perhaps no novel exemplifies more vividly the direction of American realism than Saul Bellow's *Herzog* (1964). Many critics on both sides of the Atlantic consider Bellow the most important contemporary American novelist (this, incidentally, is what Updike thinks) and *Herzog* is acknowledged to be his best work.

The starting point of this book is close to Sherwood Anderson's novellas: an eccentric, whose character is emotional rather than contemplative, is a living grotesquerie, and for all this "ordinary grotesquerie" he has been knocked off the track of American life, and this bad life is presented through his critical perception. *Herzog* is a very subjective book—it appears to be a lengthy novella about an eccentric who has gone off into his own inner world.

And at the same time the reviewers not without reason recalled the characters from Russian classics. At the beginning of the book, lying on a couch, the hero condemns and tortures himself in the Tolstoyan manner: I'm a good-for-nothing husband, father, and citizen. Moses Herzog (as the hero is named) is a historian of moral teachings, humanities predominately, he wants to find his place in the modern world, failing this there is no possibility of spiritual renewal for him. It is a novel of ideas and its morally sensitive hero was called the "Pierre Bezukhov of the thermonuclear age" by the reviewer for the *New York Times.*

Saul Bellow is directly tied to the Russian tradition.

If in Styron everyday life, hostile personalities, and morals awaken tenderness for the patriarchal locales of the South, with their Negro churches and pine trees, if in Updike the dear forested land which the pioneers discovered shows through civilization and colorless Pennsylvania, for Bellow the kind of everyday life and moral concepts which his parents (Jewish immigrants from Russia) brought to the New World are his spiritual support.

The hero remembers his penniless childhood in Canada with striking vividness and warmth. Everything is still full of reminders of Russia—the knife with the carved handle with which his father cuts overripe pears, a red blanket. His dreamer father had no luck in the foreign land. Totally devoid of practicality, he became a bootlegger; he was beaten up and robbed. Here's a typical scene. A drunken neighbor is returning home late at night singing a mournful song, and Moses wakes up in a cold room (the stove has gone out) underneath the ragged blanket which covers three brothers—Willy, Shura and himself.

Memories carry the hero forty years back. Now it is the Boom, Willy has a big business, and Shura has become a multi-millionaire: at his father's funeral he speaks solemnly and formally as he is surrounded by paunchy bankers and corporation presidents. Moses himself is not such a failure—he is a professor, a man with a place in society. But his feeling of justice has not been blunted; for him the America of the Boom is full of painful contrasts.

Chance brings him to trial when the case of the mother-murderer is examined. Then to the police station where he finds himself in a cell with a drunk and a young Negro: there is a pot in the corner, flies crawling on the ceiling. It is not so often that a fine-soulled intellectual runs up against such cruelty. But he understands perfectly well that not everyone around is free from fear of policemen's billy-clubs, poverty, the slums. And he is ashamed— which is quite a rare thing for an American—of his privileges in a world of "superabundance, crassness, or if you wish, mendacity."[†]

The book is not rich in events. After the family tragedy the hero loses his mental balance; his wife (a cold beauty given to theatrical gestures) leaves him. But that is not all—the treachery here is double—Moses's best friend, who would seem to be the model of respectability, but in fact is a charlatan and phrasemonger, had gotten together with her long before. The hero is thrown off his track; he behaves like an incompetent and—at first this is perceived as pure madness—he writes interminable letters on scraps of paper, to politicians, colleagues, former lovers, dead philosophers, what have you. These letters, naturally, remain unsent.

Of course, there is a comic effect in this: a man finding himself in a rather sad predicament, oblivious of himself, discusses elevated matters—serious things are included in the same letters with silly and parodistic ones. But one discovers a profound and paradoxical connection between the situation and the tone of the letters. A quite well-off professor, thrown out of his customary life, can look around and at himself freely; he is overwhelmed by a "Faustian dissatisfaction and spirit of universal reform." And the hero, who would seem to have gone crazy, has a broader and more healthy view of the world than do the professional pessimists of academic circles.

Bellow makes a masterful montage of reminiscences, pictures of reality, and the hero's speculations and letters. A novel which at first is so subjective and novelistic, embraces a great deal of modern life. Before us is the drama of a confused intellectual during a time of troubles.

The hero writes Eisenhower; he begins by saying the cold war was a "phase of political hysteria." And he shows that one cannot define national goals while ignoring human values. Here is a sample of his thinking, which is as old-fashioned as it is modern:

> The old proposition of Pascal (1623-1662) that man is a reed, but a thinking reed, might be taken with a different emphasis by the modern citizen of a democracy. He thinks, but he feels like a reed bending before centrally generated winds.

The sad comedy of these speculations is a result not just of his academic manner of expression. Who is writing this? And to whom?

> He took seriously Heinrich Heine's belief that the words of Rousseau had turned into the bloody machine of Robespierre, that Kant and Fichte were deadlier than armies.

This is said of Herzog. In other words, he understands the power of an idea and the social significance of words. But not long before Senator McCarthy was insulting American intellectuals as "eggheads." And a professor who wanted to do some good for his country is not in the least wrong in thinking his imagined addressee has no use for the commandments of humanism.

His tragic successor would have been interested, but not Ike. Nor Lyndon. Their governments could not function without intellectuals—physicists, statisticians—but these are whirling lost in the arms of industrial chiefs and billionaire brass. Kennedy was not about to change this situation, either. Only he seemed to have acknowledged, privately, that it existed.

Herzog does not think that a romantic can only efface himself in the presence of the modern world. On the contrary, in his eyes the threat of atomic destruction increases the significance of reason and the old values. After all, "destruction is no longer a metaphor."[†] But i he is firmly convinced that one can never correct the disorder in the world by ignoring spiritual values, he is not at all convinced that this disorder can be overcome or that by oneself one can do anything. We find in Bellow's novel the same combination we found in Styron's—a moral impulse and a feeling of helplessness. Herzog's drama is the drama of the American intellectual—has he a place in his country?

Perhaps the basic subject of his speculations in his letter to Eisenhower, among others, is the new industrial reality, the scientific and technical revolution of the middle of the century. Again he does not think of abandoning his old banner.

Romantic individuals (a mass of them by now) accuse this mass civilization of obstructing their attainment of beauty, nobility, integrity, intensity. I do not want to sneer at the term Romantic. Romanticism guarded the "inspired condition," preserved the poetic, philosophical, and religious teachings, the teachings and records of transcendence and the most generous ideas of mankind, during the greatest and most rapid of transformations, the most accelerated phase of the modern scientific and technical transformation.

The consequences of this change deeply concern Herzog. His idea on this matter borders on Riesman's speculations. But he does not pass off what exists as what is desirable or find harmony where there is none.

Thus in the letter to Eisenhower he says that now there is "more 'private life' than a century ago when the working day lasted fourteen hours." But then he adds: "The whole matter is of the highest importance since it has to do with invasion of the private sphere (including the sexual) by techniques of exploitation and domination." This refers to the monster of mass culture. But Herzog imagines something quite different, a basically humanistic resolution of the problem of leisure time.

The revolutions of the twentieth century, the liberation of the masses by production, created private life but gave nothing to fill it with. This was where such as he came in. The progress of civilization—indeed, the survival of civilization—depended on the successes of Moses E. Herzog.

Of course, here the hero is being ironic about himself. But the question remains open: how successfully can transcendental impulses compete with commercialism?

Has his time come? Or is he a hangover from a past, almost pastoral, age? Moses, as it happens, makes up his mind along these lines. And then his critique results in self-negation: business-like Yankees who are devoid of any sentiment are taken for men of the twentieth century, but with his useless emotions and powerless morality he is taken for an anachronism. Then these words are written:

> Civilization and even morality are implicit in technological transformation. Isn't it good to give bread to the hungry, to clothe the naked? Don't we obey Jesus in shipping machinery to Peru or Sumatra? Good is easily done by machines of production and transportation. Can virtue compete?

Such a rejection of morality in favor of technology would cause considerable consternation to many of the romantics whom Herzog studies. Not to mention the amazingly abstract perception of contemporary history if he is equating good and "American aid," which is far from altruistic.

In general Herzog stays within the bounds of humanism of the old school, and for all his "Faustian discontent" he does not go beyond what is customary in academic circles. When a girl Teaching Assistant writes him, "I have come around to your view, that Marx expressed metaphysical hopes for the future of mankind," he even gets angry—why "his" point of view, everyone thinks that. That is, in university circles there are many scholars who imagine Marx is a noble utopian and metaphysician just as Herzog does. But without the dialectic Herzog turns out to be helpless in the face of pessimism and despair.

He is puzzled by Heidegger's phrase that man is "abandoned" in the world. He puts caustic question marks after Kierkegaard's statement that only fear of hell can make modern man get serious. But this kind of criticism of existentialism is more amusing than convincing (all the moreso that Moses doesn't even mention the French existentialism which is most popular in America).

And all of his condemnations of pure negativism are shallow and therefore ambiguous—even a philistine could support them. For example, the passage about Western intellectuals. First they complain about industry, polluting the land. And then? "It gets to the point where they deny the humanity of the industrialized masses who are 'devoid of any originality'."[†]

One could think that the bourgeois system does not hinder workers from becoming real personalities. Marx wrote far more soberly about the English proletariat of his time, who frequently lost their human personalities. But he was a dialectician and did not take the position that the industrialized masses could not be any different than they were under capitalism.

Herzog, who is sympathetic both in his dissatisfaction and in his defense of moral values, is less so when his feeling of weakness and feeling of having a beautiful soul make him accept the status quo uncritically. A professor who has not bitten the hook of conformity, but who is not very sure of himself, and has no dialectic sometimes comes dangerously close to conformism. Bellow shows this whole way of thinking—with the contradictions, confusion, absence of "clear ideas"—remarkably graphically. Just like Moses Herzog, many American intellectuals see first one, then another side of reality—they see them mixed together, but never see them as intertwined and dynamic. One passage is particularly remarkable in this regard.

Moses is pondering the pressure from without which he experiences—he, an intellectual, a city dweller, in a centralized society after the collapse of "radical hopes."

> In a society that was no community and devalued the person. [Owing to the multiplied power of numbers which made the self negligible.] * Which spent military billions against foreign enemies but would not pay for order at home. Which permitted savagery and barbarism in his own great cities. At the same time, the pressure of human millions who have discovered what concerted efforts and thoughts do. As megatons of water shape organisms on the ocean floor. As tides polish stones. As winds hollow cliffs. The beautiful supermachinery opening a new life for innumerable mankind. Would you deny them the right to exist? Would you ask them to labor and go hungry while you enjoyed delicious old-fashioned Values? You—you yourself are a child of this mass and a brother to all the rest. Or else an ingrate, dilettante, idiot.

Reality is posited as a stable thing in his discussion. Criticism and approval do not work together, and the approval here recalls the spirit of the conscience-striken heroes of the Russian classical novel. Still, many readers of *Herzog* were attracted by its optimism—which is so unusual for the critical trend in America. Let Moses speak as a moderate progressive of a cruel era, he still doesn't want to abandon the humanistic values—all the moreso that our epoch created the prerequisite for them to become the heritage of "innumerable mankind." He doesn't want to repeat the apocalyptic speeches he is fed up with, in general he cannot stand pessimism, which is a waste. Humanity has a future, Herzog thinks, and its symbol is the humanist, not the automaton.

In American literature Bellow is praised for his feeling of the contemporary city. His hero knows how the city can crush—and not only when he lands in jail or court. He writes one of his letters on the subway in a jam-packed car. Here man, who is inclined to withdraw into himself, to surrender to the free flow of thought, constantly feels the masses, the crowds beside him.

But this man who is an eccentric and loner in a crowd feels at one with the world when he is in the empty country home. At the end of the novel we see Herzog at the ramshackle farm he bought before his marriage and abandoned not long before the domestic break-up. Everything is a mess: field mice have eaten the candles, owls have built nests in the room. But the hero feels good; he sits under the birches and at last has spiritual peace. He no longer has any reason to write letters; mental balance has been restored. Even though the cursed questions are only temporarily postponed, not solved.

Following Thomas Mann, Bellow has made the worldview the main subject of description; this is the meaning of his *Herzog*—it is virtually the first intellectual novel in the United States. American critics met it with rejoicing. This motif was sounded: after the painful impression left by the events in Dallas, Bellow had shown that America had created its own humanistic intelligentsia.

But *Herzog,* though written with marvelous craft and feeling for language, is not free of the characteristics of the centaur-novel. The letters, set in italics, are separated from the action: the detailed pictures of childhood and the academic epistles to dead philosophers and living teachers represent two poles in the novel. Herzog's way of thinking itself, with its contradictions graphically captured, is too little objectified: no matter how the author emphasizes the comicality of nonstop thinking in inappropriate situations, he is not aware enough of the naivete and inconsistencies in the novel. In the case of Mann the intellectual novel, especially *The Magic Mountain,* is structured as a novel-debate; *Herzog* is a novel-monologue and simultaneously, as the English critic Tony Tanner correctly noted, "an escape from monologue."[†] The hero tries to re-establish contact with the world in his letters, but this is more self-expression than the clarification of a hero's character and thoughts which is possible with a juxtaposition of various people and opinions. Tanner says, "Sometimes one is anxious to have some sort of meaningful interaction between the hero and his environment."[†]

Nevertheless, the book, which is academic in its material, contains the broadest generalization. This was noted by the magazine *L'Unita* when supporting the novel for being awarded the international Formentor Prize. In the newspaper's words, Bellow was nominated "for the richness of his moral and human problematics, for his 'realism,' the power with which he depicts man's 'alienation' and lack of freedom in American society (as a 'historical embodiment' of the ancient portrait of the Jew which is the basis of his characters), and finally for his ability to give these problems a general character."[*]

---

[*]*L'Unita,* May 4, 1965.

5.

The three novelists whom we have been discussing take different approaches to the depiction of the new America. But the way they perceive this new reality is totally at variance with what Trilling—speaking for American intellectuals—says in his essay, and totally at variance with Riesman's *The Lonely Crowd.*

These writers stress the unspirituality of the mass consumer society. Material progress in itself certainly does not incline them to be idyllic; on the contrary, it makes the victory of brute force especially obvious and unbearable—whether one is discussing the shots in Dallas and crime in the big cities or the rights of corporation tsars. And if critical novels are published in large editions, it proves that there are millions of intelligent readers in America, but not that the boundary between commercial and true art is being effaced.

Finally, the novel does not admit that the personality is doomed, that sooner or later conformity will be the fate of everyone. Its pathos consists precisely in the defense of the free individuality which the society of the consumer is stifling. Today's American novel, like yesterday's, is based on Whitman's feeling of personal individuality. And as the novel becomes more and more spiritual while remaining critical, it preserves the intellectual birthright which conventionally-oriented critics have been ready to deny.

In the mid-fifties, when the critic John Aldridge published his book *In Quest of Heresy* it seemed to him that conformity had crushed and stifled everything. Aldridge nostalgically recalled the time when the little journals supported the innovators in literature; but now the reader buys anything, even blank pages under a brightly decorated cover—as long as it is advertised... But if novels which contain honest and pungent ideas become best-sellers in the sixties, it is a sign of the times. Never has the American novel reached such a wide circle of readers or played such an important role: awakening a society which is mesmerized by material comforts and which has gained little from McCarthyite "brain-washing."

After the war the American novel was turned toward basic questions of spiritual life. To the questions which existentialists and Marxists pose in different ways as they respond to the movement of contemporary history.

If French existentialism took hold in the American novel, there were reasons for it.

The novelists felt alienated from their flourishing country; some eminent prose writers such as James Baldwin, spent many years away from their homeland, in France. Styron's reply to *L'Express* when asked about the position of the writer in America (March 8, 1962) is typical:

> It's hard. In France you can't imagine that; here the writer is respected as such, he is honored and he consistently feels that he is essential to the culture of his country. But the writer is received much less well in America—it's not that he is despised—but he is mistrusted. People ask themselves what is that character who

sits in his room writing good for (the majority never reads what he writes, compared to Europeans, Americans read much less); it seems to them that writing novels is a fairly easy way to make money! (Of course, I'm not talking about educated minds, but about the country as a whole.)

When he was visiting Moscow, Updike described in much the same way the distrust he causes in his neighbors.

During the post-war years in America there was no broad democratic movement; writers were paralyzed by the McCarthy commission and the inertia of the masses. But the memory of the movement of the thirties which shook America and was reflected in literature was still alive. In these circumstances a pessimistic view of a society self-satisfied with its barbarism and injustice, led American novelists to the philosophy of the absurd, and to desperate attempts to reestablish morality in a world which ridiculed morality. Let us not forget that the French existentialists—Camus and Sartre—took part in the Resistance and kept the concept of "responsibility" as one of their most important categories—and the invisible man in the novel of the black writer Ralph Ellison still feels his responsibility to suffering people after he has gone into the underground, disillusioned with society and the efforts to change it. One must take into consideration the parallel between the Resistance and the thirties, and the fact that the French existentialists strove to provide a general picture of a world where everyone is interrelated, and while doing this they did not show any mercy to American society.

But if in the American novel the contemporary hero rejects the patriarchal world of his childhood (whether it be a quiet backwater in the South, the world of Jewish or Negro poverty) he (and of course the author) constantly feels it behind him. Americans can complain about the low level of culture in their country, but they are less "cut off from their roots" than French writers. And that is why the American novel remains full-blooded and open to reality without turning into a fable or an essay. That is also why existentialist philosophy remains something inorganic in the American novel.

We have seen this in the case of Styron's novel. The reduction of the American situation to the abstract conditions of human existence, the pessimistic stance which precludes high tragedy, and the illustration of philosophical schemes. And illustration such as this is also apparent in Baldwin's *Another Country;* there the depiction of misunderstanding and silent battle between people of different races who love each other boils down to the existence of a "wall" between people and to Sartre's formula for the time of Nazi occupation—"Hell is other people."

In our time interest in Marxism has again awakened in America. The tremendous growth of productivity itself has not at all led to the liberation of man; on the contrary, the ideal mass consumer has turned out to be more standardized and limited than Babbitt; economic progress has merely underlined the narrowness of bourgeois horizons. Marx's philosophical works are perceived as modern; the same alienation that Marx wrote about in the manuscripts of 1844 has assumed its classic form in modern America.

And at the same time the Marxist ideal of a harmoniously developed personality is close to the American tradition; people who are thoughtful about the future of their country cannot overlook this philosophy.

The alienation which has developed in bourgeois society carries with it a rejection of the best features of national character. In *Capital* Marx cites the story of a certain Frenchman who felt himself a "cog" worker in Europe, but he flourished in California, learning various professions. "Because experience has shown me that I am capable of all kinds of work, I feel myself less a mollusk and more a man." The current growth of service occupations has brought to the fore a type of faceless office worker, "other-directed," far from American self-sufficiency pioneer-style. The prevalence of alienation means the preservation of the best in the national character as well.

But if the intellectuals of the thirties read Marx and sometimes expected the promised land to come the next day, the current writers and scholars (with rare exceptions) who are aware that bourgeois forms of life are too narrow and stifling for the people of the West, do not see the way to true freedom and harmony. And such novelists as Styron and Bellow, who boldly criticize American mores and Johnson's politics, cannot part from their pessimistic philosophy: we can see no mass forces in America in which criticism can find support.

The novels we have examined are also typified by these contradictions.

In the evolution of Cass and Herzog we are struck by a switch from merciless rejection to undisturbed calm. But these Dickensian notes reflect the uncertainty of the novels, just as the perplexity of a loner who is searching can be seen beyond Updike's speculations which are limited by their Protestant frame of reference.

In this moral quest—especially in Styron—one is struck by the lack of correspondence between the great sweep and the humble result.

And if Styron and Baldwin know how to look at their country through the eyes of people who are not specially enraptured by its good deeds, they are not free from American limitations. They perceive modern America, the "era of Abundance" as something stable: new horizons for humanity are not visible beyond it. The Marxist method (absolutely alien to the dogmatic pretension that the problems of America were solved a hundred years ago—we mean a method which is unbiased and consistently critical) could free them from metaphysics. And the dialectic posits that America herself be examined in its dynamism and shown as part of a changing world.

If we use Camus' ideas as a starting point, we can better understand the new type of novel which has arisen in America.

He wrote: "The American novel strove to find its unity by reducing man to the elementary or to his external reactions and environment." If Proust chose the internal life, the Americans turned to a depiction of the automation of everyday things, a mechanical external life—to the point of speech repetition in dialogs. "Even in Faulkner, the great writer of this generation, the interior monologs reproduce only the surface of thought." And this, Camus thinks, was in effect a condemnation of reality, a stylization of it. He concludes his speculations on American prose with words about the simple-hearted "innocent" hero typical of it: "He is a symbol of this despair-filled world where unhappy automatons live in their mechanical connections—an artistic world which American novelists have help up to the modern world as a pathetic and fruitless protest.

Of course this juxtaposition of one-sided Americans to Proust, who was not limited in this way, remains a whim of Camus' thought. Naturally, the prose of Anderson and Hemingway which is transmitted through repetitions of the automatic everyday actions, was predominantly psychological and lyrical, not at all a literary variant of the puppet theater. Naturally it did not lose sight of the fact that a whole man was behind a half-alive automaton or striking grotesque—Mark Twain's river of clear rivers, open spaces, and free manners was close to their prose. But Camus was saying what even the American writers of the new generation felt: they felt cramped in the limits of Hemingway's universe; the limitation of the world by these boundaries turned into an obvious stylization—this is how Hemingway's *Across the River and Into the Trees* was perceived; writers strove to broaden the frame of the lyrical novel, going deeper into the inner worlds of their heroes and getting more and more receptive to the life of ideas (the experiments of Camus in *The Stranger* and *The Plague* profoundly interested them).

The American intellectual novel is taking shape before our eyes. It isn't hard to see that the novels are taking up tasks which are new to them, and there is no finality or completeness in their books. But they present a quality which the masters of the Western novel-allegory and the novel-fable do not have...

Of Roger Martin du Gard, Camus wrote: "It is the third dimension which gives depth to his works, makes them somewhat unusual in modern literature." He explained that "passionate or inspired shadows" had replaced living heroes in modern literature, and the Europeans, it seemed, had "lost the secret" of a full-blooded depiction of man (that which the author of the *Thibaud Family* had to perfection).

But this certainly cannot be said of the contemporary Americans. In the postwar novels we see not shadows, but living people; the tragic atmosphere does not preclude humor; the novel preserves its character as a discoverer of the world. It was this combination of freshness and sensitivity to modern misfortunes in the American novel which conquered the Europeans. And it would have lost its own face it it had become cosmopolitanly intellectual and forgotten about its country while doing all this thinking.

It is interesting that last year a novel full of American originality, Truman Capote's *In Cold Blood,* achieved world-wide popularity. A town lost on the Western prairies, a viciously senseless and inevitable murder. This documentary novel recalls Hemingway's famous story "The Killers." But if there the heroes were ominously programmed marionettes, the half-breed Perry Smith, driven to the wall by failures and disillusionments, a son of his time, a dreamer and gold prospecter at heart, is understood and felt as a tragic character. Profoundly American in its situations, grotesque heroes, its pure and simple style, this novel approaches the European novel. And the dreams in which the citizens see murdered bodies, nightmares, ghosts, and the Dickensian humor (a saucy postmistress makes fun of the frightened town)—all this bears witness that the horizons of the lyrical novel are growing broader.*

But in this book—which is very whole—there is no striving to draw a line from what is depicted to the spiritual life of our epoch. In the other American novels which have won world fame one does find this striving; the features of the centaur-novels show through in these books of the first postwar decade too.

In Mailer's and Jones' soldier novels the spiritual theme does not get lost behind the seemingly naturalistic details (or so shortsighted critics thought then), behind the senseless marches, soldiers' fights, and barracks manners. In *The Naked and the Dead* the cruel descriptions are interspersed with the intellectual duels of General Cummings and the rebellious Lieutenant Hearn. In *From Here to Eternity,* beyond the simple-hearted hero, disobedient Prew, one feels the author with another sensibility and totally different historical experience: that is why the reality of the postwar world arises behind the everyday life of a prewar barracks.

Even closer to the novels we have examined is the remarkable book of the Negro writer Ralph Ellison, *The Invisible Man.* It is with good reason that Faulkner and Langston Hughes valued it so highly. Negro life, Negro characters are shown brilliantly; the patriarchal believers, the respectful time-servers made wise by experience, and the lonely rebels. But against the background of this real and colorful life, its tragic aspects presented first of all, the hero, a lonely youth trying to find himself, is an "invisible man," because he does not exist, he is as if invisible to whites—at times he seems fleshlessly-spiritual; and his speculations on the rights of the grain of sand against the flood of history look like variations of the themes of French prose. This book was published in 1952 when there was not even a hint of a Negro Revolution, and the fact that its hero goes from rebellious moods to despair is understandable (all the moreso that he himself dreams of returning from winter hibernation to action).

The very searching and impulses which underlie Styron's, Updike's and

---

*Unfortunately this is not very noticeable in the Russian translation: no more than a third of Capote's novel was published under the title *An Ordinary Murder.* [Author's note.]

Bellow's novels, though they are much indebted to modern European thought and art, have firm American roots. The novelists themselves realize this perfectly well.

Updike recently wrote *(America,* No. 11): "In my opinion there is a basic tension which has been caused by the variety of trends in American literature—its tendency toward its refined European heritage on the one hand and toward mysterious unexplored open areas on the other."*

Of course in the history of American literature this tension has more than once led to artistic synthesis. The original and philosophically dense prose of the romantics—above all *Moby Dick* and *Walden*—remain models for the contemporary generation of novelists as they were for the generation of the twenties.

In the best work of that period closeness to its roots and the joy of discovering a new reality were combined with boldness of thought and psychology in which the Old World and the crisis of Western civilization were both treated. But that time also produced such perfect things as *Winesburg, Ohio* and *The Great Gatsby* which were not understood in all their profundity for a long time.

Foremost in the novel of the sixties is the searching, the impulse, transition. The synthesis has not yet been found. Contemporary American prose is not only the new reality of its country, but also new spiritual persepctive.

Various literary and historical epochs were reflected in the centaur-novels.

One Italian critic wrote of Updike's *Rabbit, Run:* "Thank God standardization has not reduced personality to such levels yet, but it would seem that our time has not yet come." The Americans are among the first to capture important characters in the historical development of the West. We remember what Faulkner said of his Percy Grimm—he was a model for a Nazi before Hitler.

If American novelists know no equal in depicting cruelty and primitiveness in the modern world, they are particularly attracted by the high psychological culture of the Old World. That same book *Rabbit, Run* is written by an author who Proustianly cultivates memory of the past; and the other centaur-novels do not do without retrospection and interior monologue—the almost universal forms of contemporary prose in the West.

But in our day such a fresh posing of moral problems and persistent echo of the Russian classics are not at all so common.

The Negro novelists—Ellison and Baldwin—speak for the oppressed—both black and white. These important talents have blood ties with Dostoevsky—no

---

*Retranslated from a Russian-language magazine prepared by the United States for cultural exchange distribution in the Soviet Union. *[Editor's note]*

one has ever felt the tragedy of insulted virtue and offended pride as he did. The author of *Crime and Punishment* inspired Styron too. Bellow in depicting a moral crisis was striving to touch on Tolstoyan territory.

This echo is helping the American intelligentsia to find itself—contrary to the rapture with prosperity and laudatory official rhetoric. Literature is again discovering the moral truths which were the life-blood of the Russian classics. In its best examples the novel of the sixties continues its job, becoming a school of critical thought and uneasy conscience for Americans. That is why in his programmatical essay Saul Bellow recalled the famous words of Leo Tolstoy—that Truth was his most beloved literary hero.

MENDELSON ON UPDIKE

Moris O. Mendelson (1904-   ) is one of the older Soviet critics of American literature, and one of the few who has actually been to the United States. He joined the Party when he arrived here in 1922, and he emigrated to the Soviet Union in 1931. He has written prolifically, beginning in 1939 with a book on Mark Twain (later editions published in 1958 and 1964). Other books include *Walt Whitman* (1954), *The Life and Works of Whitman* (1965), and an important volume called *The Modern American Novel* (1964). He has written on Hemingway, Faulkner, and Dreiser as well as many other twentieth-century authors.

The section translated here is part of a much longer article from the book *Problems of Twentieth-Century American Literature* (Moscow, 1970), edited by Mendelson, A. N. Nikolyukin, and R. M. Samarin. Apart from Mendelson's article and Nikolyukin's (translated above), the section of this book devoted to recent literature contains: R. M. Samarin, "The Modern Militarist Novel in the USA," J. N. Zasursky, "American Mass Fiction of Conformity," M. M. Koreneva, "Passions According to Tennessee Williams," and O. M. Kirichenko, "Some Trends in Modern American Poetry." Mendelson also contributed a sixty-page article on Fitzgerald, and other critics contributed pieces on Willa Cather, Edith Wharton, Vachel Lindsay, Ring Lardner, Ellen Glasgow, and Thomas Wolfe. The volume also contains V. A. Libman's bibliography of Russian translations of twentieth-century American literature. This helps to make it one of the most important books on American literature yet published in the USSR.

M. O. Mendelson

SOCIAL CRITICISM IN THE WORKS OF
BELLOW, UPDIKE, AND CHEEVER
(On Updike's *Couples*)

The picture of American literature during the sixties is one of extreme variety of color and glaring contradictions.

The realistic trend and the modernistic trend develop simultaneously; books which are openly conformist and reactionary are published alongside works which are sharply critical. Sometimes the same writers come out first with vivid, socially-significant works, and then turn out to be prisoners of retrograde views. For example, the melancholy path of John Steinbeck in the last years of his life is well known—from the marvelous novel *The Winter of Our Discontent* to his shameful defense of the actions of the American imperialists in Viet Nam. In the past decade Saul Bellow, or say, Arthur Miller have published works which are generally antibourgeois in tendency, but occasionally they have aligned themselves with undertakings which were initiated by anti-communist elements. Norman Mailer shows provocatively anarchistic and clearly modernistic inclinations which are a serious shortcoming in his work, but occasionally he throws down his own kind of challenge to those who have power in the United States. John Cheever often composes "diverting" novellas, but he also prints profoundly satirical works. In the works of Cheever the realist—for the basic trend of his works is realism—one perceives an acknowledgement of the amorality of capitalistic higher circles in the United States, and still he has given in to the influence of circles which pursue aims hostile to socialism. Having published the solid exposé novel *From Here to Eternity* at the beginning of the fifties, subsequently James Jones has created a series of surprisingly weak books. If Jones at least remains a productive author, J. D. Salinger has been almost silent for many years now. In his novel *Couples* John Updike raised a problem of great social significance, but, alas, he made his book a semipornographic work.

In a moment of anger this same Updike spoke of the "downright trashiness of present American fiction."* In one review he characterized the latest representatives of American literature as a "scraggly association of hermits, cranks, and exiles," maliciously calling Mailer and Jones "homegrown cabbages loyally mistaken for roses."**

---

*Quoted from a review of Borges. Cited from *New Republic* (Dec. 11, 1965), p. 23.

**John Updike, *Assorted Prose* (New York, 1965), p. 319, p. 318. [In a review of Nabokov's *The Defense. Ed.]*

64

Deepening and developing Ernest Hemingway's well known skeptical judgments of American literature ("We have no great writers . . . When our good writers reach a certain age, something happens to them")[†] Updike writes mournfully: "When ever in prose has slovenliness been so esteemed, ineptitude so cherished . . . . The study of literature threatens to become a kind of paleontology of failure."[*]

We are not inclined to agree completely with Updike's judgments.

There is no doubt that in the fifties the "cold war" undertaken by the higher-ups in the United States of America and the oppression of McCarthyism had the most disastrous effects on the literary life of the country.

True, one can name a few talented novels and, especially, dramatic works, which were published on the other side of the ocean during the first half and the middle of that decade (among them Hemingway's story *The Old Man and the Sea,* Jones' above-mentioned novel, Salinger's novel *The Catcher in the Rye,* the plays of Miller and Tennessee Williams). However, on the whole American literature of this period demonstrably went in an obvious backward direction (especially in comparison with the forties or even more with the thirties when such masterpieces as Steinbeck's *The Grapes of Wrath,* Hemingway's *For Whom the Bell Tolls,* Faulkner's *The Hamlet,* Maltz's *The Underground Stream,* or Wolfe's *You Can't Go Home Again* appeared). In the fifties conformity was possibly more widely developed in the literature of the United States than at any earlier time. Decadent tendencies made themselves felt with increasing influence. Though it grew quantitatively, on the whole ideologically criticism became more degraded—formalistic, Freudian, neo-mythological trends and such like became dominant.

All of this is beyond argument. Nevertheless, let us recall that already on the eve of the sixties there were glimmerings of a change for the better—in one degree or another they can be felt to this day.

The reasons for this well known improvement in the situation of American prose, drama, and poetry must be sought above all in contemporary social conditions. A role is played by the continually intensifying battle (which began in the mid-fifties) of the American Negroes against racial oppression, the growing protest movement in various levels of the country's population (particularly among the students) against the power of reaction, against bourgeois ideals, direct statements against the war in Viet Nam, and the demands of the poor for betterment of the conditions of their existence.

It is true that modern American prose abounds in truly scandalous examples of the degradation of art. There is a furiously growing undergrowth of novels which glorify the bosses of capitalism and murderers in military uniform. An incredibly large part of the production of American publishers is

*Assorted Prose, p. 264. [From a review of Letters of James Agee to Father Flye. Ed.]

made up of works which as a matter of principle deny the ability of man to be man, which persistently urge the reader to believe that everything on earth is chaos and absurdity, that the human soul is only an embodiment of something cut off and devastated.

Updike noted correctly that American critics often defend talentless, craftsmanlike works. Not without basis, he mourns the inability of the multitude of writes in the United States of America to develop their gifts (Van Wyck Brooks often pointed this out).

And today as a whole the American novel cannot be compared in its ideological-artistic merits with the works of the big masters of American prose during the twenties and thirties of our century.

However, this state of affairs and in general the complexity of the situation which has come to be in the literature of the United States of America should not prevent us from seeing that the sixties is a time of change for the better compared to the previous decade. Probably the earliest graphic example of this is Faulkner's novel *The Mansion* (1957) which was published on the eve of this decade, a novel in which (contrary to his prejudices) the writer was able to show with great mastery that among the opponents of the "Snopesism" that he so hated (that is, soulless money-grubbing in its specifically American form) the foremost place was occupied by the Communists.

The end of the fifties and especially the succeeding decade are marked by a beginning of the creative activity of quite a few gifted American novelists, dramatists, and poets. Some of them belong (or belonged) to the older generation—Faulkner, Steinbeck, Caldwell, Hughes. Others became known only after World War II or even quite recently.

In any case the names of Bellow, Updike, Cheever, Mailer, Jones, Killens, Maltz, Bonosski, Grau, Heller and Malamud in prose; Miller, Williams and Albee in dramaturgy; Lowell, Ginzburg, and Levertov in poetry—there are the names of the writers—some of whom (we cannot pass over this in silence) sometimes expressed erroneous opinions on important problems of social life, but who are gifted writers more or less inclined to be critical of bourgeois principles of life, authors who have already done quite a bit and promise more.

Of the writers named (and the list could be expanded) this essay will examine the works of the three prose writers, primarily recent, who it seems to us, have an especially large place in American realistic literature of the last few years.

We have in mind Saul Bellow and John Updike as novelists (their short stories are less interesting) and John Cheever as a story writer.

None of these three authors can be called a member of the most progressive ideas of our time. Yes, Saul Bellow has expressed more than dubious opinions fairly often. Some extremely negative sides in the ideological positions and in the works of Updike and Cheever are readily apparent.

Nevertheless, socio-critical motifs sound persistently in the works of these artists. It is, of course, extremely important to point this out. This task is of no little significance, particularly since American bourgeois critics are most often inclined to consider the work of Bellow, Updike, and Cheever devoid of any significant social meaning. Emphasizing the formal merits of their books, acknowledging at times the artistic value of individual novels or stories of theirs, the literary scholars of the United States are unanimous in depreciating the social significance of the works they analyze.

Herzog, Bellow's best novel (and the one most saturated with social ideas), in which the traditions of critical realism were most clearly apparent, though it got a big press was nevertheless examined as only a mirror of the hero's actions, a hero who was not completely normal and who was extremely limited by belonging to a narrowly Jewish background. American critics see in Cheever primarily a humorous writer of manners. And Updike is often evaluated as a very talented master of words who, however, has nothing to say.

Thus the critic George Steiner wrote of *The Centaur:* "The point to be made about John Updike is tiresomely obvious. The disturbing fact is that one should want to keep making it with each successive book . . . . It is, of course, the gap between formal, technical virtuosity and the interest or originality of what is being said."*

Of the Farm was also perceived by the critics as a work which was truly brilliant in form, but with a total absence of content. It's amusing that in emphasizing this old idea of the poverty of Updike's work in socially significant content from the beginning of his career and even in *Of the Farm,* the magazine *Time* tried to use the writer's own wife's opinion for support. She supposedly said "nothing happens" in *Of the Farm.* **

Let us add that it is not only the conservative press in the United States which is inclined to underestimate the social resonance of Updike's works, but at times even the progressive press. Thus in one of his articles the progressive American publicist Joseph North noted in passing: "No matter what Updike says, life boils down to a quarrel with his mother-in-law."*** North apparently had in mind *Of the Farm* where a middle-aged woman's relations with her son's wife play, as we know, a large role. But after all, this work did not demonstrate that life "boils down to a quarrel with one's mother-in-law." Not at all! At the basis of the novel *Of the Farm* are important observations which touch the life of society.

---

*Kenyon Review (March 1966), p. 268.

**Time (April 26, 1968), p. 55.

***Retranslated from *The Worker.* Editor's note.

* * * * * * * * *

Updike's novel *Couples,* published in 1968, unfortunately does not give one the right to speak definitely of the later development of his work along the lines suggested in *The Centaur* and *Of the Farm.* The new novel leaves a dual impression. On the one hand it seems to bespeak an increased concern of the writer with what is happening in his country, and Updike's criticism sometimes becomes more determined than before.

The writer is not deceived by the material well-being of his heroes. He is not able to comprehend completely the reasons why almost all of the "couples" he depicts live a disgusting life, but at least he doesn't try to prettify the real picture. At the same time the circle of life-phenomena which the author touches on seems annoyingly narrow. A writer who inherited so much from such different artists as Faulkner and Hemingway, the careful eye, the extraordinary gift of expression, the compendious laconism, now offers the reader an obviously padded work full of annoying repetitions, weak stylistic innovations, and simply devoid of psychologically vivid and profound characters. Tiresome, for example, is the detailed description of the parties which these well-to-do provincial Americans arrange without end. The couples are bored with life, they thirst for amusement, but the reader can hardly be attracted by a detailed acquaintance with their not particularly inventive games. Finally, the novel is full of coarsely naturalistic details of the sex life of the heroes and sometimes it borders on pornography.

However, one cannot not take into consideration the fact that the main theme of *Couples* is the total moral collapse of well-to-do Americans, their spiritual degeneration and bestialization.

The two epigraphs of the novel say much. One of them is taken from *The Future of Religions* by Paul Tillich, who has written a great deal in the United states on religious themes. Tillich draws a parallel between contemporary America and decadent Rome. He notes that in our day Americans like the Romans tend to be indifferent to the life of society, a "mood favorable for the resurgence of religion but unfavorable for the preservation of a living democracy."*

The second epigraph is taken from Blok's "Scythians." Updike passes over the call for the "old world" to come to its senses and come to the brotherly "feast of work and peace" which the poem contains. He cites only

---

*It is notable that Updike is not at all certain that the United States has a place even in the "resurgence of religion." Once he said that the Christian religion "is patently shameful, for our life is shameful" *(Time,* April 26, 1968, p. 54). *[Editor's note:* The last quote here is retranslated. Updike said: "They were trying to make Christianity less than a scandal, as Kierkegaard called it. Well, it is a scandal; it's obviously a scandal because our life is a scandal." And it is on page 74, not page 54.]

the threatening lines addressed to the "old world":

> We love the flesh; its taste, its tones
> Its charnal odor, breathed through Death's jaws...
> Are we to blame if your fragile bones
> Should crack beneath our heavy, gentle paws?

It occurs that Updike like some other contemporary American writers (we could name at least James Jones, author of the novel *Some Came Running* [1957] where direct analogies between the United States of our day and degraded ancient Rome arise) is so worried by the fate of his morally degenerate homeland that he looks into the future with obvious horror. Though in *Couples* there are no direct authorial statements on the theme that in the America of our time there is something very similar to Rome on the eve of its doom, one feels that in certain corners of Updike's psyche this thought keeps coming up.

In their essays the American literary scholars, who have written a great deal about Updike's latest novel, scarcely touch on the threads which tie *Couples* and Sinclair Lewis's famed novel of a half-century ago, *Main Street*. However, in a definite sense Updike develops—at a new stage—some of Lewis's motifs.

Let us recall that in his time the author of *Main Street* literally stunned his contemporaries in the United States (and far beyond its borders) with his satirical unveiling of the intellectual and esthetic squalor of the "main people" of his native land. Looking at the United States (not just small American towns like Gopher Prairie which Lewis portrays, but at the "mainstreets" of the country as a whole) through the eyes of Carol Kennicot, who is perhaps not a very far-sighted woman, who is weak-willed, but who still has a living soul, the reader is convinced that rich America is ruled by a wholehearted craving for material well-being (all the interests of the inhabitants of "mainstreet" are subordinated to this) and that besides this, in essence the well-off Americans live a parasitical life—at the expense of the lower classes.

One can point out direct echoes of *Main Street* in *Couples*. Let us recall how Carol is depressed by her awareness that in the typical American town where she settled after her marriage there is nothing which makes the eye happy, that the homes of the local rich people are simply ugly. Piet Hanema, the central hero of *Couples*, is asked, "Why do you build such ugly houses?" And he confesses that there really is nothing attractive about the homes he has built. "I hate my houses," Piet exclaims, "God, how I hate them."

But this is only a detail, and not a totally decisive one. The main thing that Updike has shown is that the residents of typical American towns have become much worse morally than they were half a century ago.

True, in some of his works even Lewis gave us to understand that many Americans from the upper classes not only do not know spiritual demands but are dissolute. Thus, in *Arrowsmith* we read that when the main hero got better acquainted with the "high society" of a certain town where he once lived, he heard something about husbands who " 'spent time' in Chicago, about wives who met young men in New York hotels, and beneath their refined conjugal peace he sensed a seething dissatisfaction."[†]

However, in Lewis's novels this theme did not occupy a particularly significant place. Throughout his creative life that author displayed a well known restraint in discussing it. Not Updike. And the point here is not just the writer's extremely (extremely!) frank treatment of the most intimate facts of his heroes' lives (as we find in very many of his contemporary colleagues in the USA), but also the growing trend (which this writer has noted) of the "main people" of the USA over the last few decades toward maximally amoral behavior.

Let us recall Herzog's self-critical remark that sex plays an extremely big role in his life because under conditions in America it is very hard for him to take part in politics (politics, it goes without saying, in the highest meaning of the word, and not that which is the profession of sly and selfish politicos). And it is as if Updike has made it his goal to prove the correctness of the observation made by Bellow.

In the town of Tarbox where the action of *Couples* takes place, the "cream" of local society are almost totally absorbed by sex, they eagerly change partners, they are busy with pathological "amusements" in the sexual sphere, they give themselves over constantly to new forms of debauchery.

One American critic correctly characterized the heroes of the novel: "They seldom talk about art, literature, philosophy, or even politics. Most of them seem rather unattractive at the outset and grow more so as the novel goes on."[*]

The open contempt for social problems, including the most urgent problems of society, is symbolized in the expressive—and even terrible—scene of the party which the "couples" give on the day of John Kennedy's assassination. As the writer says, they are truly "corrupt couples." And it seems to the novel's main hero Hanema—a man who is to some extent better than his lovers and their husbands—that the "couples" are dancing on the "polished top of Kennedy's casket."

We must add that although of all of the novel's personages Updike is most sympathetic to Piet Hanema, this hero too is not characterized by rich and vivid inner content. As a result, the isolated acute observations he makes about the state of affairs in the United States often seem injected from without—they correspond poorly to Hanema's spiritual possibilities.

And still much in the book makes one stop and think; it has pages which make one react as if touching a naked electric wire. For example, the following words, which express the writer's views, are put in the mouth of the main

Saturday Review (April 6, 1968), p. 21. [Granville Hicks' review. *Ed.*]

hero:

> I think America now is like an unloved child smothered in candy. Like a middle-aged wife whose husband brings home a present after every trip because he's been unfaithful to her. When they were newly married he never had to give presents . . . God doesn't love us any more. He loves Russia. He loves Uganda. We're fat and full of pimples and always whining for more candy.

Talking to a reporter Updike remarked that the couples he had depicted were a "microcosmic middleclass America who do breathe the same moral atmosphere we do, from Berkeley to Boston."*

The author of *Couples* clearly understands that the residents of Tarbox (it is often called Sexbox) are not monsters of unknown origin, not exceptions. In the human fall which Updike describes there is something which is in the highest degree instructive.

Lewis began his *Main Street* with these words:

> This is America—a town of a few thousand, in a region of wheat and corn and dairies and little groves.
> The town is, in our tale, called "Gopher Prairie, Minnesota." But its Main Street is the continuation of Main Streets everywhere. The story would be the same in Ohio or Montana, in Kansas or Kentucky or Illinois, and not very differently would it be told Up York State or in the Carolina hills.

Not a single critic has succeeded in refuting Lewis's assertion.

As we have seen, Updike said something very similar to the declaration of the author of *Main Street*.

Basing themselves on the shortcomings of *Couples,* on the well known imprecision of the author's thought, some contemporary critics in the United States are trying to create the impression that Updike depicted only a very small circle of Americans and reflected untypical and uncharacteristic phenomena. They do not point out, they do not want to point out, that for all of the book's stinging aspect it is nevertheless a mirror of the moral rot taking place in the ruling class of the USA as a whole—a process, to use A. I. Herzen's remarkable words, of "moral murder." The author of *My Past and Thoughts* said that the period of Tsar Nikolai I "killed" not only physically, "not just with its salt mines and white straps," but also with "its suffocating, humiliating atmosphere, its, so to speak, negative blows."** How many of these "negative blows" the capitalistic America of our day inflicts on the souls of its most prosperous, seemingly "well-off" citizens!

We must again emphasize this: neither of Bellow nor of Updike (and the same goes for Cheever) can it be said at all that they start from a completed system of anti-capitalistic principles. They are even further from accepting socialism as the means to make society healthy again.

But these writers' rejection, in their best works, of the peculiarities of the spiritual life in capitalist America is an irrefutable fact. And this should be judged according to its merit.

New York Times Book Review (April 7, 1968), p. 34.

**A. I. Herzen, *My Past and Thoughts,* Parts 4-5 (Moscow, 1967), p. 428. [Herzen was a nineteenth-century Russian social thinker. *Ed.]*

NIKOLYUKIN ON MAILER

A. N. Nikolyukin is a specialist on American romanticism who began writing at the start of the sixties. His major work is a book called *American Romanticism and Modernity* (Moscow, "Academy of Sciences," 1968). The first extensive study of American Romanticism, it contains essays on Freneau, Brown, Irving, Cooper, Melville, Hawthorne, and Poe. Nikolyukin has also published a number of reviews of American literary criticism and co-edited an important volume of essays entitled *Problems of Twentieth-Century American Literature.*

Apparently the earliest mention of Mailer in Soviet criticism is Raisa Orlova's long review article (1960) on American war novels, including *The Naked and the Dead, From Here to Eternity* (published in 1971 in an abridged version in the USSR), and works by Hersey, Appel and others. Next Mailer was discussed along with James G. Couzzens, Kerouac and others in V. Nedelin's "In the Gloom of Psychoanalysis: Freudianism and the Seekers of Anti-ideology" *(Foreign Literature,* No. 10, 1963). In Mendelson's bulky *The Modern American Novel* (Moscow, 1964) Mailer gets three pages, compared to forty pages on Albert Maltz. *An American Dream* was negatively reviewed by Tugusheva in 1967. However, the Soviet attitude to Mailer changed in the later sixties, in connection with his publicistic writing. Notes and reviews on *Cannibals and Christians(Foreign Literature,* No. 2, 1967; *Foreign Literature Abroad,* No. 2, 1967) and *Why are We in Vietnam? (Foreign Literature,* No. 12, 1967) appeared. Brief excerpts from *The Naked and the Dead, The Armies of the Night* and *Cannibals and Christians* were printed in the *Literary Gazette* in 1968. Then a severely abridged translation of *The Naked and the Dead* came out (1970), followed by an abridged version of *Miami and the Siege of Chicago* in *Foreign Literature* at the beginning of 1971.

The essay translated here is from *Problems of Twentieth-Century American Literature* (Moscow, "Academy of Sciences," 1970), pp. 30-48.

A. N. Nikolyukin

REALISM AND MODERNISM IN THE WORKS OF NORMAN MAILER

Among modern American writers Mailer stands out for the determina-
tion, carried to the point of anarchical riot, with which he undertakes to
solve the most urgent problems of contemporary American life: the crisis
of the bourgeois system, the struggle for Negro civil rights, the problem of
violence—the tragedies of today's America stunned by the shots fired in Dallas,
Memphis, Los Angeles and far-off   Vietnam. And though his views have a
vividly marked bourgeois character, this anarchical protest attracts readers in
the United States and beyond its borders to Mailer's works.

Norman Mailer, who won fame soon after the end of World War II with
his novel *The Naked and the Dead* (1948), has created two novels in recent
years—*An American Dream* (1965) and *Why Are We in Vietnam?* (1967)—as
well as several publicistic books in which the writer's socio-political views are
expressed—*Cannibals and Christians* (1966), *Armies of the Night*   (1968).
Mailer changes his political views and evaluations so quickly that it is hard to
keep track of the mental gymnastics of a man who is simultaneously a defender and opponent of Presidents Johnson and Nixon, a preacher of the "sexual
revolution," an opponent of American aggression in Vietnam—but also, along
with this, a vicious anti-communist.

Attempting to characterize the writer's contradictory credo brings to
mind Erskine Caldwell's characterization of the contrasts inherent in contemporary American life: "Total movement. Total petrifaction. Open all night.
Closed for the season. Welcome no matter who you are. White only. Colored
entrance. Incredible wealth and desperate poverty.   Aggression and reaction.
Pious religiosity and unbridled dissolution... Programs of calculated hate and
plans for devoted friendship!"[1]

In his first novel, *The Naked and the Dead,* Mailer created masterful
sketches of the upper and lower echelons of the American army during the
war with the Japanese in the Pacific. The military machine grinds down the
soldier morally, reducing him to a state of psychological nonexistence.
Mailer's book shows the laying of the foundations for militarism, barbarism which has now been seen in such a miserable light in   Vietnam. Today,
therefore Mailer's novel is perceived as a prediction of the dirty war in Vietnam. The strongest indictments in the novel are the portraits of General
Cummings and Sergeant Croft; they have remained among the best accomplishments of American anti-war prose in our time, along with certain heroes

---

[1] E. Caldwell, *Vdol' i poperek Ameriki* (Moscow, 1966), p. 21.

of James Jones and John Hersey.

But already in this the most realistic of all of Mailer's novels the modernist treatment of man makes itself felt, especially in the pictures of the ordinary soldiers. In Chapter Seven of the novel, which is devoted to a description of the battle with the Japanese, the American soldiers are depicted as lost creatures; the fear of battle awakens the basest feelings and thoughts in them. With such material a realistic writer could have created a satirical picture, but in these scenes Mailer does not raise himself above his heroes; in their insignificance he sees what seems to be the norm of human existence—a senselessness which is revealed at the most crucial moments in life, one of which is war. Thus realistic scenes of the battle on a far-off Pacific island are combined with a modernist conception of the helplessness of man in this world. The entire novel is interpenetrated by the existentialist motto, "Live dangerously." This feeling is expressed in various ways in Mailer's characters. Sergeant Croft feels a secret and dark satisfaction when someone from his platoon is killed, "as though the death was inevitably just."[2] "The natural role of twentieth-century man," General Cummings repeats twice, "is anxiety."[3]

General Cummings takes the next further step in justifying what Sergeant Croft simply feels from "within." In the novel he speaks as a preacher of American fascism—one who has taken into account the struggle with communism and Hitler's mistakes and applied the Nietzschean doctrine of the "superman" to the army.

In his lecture to Lieutenant Hearn he states the basis for the necessity of fascism in America: "The concept of fascism, far sounder than communism if you look at it, for it's grounded firmly in man's actual nature, merely started in the wrong country, in a country which did not have enough intrinsic potential power to develop completely."[4] And then Cummings introduces the Nietzschean foundation into this discussion: "There's that popular misconception of man as something between a brute and an angel. Actually man is in transit between brute and God . . . . the only morality of the future is a power morality."[5]

Satire directed against the American army is especially clear in the figure of General Cummings; he declares the fundaments on which the power of the U.S. is built, "The Army functions best when you're frightened of the man above you, and contemptuous of your subordinates."[6] This is the moral-

---

[2] N. Mailer, *The Naked and the Dead* (New York, 1948), p. 444.
[3] *Ibid.*, p. 177, 231.
[4] *Ibid.*, p. 321.
[5] *Ibid.*
[6] *Ibid.*, p. 176.

ity of brute force and military servility. In his instructions to Hearn the General repeats, "The average man always sees himself in relation to other men as either inferior or superior."[7]

The naturalistic picture of the decomposing bodies on the battlefield leads to the concept of human insignificance. "We're all carrion, stinking carrion!" exclaims one of the soldiers on seeing the maggot-filled corpses which for him become the whole embodiment and sum of the meaning of human existence. Here we can already see the future Mailer with his preaching of existential freedom—which leads to a pathological desire to kill.

The Naked and the Dead is rightly considered the first significant American work about the Second World War. Much in Mailer's novel comes from the early Dos Passos, before the evolution which led the latter into the camp of socialism's enemies. Characteristic in this respect are the biographical chapters—reminiscences under the subtitle "The Time Machine." As the American Marxist critic S. Finkelstein notes, the vivid portraits of dozens of soldiers and officers and the biographical sketches cut into the narrative "give the impression of showing American society itself in uniform. And indeed the army of a nation at war is that nation turned inside out, with its secrets exposed."[8] In the novel we see the U. S. Army at its most repulsive. The realistic power of Mailer's early novel helped it to stand the test of time.

Between *The Naked and the Dead* and his books of the sixties Mailer created two novels—*Barbary Shore* (1951) and *The Deer Park* (1955). At the center of *Barbary Shore* lies the conflict between the former Communist (who though leaving the Party does not want to betray the ideas of socialism) and a paid FBI agent named Hollingsworth who is ready for any treachery. As M. O. Mendelson notes, in *Barbary Shore,* "The author demonstrated his Trotskyite sympathies, and simultaneously a simple inability to collect his thoughts. In this and several of Mailer's other books (particularly *The Deer Park)* we see literary impotence which is almost incredible in such a seemingly experienced writer."[9]

The most talented thing that Mailer did in the fifties was his first book of publicistic articles *Advertisements for Myself.* In the most famous essay in the book, "The White Nigger," he creates the figure of an American existentialist hipster who expresses both protest against conformity in the circumstances he lives in, and a sermon preaching violence, irrationalism, and sexual freedom. Mailer's "The White Nigger" reflects the beginning of the disintegration of the beatnik movement as a definite (though extremely limited) kind of social protest.

Ironically paraphrasing Thomas Paine's famous words about the heroic epoch of the American Revolution, "These are the times that try men's souls,"

---

[7]*Ibid.,* p. 176, 322.

[8]S. Finkelstein, *Existentialism and Alienation in American Literature* (New York: International Publishers, 1965), p. 270.

[9]M. O. Mendel'son, *Sovremennyi amerikanskii roman [The Modern American Novel]* (Moscow, 1964), p. 423.

Mailer talks about today's America, "These have been the years of conformity and depression. A stench of fear has come out of every pore of American life."[10]

The moral credo of the hipster which was later embodied in Mailer's novels is expressed in "The White Nigger":

Hip abdicates from any conventional moral responsibility . . . . men are not seen as good or bad [. . .] * but rather each man is glimpsed as a collection of possibilities, some more possible than others [. . .] * and some humans are considered more capable than others of reaching more possibilities within themselves in less time . . . . What is consequent therefore is the divorce of man from his values, the liberation of the self from the Super-Ego of society. The only Hip morality [. . .] * is to do what one feels whenever and wherever it is possible.[11]

Thus he creates a philosophy which justifies any human acts in the sphere of social relations and "individual violence" as an expression of the protest of a personality against the "collective violence" of a state, against the members of society. This philosophy has only one rule—the immediate realization in action of the will of the personality. The denial of moral responsibility leads the "white nigger" to the assertion that it is impossible to foresee the results of our acts, and therefore we cannot know whether we are doing good or evil. The White Nigger is a man outside the law and morality, an underground man, who looks spitefully out of his underground at the hateful and doomed world of contemporary civilization. The Soviet critic V. Nedelin has written the most expressive characterization of this Mailer hero (though, one must admit, Mailer did point out some real features of American reality):

Arrogantly rejecting everything and everyone, without hurrying, with a bitter sneer he wanders about the streets of gigantic cities ready to meet death around any corner or to take a flaring match with which any passerby has lighted a cigarette as a call from fate ordering him to burn down the city. He is ready for anything. He is the only free man, he bears in himself all the fury and love, all the simple-heartedness and all the demonism, all the doom, grief, and irony of today's world.[12]

The ideas expressed in Mailer's publicistic works were soon embodied in the novel *An American Dream.* The book elicited extremely sharp reaction from the American press. But does *An American Dream* only show that "in our culture a writer very soon perishes"[13] as one of the American reviewers

---

[10]N. Mailer,*Advertisements for Myself* (New York, 1959), p. 338.

[11]*Ibid.,* pp. 353-54. [Brackets mark omissions not noted in the Russian translation. *Ed.]*

[12]*Inostrannaia literatura [Foreign Literature]* , No. 10 (1963), p. 209.

[13]*The Progressive* (Feb., 1965), p. 51. *[Retranslated.]*

of the novel wrote? Even Hemingway said that something happens to American writers at a certain age, "They write when they have nothing to say, when the well's gone dry . . . Once they've betrayed themselves they try to justify the betrayal, and we get the usual dose of scribbling."[14][†] But doesn't Mailer's book reflect certain general and deeper tendencies of American reality, including American culture?

Bourgeois historians of American literature see the concept of the ideal American society—the so-called American dream—as the basis of the national tradition in literature. Frederick Carpenter, author of *The American Dream and Literature* (1955) considers that the manner of thinking and feeling to which this national tradition gave birth defined the form and content of American literature. He examines the history of American literature from the War of Independence to our day from this point of view.

And what had the "American dream" turned into by the middle of the twentieth century? With a title which promised so much, it seemed, Mailer was called to give an answer to this question. If at the beginning of the nineteenth century the "American dream" still had some socio-historical basis (though the most prescient minds saw its illusoriness even then), in the era of Imperialism and socialist revolutions the reactionary utopian essence of this idea became obvious. However, the number of preachers of the "American dream" not only did not decrease in our time, on the contrary, it rather increased. Grafting the most whimsical views onto this abstract concept, they use the idea of the "American dream" to pursue concrete political, philosophical and esthetic goals.

The hero of Mailer's first novel, General Cummings, saw the concept of "healthy" fascism as the embodiment of the "American dream." "America is going to absorb that dream, it's in the business of doing it now," he says to his subordinate Hearn.[15] The hero of *An American Dream,* Stephen Rojack, is the embodiment of the idea that this dream can be fulfilled only by a man who frees himself totally from the burden of morality and responsibility and enters the world of existential freedom, striving to turn his repressed impulses and drives into life. Crime without punishment—that is the ideal of the new man in the new world. That is the last word in American existentialism, that is the "attractive" prospect which it opens up before a surprised humanity!

Stephen Rojack is an intellectual murderer. He is a professor of existential philosophy at NYU and author of the popular book *The Psychology of the Executioner*—a study of various types of executions in various countries. Preaching freedom of action, "the freedom to make choices" as the existentialists say, Rojack—like his prototype the "white nigger"—tries to resurrect

---

[14]E. Hemingway, *Sobranie sochinenii [Collected Works]* (Moscow, 1968), II, 307.

[15]*The Naked and the Dead,* p. 321.

the teaching of the well known Marquis de Sade. In Mailer this doctrine assumes a universally sexual form: "All men and women have absolute but temporary rights over the bodies of all other men and women."[16] Using precisely this power, Rojack strangles his wife, throws her body onto the street from the tenth floor, and then immediately, before the police arrive, possesses the maid, and then seeks inner harmony in the arms of a popular nightclub singer named Cherry. In these scenes cruelty and violence are blended with the peculiar existential irony with which the author views his heroes. It is sometimes hard to say if he is condemning Rojack or admiring him. The writer leaves "freedom of choice" to the reader.

From the very beginning the philosophy of death occupies a major place in the novel. After a series of failures in life, Rojack notices his growing desire to commit suicide, which then unexpectedly finds outlet in the murder of his wife, for "murder contains something of exhilaration and sex"[17] in it. But suicide, Rojack reasons, is insufficiently sexual, and therefore it does not attract him as much as murder, which "gives one a feeling of relief and calm," a kind of physiological outlet essential for a man who has stored up too much energy.

Bourgeois criticism views *An American Dream* as a reflection of the "sexual revolution" which America is currently undergoing. However, by no means does this always presuppose a positive evaluation of Mailer's novel. On the contrary, the reviewer for *The Spectator*, A. Alvarez, condemns the "sexual exhibitionism" of Mailer who "writes as if he had just invented the orgasm."[18]†

The problem of crime without punishment posed in *An American Dream* is connected to Mailer's concept of the role of violence in contemporary society. In an interview published under the title "Living Like Heroes" he said:

> I believe there is a way in which a man's personality can die before his time, and that is worse than being killed in a concentration camp, because—and this is where I am optimistic—if a man is killed in some most unjust way, then this will be taken account of in eternity; but if one's death isn't dramatic, if one is extinguished day by day by the society in which one lives, then one loses one's chance of eternity.[19]

The contemporary world is divided into those who beat and those who get beaten, Mailer says with cynical objectivity. Some like to do the beating, others prefer to be beaten. Different people like different things. Such is freedom of choice, such is the contemporary alternative in Mailer's book *Canni-*

---

[16]N. Mailer, *Advertisements for Myself,* p. 354.

[17]N. Mailer, *An American Dream* (London, 1965), p. 16. [Retranslated. Mailer actually says, "Murder, after all, has exhiliration within it," and "murder offers the promise of vast relief. It is never unsexual. " Editor's note.]

[18]*The Spectator* (May 7, 1965), p. 603.

[19]*New Statesman* (Sept. 29, 1961), p. 444.

bals and Christians. Here the writer tells about the "existential effect" of narcotics on him. Smoking marijuana man feels the significance of each separate moment of existence. Infinite nothingness opens up before him, and, continues Mailer: "The nothingness in each of us seeks to attack the being of others, the way our being in turn is attacked by the nothingness in others. I'm not speaking now of violence or the active conflict between one being and another. That still belongs to drama. But the war between being and nothingness is the underlying illness of the twentieth century. Boredom slays more of existence than war."[20] *An American Dream* was written based on these philosophical positions. Its cruel existentialist heroes are unthinkable outside the contemporary epoch, just as it would be impossible to imagine the face of present-day America without those who created it—that participant in World War II, former Congressman Rojack and his father-in-law, the financial magnate Kelly.

Rojack's flight from inner isolation leads him to the end of the novel in the jungles of South America, to primordial nature. In his vain quest for the "American ideal" he reaches toward ever newer horizons; he imagines fabulous cities where at last he will be able to find himself. He first sees these fabulous cities when he is strangling his wife Deborah, and then again when he is raping the German maid, a former Nazi. Finally, the dream of fabulous cities takes him from New York to the deserts of Nevada where at 5:00 A. M. the sky is illuminated by the white flash of an atomic explosion on a test site. This kind of life—bordering on death (thus he is so concerned with the problem of cancer as symbolic self-destruction)—leads Rojack to himself, and the author as well, who once declared that he would "lose my sense of life if I stayed sober very long."[21†]

Then the illusion of America, the "land of freedom and happiness," turns into a flight from it. And this is the real embodiment of the "American ideal" today. Mailer's novel thus definitely sums up the two-hundred year-old quest for the "American dream" begun as early as the "fathers of the American Revolution" and so depressingly completed by their wayward children of the twentieth century.

The reviewer of the *New York Times Book Review* juxtaposes *An American Dream* with *An American Tragedy,* as a sequel to Dreiser's novel, one written forty years later. "But while Dreiser's Clyde Griffiths languishes, a passive victim of the system to the last, Rojack finds the beginnings of liberation in his deed."[22] "Tragedy" is transformed into "dream" thanks to the energetic acts of Mailer's hero. Thus bourgeois criticism adapts Mailer to its theories, and attempts to oppose Dreiser's failure-hero to Mailer's murderer-optimist as the latest achievement of American genius.

---

[20]N. Mailer, *Cannibals and Christians* (New York, 1966), p. 214.

[21]*Cosmopolitan* (August, 1963), p. 63.

[22]C. Knickerbocker, *New York Times Book Review* (March 14, 1965). p. 36.

For all the emotional tension of the narrative manner, in many respects *An American Dream* definitely shows the writer's retreat from the realistic manner of his first book. In Mailer the treatment and understanding of man as he flails about the jungles of New York begins to look like modernistic disintegration of consciousness. Man stands on the edge of an insane world and can no longer distinguish between the normal and the schizophrenic. This process so interfuses *An American Dream* that it extends not only to the novel's system of imagery, but is also reflected in the style, the narrative language. Like William Burroughs' modernistic novel *Naked Lunch* which had appeared a few years earlier (it was the most obvious embodiment of the crisis of the neo-avantgarde), whole pages of *An American Dream* read like the stenographic record of a paranoiac's delirium. In the final analysis this psychic seismograph pouring out in an uninterrupted flood reflects definite life impressions and emotions, but in an extremely obscure, modernistically distorted form.

The novel culminates with a scene in which the hero wanders through the Nevada desert. At the side of the deserted road he sees a telephone booth and a telephone with a rusted dial in it. He calls Cherry, the only creature to whom he is tied by any warm human relations. And there in the moonlit desert, symbolizing the loneliness of man in our world, the voice of his beloved rings out: " 'Hello, hon. I thought you'd never call... Marilyn says to say hello. We get along...' Hung up and walked on back to the city."[23]

In coded form this final scene is supposed to mean that when he cuts himself off from people Rojack senses isolation, the superfluousness (to him) of the society he has lived in until now; and he has entered into direct communion with the supernatural world, after which he has again returned to living people.

The ironic element we see in this scene is characteristic of Mailer's narrative manner. It is as if irony helps the writer to destroy reality's defined contours, which he hates. Much in the novel is intended to create in the reader a sense of the unreality or the undefined nature of what happens in the realm of the feelings and real human interrelationships. Defined existence gives way to a flow of being which cannot be stopped and molded, for by stopping on one instant or fact the writer can lose this eternal flow of existence which he considers the main thing in an artistic work. This is the esthetic conception of the book; it destroys the real picture of reality in its effort to transmit fleeting human impressions.

In *An American Dream* there is a scene when Rojack is walking on the parapet of a thirty-story building, balancing on the brink of life and death. Twice the writer returns to this situation, as if striving to emphasize its central meaning in the novel. Like a tightrope walker, Mailer himself balances between exposes of and glorification of the rottenness of modern America.

---

[23]*An American Dream,* p. 271.

Having begun his political career like Rojack by supporting the progressive bourgeois politician Wallace for president in 1948, Mailer constantly vacillates in his social and political sympathies. In his work he jumps from realism to modernism (which cannot satisfy him either). If in the press recently one can read more and more often about him being persecuted by the powers that be for his part in anti-war demonstrations, his declarations against the Vietnam adventure, in the realm of art Mailer's protest manifests itself in the form of an existential "shocking" of his readers.

With "existential whimsy" as he himself calls it, Mailer approaches even the major problems of contemporary life, including the problem of the Vietnam war. The title *Why Are We in Vietnam?* was intended to create a sensation, it was a calculated use of the big and important theme which now concerns all humanity. But the reader will be disappointed if he believes this attractive title.

Mailer's book is devoted not to the Vietnam war, but to hunting—a theme about which many of the books of Cooper, Melville, Faulkner and Hemingway are written. However, it would be in vain to search for the democratic traditions of these writers in Mailer's book. The Texas millionaire Rusty Jethro heads for Alaska to hunt bear. With him is his sixteen year-old son Ronald, who calls himself D. J., and his son's friend Gotfried Hyde, usually called Tex. The story is told by D. J. who says of himself that he is a disc-jockey whose record program reaches the whole world. At fifteen he had read the Marquis de Sade and the novels of William Burroughs about homosexuals and now he hurries to share his knowledge with the whole world.

The novel opens with a radio show from Dallas, Texas, run by D. J. What does this voice from the city which has become famous all over the world for the "crime of the century" want to tell the world? He announces that somewhere in the sky "for each of us there is a record player which takes down all our words and deeds."[†] It is for this "higher reason" that D. J. conducts his program. Each chapter is preceded by an introduction like the chapters called "The Time Machine" in *The Naked and the Dead*. Citing the artistic manner of James Joyce, the writer now strives to escape the framework of realistic narration and "smooth out" the time of the action. In *Why Are We in Vietnam?* one can observe the disintegration of artistic form in the novel as a result on one hand of the modernistic play with the novel (the narration is done with intentional indefiniteness), and on the other hand a parody (and self-parody) of the style of the modern American novel.

The events described in the novel are as if seen by an adolescent who is discovering the attractive and seductive sphere of sex for the first time. The description of life in the family of the Texas Jewish millionaires is done with a special sexual jargon. If we agree to view all Mailer's sexual lexicon as professional medical terminology, one can see in the book, as in Burroughs' novels, a semidelirious study from the realm of sexual psychopathology.

While the novelists of the past or the best writers of our day have created or are creating the image of the social man, Mailer strives to create the "sexual man." It is not important to the writer who his hero is and what his position in society is, but what he is in a sexual respect. Not in vain did the American reviews consider that in his novel Mailer had broken all records for the use of indecent language. The reviewer for the *New York Times Book Review,* Anatole Broyard, wrote of the novel:

> In the good old times novelists treated sex as a meaningful manifestation of character conditioned by the entire development of the action. Now in books one finds sex without any connection to the action at all, not even connected to bed, like the words that are written on fences.[24†]

Even the Negro problem comes up in the novel in sexual form. D. J. considers that soon the time will come when sex matches will be held on TV, and anyone can watch the spectacle, as they now watch hockey or football. Perhaps he or his friend Tex will make the semifinals and compete with some white or black beauty. "Only thing holding this scheme back," worries D. J., "is the problem of integration."[25]

D. J.'s ideas about sexual freedom are not new. America is flooded with pornographic books glorifying "love for all," so called "voyeurism." A few years ago *Roman Orgy* was a bestseller in this line, the author of it hid beneath the pseudonym Marcus von Heller. Of such novels with flashy titles like *The Hot Flesh of the Young, The Bed of the Forbidden, Naked Nymphs on the Rancho,* the well known American publicist Herbert Aptheker wrote: "There is no doubt that in our country the debasement of man to the level of an animal is done systematically and with premeditation. The set goal is the befogging of the consciousness, the increasing of the senselessness, the negation of science, logic and truth. This brings with it cynicism and sadism. And in the final analysis—fascism."[26]

D. J. is his father's son and only repeats in a new form what Rusty maintains—his basic ideas about modern life are reducible to the rules:

> White women and Negroes are free and live with each other. The Yellow race, Africans, and adolescents including his own son are no longer subservient. Europeans hate Americans. Communism attracts the sympathies of all failures...[27†]

---

[24] *New York Times Book Review* (Sept. 17, 1967), p. 4. [Or, to give it in the original:

> In the goody-good old days, the novelists were forced to treat sex as a meaningful act. To be punishable, it had to be part of the development of character, to occur in a context of inevitability. Now sex occurs in no context whatever—not even a bed—and it is about as meaningful as Berkeley students shouting four-letter words over a loudspeaker.

Editor's note.]

[25] N. Mailer, *Why Are We in Viet Nam?* (New York, 1967), pp. 109-110.

[26] G. Apteker, *Voina protiv razuma [War Against Reason], Literaturnaia gazeta [Literary Gazette],* Sept. 17, 1969, p. 8.

[27] *Why Are We in Viet Nam?,* p. 110. [Again Nikolyukin cuts the original

82

A collection of hackneyed ideas excuses the contemporary businessman from the necessity of thinking.

The young hippy D. J., when examined, turns out to be an oversimplified edition of the master of American life—the Texas millionaire. However, the writer tries to present his hero as a more significant, literarily acclimatized hero. If in the beginning D. J. compares himself with Huck Finn, then later he plays the role of Holden Caulfield, or the two-faced, eternally changing Dr. Jekyll (thus, in a specific case, he decodes his initials). D. J. agrees to be whoever one wants—even Jack the Ripper, only not himself. Discussing the idea that someone there, above, is registering everything that happens here, he says:

> I, Ranald, S-and-S Jethroe, working as D. J., may be trying to trick Number One Above, maybe I'm putting false material into this tape recorder, or jamming it—contemplate![28]

The likening of the hero to the hippies doesn't explain much, because this concept has long ceased to mean anything definite. At one time the "hippy" was identified with a non-accepting youthful audience. Now one can find the assertion that a hippy is simply anyone who loves mass performances of modern dances. The original hippies when journalists started the uproar over them in the mid-sixties have dispersed; the "flower children" returned to school when the next semester began. Those who were left no more corresponded to the notion of "hippy" than those who abandoned their ranks. And still the movement exists. They are directly guided by the well-rooted representatives of the Bohemia who talk so much about "the movement." The name the "loving crowd" is as appropriate to the movement as any other. Yes, the "loving crowd" is tied to the American Bohemia, and it flourishes where life is easiest. For example, in California, especially among the "teenagers" (youths from thirteen to nineteen), and not just those who have dropped out. Children from respectable families also belong. Among them are also college teachers who wear long hair and whose wives love to show off their clothes and all of those who read the student magazines of San Francisco and Berkeley.

Soap bubbles burst in each of the eleven chapters which make up Mailer's novel. It seems the author has pretentions to nothing more than tricks like the initials D. J., nor does he pretend to deal with serious political questions. The whole world and all its problems—is nothing more than a soap bubble, and the faster it breaks the funnier it will be!

---

without noting it. The original reads:

(1) The women are free. They fuck too many to believe one man can do the job. (2) The Niggers are free, and the dues they got to be paid is no Texas virgin's delight. (3) The Niggers and the women are fucking each other. (4) The Yellow races are breaking loose. (6) The adolescents are breaking loose including his own son. (7) The European nations hate America's guts. (8) The products are no fucking good anymore. (9) Communism is system guaranteed to collect dues from all losers.

[28]*Why Are We in Vietnam?* p. 26.

The basic changes in the work of Mailer over the last two decades are indubitable: the realistic tendencies which appeared in *The Naked and the Dead* give way to modernistic experiments in *An American Dream* and a progressively disintegrating form in the book about Viet Nam.

But what kind of novel is this in which the heroes leave for Vietnam on the last page? Yet another book about the currently popular hippes in America, or a meditation on what led America to shame in the Vietnam war? Isn't the unbridled and indecent story about hunting in the mountains of Alaska reminiscent of what the Americans are doing in Vietnam? After all, D. J. and Tex head for Vietnam as if on holiday, as if on a merry hunt for a new big grizzly. And in general if people like the millionaire Rusty govern the country, is it surprising that they scorch the Vietnamese land with napalm, that they kill women, children, old people? To all these questions the writer gives no direct answers, but they are felt in the context of the novel.

In recent years Mailer has come out rather actively against American militarism. His participation in the fall of 1968 in the march of the freedom fighters on the Pentagon is a very clear example of Mailer speaking out against the dirty war in Vietnam. In the spring of 1968 Mailer's novel-reportage about this demonstration of thousands against militarism and the war—*Armies of the Night*—was published. It is the story of how on October 21-22 in 1967 thousands of participants in the anti-war movement (the "new Left") organized the "march on the Pentagon." As a result of the clash with the police many hundreds of demonstrators were arrested, including the author himself.

Publicistic and novelistic forms are intertwined organically in the book. Its subtitle—"History as Novel, Novel as History" is called upon to reflect unity. The anti-fascist tendencies of *The Naked and the Dead* are echoed here in the anti-militaristic declarations of these days. It is a book about the American opposition, about the intelligentsia, the students, the Negroes, the youth who personify protesting America today. However, it is not accidental that in Mailer the working class is absent. Apparently here we have the fashionable conception of bourgeois sociology, of "left" radicalism, tied today to the name of Herbert Marcuse—about the contemporary proletariat's loss of the determining role in social development.

The movement of the American "new Left," to which Mailer himself sometimes belongs, occasionally condemns the capitalist system as a whole; but their positive program is characterized by extreme vagueness. However, there are also people in the civil rights movement who, as they participate in the battle for negro civil rights and speak against the war in Vietnam, are gradually freeing themselves from ideological errors.

Characterizing the "new Left" movement, the General Secretary of the Communist Party of the USA, Gus Hall, talking to the *Pravda* correspondent said:

> They are people rising up against the existing order of things, but they are still not conscious, ideologically tempered fighters... In other words, they are people who see the diseases of the system, but they still do not understand that all of these

diseases are part of the system, a product of the system. They rise up against these diseases, evils, but not against the system itself; and they are not yet real revolutionaries. I consider that patience is essential, understanding of the positive sides of this youth movement is essential. From a movement of rejectors like this one can borrow the resources for a revolutionary movement; it can grow and it can direct these moods. And instead of condemning these people, I consider that we should consider it our role to win them over to the Marxist-Leninist revolutionary position.[29]

In Mailer's most recent publicistic books, *The Presidential Papers* and *Cannibals and Christians,* one of the most sensitive problems of America in the middle of the twentieth century keeps coming to the surface constantly— the Negro problem. Not in vain did the special commission created by President Johnson to establish the reasons for the race disorders in America conclude in the spring of 1968 that the country was on the way to creating two societies—one black, one white, separate and hating each other.

The Negro problem has the attention of all thinking America. Debates go on in university auditoriums, campgrounds, on the streets of the cities caught up in Negro disorders. In a special issue of *Newsweek,* under the title "The Negro in America," the editor, Osborn Ellison, admits that the reason for "race disorders" was that America can not guarantee many citizens, especially the Negroes, that degree of equality which the "American idea" (i.e., official propaganda) declares: " . . . whites have yet to show their committment to social justice for the Negro. And Negroes, out of deepening despair that whites will ever do so, are falling more and more into a mood of angry disillusion called 'thinking black'," writes Ellison, and this means "Huey Newton and his rage—a rage so blinding he can look on white America comfortably only through the cross-hairs of a gun. 'A gun makes me immediately equal to anyone in the world,' he declared . . . The old leaders are neutralized, so despondent is their mood . . . . into their places come the new leaders, most of them young, some of them mad, others quite lucidly sane, and all of them united on the point that black pride and black power in some form are the absolute prerequisites for black equality. And the new leaders, unlike the old, can speak to the angry, alienated ghetto underclass."[30]

Reflecting a similar mood, the well known Negro writer James Baldwin writes: "White America appears to be seriously considering the

[29]*Pravda* (July 5, 1968).

[30]*Newsweek* (November 20, 1967), pp. 23-24. [Actually the passages quoted are from pp. 37-38, and they include parts of the general article as well as Ellison's editorial remarks. Nikolyukin omits "others quite lucidly sane" and puts quotation marks around "black pride" and "black power." Editor's note.]

possibilities of mass extermination..." ("A Question of Committment").[31] This is the source of the direct calls for Negroes to be against all whites in general, attempts to substitute purely nationalistic demands for the social and political demands of the American Negroes who fight for their civil rights.

We find an especially sharp posing of the question of "two races in every city" in the statements of today's Negro nationalists. Thus the Negro poet and dramatist Leroi Jones said after the bloody events of the Newark summer of 1967:

> The black man was here on this planet first, and he will be here long after the white man is gone . . . I don't think we need any white people in there except at the request of the black people. Otherwise it's some kind of unnatural situation. In Newark, people come in this town during the day and make money and take it out again. That's unnatural. It's just another colony...

And to the question of the interviewer "Will Newark become an all-black town?" Leroi Jones answered: "I think so, because as the political strength comes, a lot of people who would not even consider being ruled by black people, even if it was done under their so-called American system, would just panic."[32]

Comparing the Negro movement with the struggle of the "new Left," Gus Hall said:

> Here again we run into an analogous situation. The movement has its place, but it does not always develop along class lines. Among a certain part of the Negro movement, for example, elements of nationalism can be observed. Nationalism plays an extremely important role in this stage of the movement, and in our opinion it is a positive factor playing a positive role. It is this nationalism that united the Negro people in the struggle against the system of de facto slavery imposed on it by capitalism.
>
> But in this case too it is clear that there are definite elements which are arriving at erroneous conclusions, conclusions about the necessity of complete separation from the whole country; they come to the conclusion that they must oppose all whites as a whole. These elements do not understand the role of classes, they do not understand the significance of the class struggle and the fact that precisely capitalism generates the existing system of oppression and exploitation.[33]

Norman Mailer too has taken part in the discussion of "black power" which has developed in the last few years around the "new Left." In an essay which appeared in the *Partisan Review* he wrote:

> ...this Negro does not want equality any longer, he wants superiority, and wants it because he feels he is in fact superior . . . a feeling of vast superiority is beginning to grow in the black man, and the antenna of his superiority lead not to

[31] *New York Times Book Review* (June 2, 1968), p. 2.

[32] *Evergreen* (December, 1967), pp. 96-97.

[33] *Pravda* (July 5, 1968).

developing the Negro to a point where he can live effectively as an equal in white society, but rather toward developing a viable modern culture of his own, a new kind of civilization. This is the real and natural intent of Black Power.[34]

As is clear from this statement, Mailer seems to join with the position of the Negro nationalists and their demands for the separation of white and black. The events of recent times, especially the united conference in Oakland, California—organizers and participants of which were the Negro nationalistic organization called the Black Panthers, the Students for a Democratic Society, and the Communist Party of the USA—have shown that the slogans of opposition to reaction and racism are more and more unifying the representatives of the most varied social organizations in America. "The conference demonstrated the retreat from nationalism," noted H. Aptheker, a participant and one of the leaders of the American Communist Party, "a turning to the understanding of the basic significance of the working class, to an awareness of the invaluable importance of theory in general and Marxist theory in particular, and also the necessity of maximally broad unity of all democratic, anti-racist and progressive forces, independently of the color of their skin."[35]

In his books Mailer strives to impress upon his readers the constantly changing face of the country, the antagonism of the Negroes and whites, to convey the anarchism of the "new Left" and the eccentricity of the preachers of the "sexual revolution." This is an effort to chase after the most fashionable winds of American life. Mailer's "left radicalism" often in fact turns into conformism, acceptance of the contemporary bourgeois America which the writer is ostensibly rejecting. The spiritual poverty of America has found its reflection in the latest novels of Mailer. More than that, they themselves bear the stamp of this impoverishment of spirit.

The crisis of the American spirit and, speaking more broadly, the inability of bourgeois America to produce ideas which would attract the younger generation which is beginning its life in the second half of this century is becoming more and more obvious every year—and not just in the United States but on the other side of the Atlantic.

One of the most successful representatives of the French "new novel," Michel Butor, in his book *Mobile; étude pour une représentation des Etats-Unis* (Paris, 1962) created the image of a country racing recklessly ahead and nevertheless standing in place, an image of an America which has become spiritually poorer in comparison with past periods, periods which are introduced into the pages of this novel-reportage freely in the form of ancient Indian chieftains, the first European colonists, the first scientists and writers of America, the historical documents of long past days.

In this novel the measured and unhurried diction of the great Americans of the past—the letters of Thomas Jefferson, the autobiography of Benjamin

---

[34]*Partisan Review* (Spring, 1968), pp. 219-220.

[35]*Pravda* (October 30, 1969).

Franklin—are juxtaposed to the spasmodic sentences which do not permit an image to be made, to the plays of associations and American "progress" as ends in themselves. Even the arguments between the two sides in the trial of the "Salem witches" become sensible when compared to today's soulless age.

From the past to the present, from modernity to the bygone, such is the changing, fragmented form of Butor's narration. "What attracted Butor specifically to this form?" asks the Soviet scholar of the new novel, T. B. Balashova. "Of course, first of all the possibility of switching movement— all the roads of America and the roads of history. The movement during which the contrasts, brought close by the speed, speak for themselves; and the race of time becomes the march of History. The evolution of the centuries, the evolution of humanity interests the author of *Mobile.*"[36]

The stylistic devices of Mailer's most recent books are rather close to the techniques of the "new novel." Turning to the past allows one to emphasize the contradictions of the contemporary development of the USA more graphically. And although the national peculiarities of the novel in France and the USA leave a decisive stamp on each of the separate books, the points of approach in the artistic interpretation of reality, especially on similar— American—material, allow us to see more clearly the socio-critical motifs in the works of contemporary authors of various countries, and along with this their limitations.

At the end of 1968 Mailer published a new publicistic book on the pre-election conventions of the Republican and Democratic parties, which took place in the summer of that same year. *Miami and the Siege of Chicago* is the title of this reportage on the events which had strong repercussions in the world press in connection with the presidential elections. Here with especial lucidity the crisis of the neo-avantgarde became manifest, its ideology and practice, the embodiment of which is Mailer himself. And the press keeps bearing new stories about Mailer making a movie about the "sexual revolution" or writing about the flight of the first Americans to the moon.

---

[36]T. Balashova, *Frantsuzskii roman 60-kh godov [The French Novel in the Sixties]* (Moscow, 1965), p. 78.

LEVIDOVA ON McCULLERS

Inna M. Levidova is the head bibliographer at Moscow's Library of Foreign Literatures. She is author of a three-part annotated bibliographical survey called *Artistic Literature in the USA* (1958-60, 1961-64, 1964-67), one of the few sources—titles printed in English—that gives one an idea of the kinds of acquisitions made by an elite library in the USSR. Levidova has compiled other bibliographies, including those devoted to Sinclair Lewis and Arthur Miller. Her brief survey of Soviet criticism of *The Centaur* is published below. She has written a number of articles and reviews on modern American poetry and fiction, including "On American Poetry in Our Day" *(Foreign Literature,* No. 9, 1966) and "The Novel at the Center of Arguments" *(Questions of Literature,* No. 5, 1967). Of particular interest for the beginning of the sixties and the new Soviet attitude toward American literature was her "Lost Souls" *(Questions of Literature,* No. 10, 1960), a very long article (and the first to discuss such subjects seriously) on Kerouac, Salinger and Capote. She has also written intelligently on Steinbeck, Faulkner, Malamud and Baldwin. American specialists who have read this anthology in manuscript (and a few other translated items available) have singled out Levidova's work as not less tendentious than other Soviet criticism, but particularly well informed and logical. Presumably her easy access to the collection at the Library of Foreign Literature is one reason for this. Judging by her work it would seem Levidova has visited the United States, because she avoids the amusing errors about *realia* which certain other Soviet critics make.

McCullers was first mentioned in a brief note on *Clock without Hands* in *Foreign Literature* (No. 1, 1962), followed by a long review in *Questions of Literature* (No. 10, 1962) by Raisa Orlova. Three of her stories appeared between 1964 and 1966, and E. Golysheva's translation of *Clock without Hands* appeared in an edition of 115,000 copies in 1966 (Moscow, "Young Guard" Publishing House). Levidova's survey-review was published in *New World* (No. 10, 1966).

I. Levidova

CARSON McCULLERS AND HER LAST BOOK

The literature of the South is a "country within a country" in the national literature of the United States. It is easy to recognize a book by a true Southerner—the colors are thicker, the shadows deeper, the lines sharper and more whimsical. Cruelty and humor, coarse earthiness and poetic phantasmagoria, the naivete of folklore and psychological complexity—many things blend together completely in this bright, explosive tradition with its dazzling surprises. On the whole it is a very young tradition, the age of Faulkner and Thomas Wolfe, but in its distant origins it is tied to the romantic-grotesque element in Edgar Allen Poe.

Among contemporary Southerners (some of whom—Faulkner, Truman Capote, Flannery O'Connor—are already known to the Russian reader) Carson McCullers occupies a special place, though the critics have often compared her to these writers, as well as many others, beginning with Flaubert. It seems to me that Carson McCullers' peculiarity consists of the fact that unlike the other Southerners, she is a reflective artist, quiet, strictly limiting herself to her definite themes and repeating motifs. But this is not rarified "chamber" literature; within the bounds of her artistic and real-life experiences she "digs" deeply, she has a steady eye and an uncompromising intellect.

McCullers' work has always caused controversy. And even now when her reputation is established and superlatives are regularly found on the dust-jackets of her books, there are critics who absolutely refuse to accept the world she creates: "The strange, fierce landscape of Carson McCullers, "a world inhabited by people who are lost, prodigal, unfortunate, demonic..." But regardless of how one relates to it, this world does *exist;* it has become part of the spiritual life of those who have discovered her works.

It is not surprising that the publishing house "Young Guard" decided to publish a translation of *Clock without Hands,* Carson McCullers' last novel, finished in 1961 after ten years of work interrupted by long and painful illnesses (now the author is an invalid, she can hardly get out of bed, but she continues her literary work). Begun in the fifties when in the American South the first steps in the movement for civil rights were just underway, and published in an era of many thousands of marches, true battles for democracy —this novel is interesting in itself and as a landmark in the development of Carson McCullers the writer. But it is a shame that our first meeting with this artist did not take place on the pages of her first, and in the opinion of many most significant work, the novel *The Heart is a Lonely Hunter,* with which in 1941 the twenty-two year-old Southerner who had recently arrived in New York immediately found a place in the most important American prose of the twentieth century. It was an imperfect book, perhaps somewhat too over-loaded, here and there compositionally weak—but a work which truly caught one up in its stern penetrating lyricism, power, and the precision of the author's psychological imagination, her ability to depict everyday life in all its concrete, tangible details—without weakening the unity of conception.

The book is set in an unnamed industrial town in Georgia (Carson Smith, the future Carson McCullers, was born in just such a town—Columbus) at the end of the thirties. The Depression has put its dirty-gray mark on the life of the inhabitants of the suburbs, on the workers, on the factory hands, on the poverty of the Negroes. A war is on in Europe; and though few of the ordinary people give any special thought to it, a dull menace hangs over the town. Unrelenting social enmity softly bubbles under the surface, occasionally breaking loose in ugly bloody encounters. All this is not background of the book, but its essence, its atmosphere; but the heart of the novel lies in some-thing else. McCullers had originally called it *The Mute;* the title *The Heart is a Lonely Hunter,* which in itself sounds somewhat mannered, was given to it by the publishers (probably from a line in a poem called "The Lonely Hunter" by a now-forgotten poet from the beginning of the century, F. MacLeod). And the title turned out to be quite exact—this is precisely what the book is about. There are several main characters: fourteen year-old Mick Kelly, the old Negro doctor Copeland, Jake Blount—a half-alcoholic tramp and self-appointed socialist agitator, Biff Brannan—owner of the New York Cafe. And each of them thrashes around in the cage of his spiritual loneliness, desperately seeking a path to other people, to meaningfulness and fullness of being. Temporarily at least Mick, the daughter of a watchmaker with a large family who can hardly make ends meet, has a retreat which she jealously hides from others—an intense and beautiful world of music which she listens to outside the windows of other people, trying to compose some herself, without knowing the notes. (McCullers studied to be a pianist; music plays a special role in her books right up to the last one.) Dr. Copeland and Jake Blount passionately hate social evil; they are possessed by the need to help their unfortunate brothers. But they are both tragically isolated in the town, and though they are so close in their views, their relation to each other is one of sharp and blind antipathy. Biff Brannan, more contemplative in char-acter, is an "observer of life" who keeps his establishment open all night with no profit for himself; there is not a soul who is close to him and he wants somehow or other to be in the very thick of human existence. But then it happens that this small group of different and disunited creatures, with no previous agreement, concentrates its sympathy, trust and its need to express itself and communicate with someone, on the deaf-mute John Singer who appeared in the New York Cafe one spring morning and became a regular customer. He is an engraver who works in a jewelry shop, is always smartly dressed, calm, friendly; he reads lips with facility and answers his interlocutors tersely—with gestures or a couple of words written in a notebook. In a little more than a year he becomes trusted, an old friend and almost Mick's, Blount's, Copeland's and Brannan's teacher about life. But then one day Singer leaves town for a few days. When he returns he takes a revolver out of his boss's shop, goes to his own room, and shoots himself in the heart. His death is a terrible and totally unexpected blow for those around him. But it does not surprise the reader, because from the very first lines the reader learns John Singer's pre-history and secret. He is not at all a sage, not a teacher of life; he does not know himself why people are so drawn to him, and he understands far from everything people tell him—and is not even terribly interested in it.

Singer has his life's center—his friend, also a deaf-mute, the Greek Antonapoulos with whom he lived for ten years until he had to be sent to another town to a mental hospital for chronic cases—Antonapoulos was mentally retarded and his illness kept progressing. But to Singer this Buddha-like, lazily grinning Greek seemed the embodiment of wisdom and condescending goodness; only with him did he share his thoughts and impressions. But after Antonapoulos's departure his image assumes a finally set form in Singer's memory. Visiting his friend, sending packages to this glutton with the sweet-tooth were the only joys of the deaf-mute engraver. And when Antonapoulos died there was no longer any reason for Singer to go on living.

After Singer's suicide his "circle" feels orphaned and betrayed. They all scatter in various directions. For Mick this first loss coincides with a radical change in her life. Her childhood has ended; Mick is a salesgirl in a department store; the music which had sung in her seems to have gone silent...

In this externally formless book, tightly packed with the details of everyday existence, it is not difficult to find the *skeleton*, the symmetry of the inner conception. We see six people connected—and more surely disunited—by complex relations, the "common denominator" of which is spiritual isolation, the inability of a man to get through the barriers separating him from another—or other people, the ubiquity of human loneliness. *The Heart is a Lonely Hunter*, like all of McCullers' novels exists in two organically united planes—psychological and social realism, and allegory, fable. The allegoricalness of the book is underlined by a whole series of devices; it was the "oral" repetitions, the role of numbers, and the intentional "roundedness" of plot situations that provided material for the numerous interpretations of the novel—religious, mythic, Freudian, political. Apparently closest to the truth is a *moral* interpretation of the novel. Man tries to save himself from loneliness by love. But love is not simply blind, it is almost always directed at an object which by its nature cannot give the lover happiness and harmony. Love does not pierce the wall, but by its very presence it helps the personality find itself and feel even if only for a short while, genuine fullness of being. The bitterest irony is in the fact that the lonely, lost, and despairing ones go with the burden of their sufferings and thoughts to the deaf, the dumb, and the *indifferent*. Even more ironic is the fact that this chosen one who seems clairvoyant and compassionate to them has devoted himself completely to a fictitious creature, the product of his own loneliness, and who is in reality quite simply a repulsive idiot. Chaos reigns in the world, and the same kind of chaos rules in human souls as well.

And still, contrary to everything, over a world which is ominous, depressingly banal, absurd, which is choking in the grip of its age-old misunderstanding and fatal alienation, rises the eternal and irreplaceable power of goodness—love, self-sacrifice, the striving for beauty, the striving to get closer, even if only for a single instant, to a comprehension of the meaning of human existence. McCullers is able to tell about this with the amazing charm of conviction, without a bit of sentimentality or rhetoric. That is why although much has changed since then in the spiritual make-up of America, her first book lives on even now; that is why it did not end in the vast heap of "black" novels and plays which asserted the universal absurdity of being. Basically, all of McCullers' subsequent work developed as a study of this, the writer's basic theme which she varies in the few books so far published—two short novels, a long story, a collection of short stories. She is attracted to unusual characters, grotesque ones who do not fit the concept of "the norm." In her best work, *The Ballad of the Sad Cafe,* the three heroes are locked together—like the prisoners who work on the roads near the unnamed town, the setting of the story—by one chain of incomprehension, love and hate. Miss Amelia Evans is a shopkeeper, a rich woman, owner of the biggest house in town, a masculine creature of masculine character and habits. The object of her most recent and all-devouring affection is her cousin Lymon, a capricious, treacherous hunchback. The object of cousin Lymon's rapture and devotion is Marvin Macy, a loafer, thief, hooligan, and ex-convict. In the past he had married Miss Amelia, with whom he was passionately and timidly in love, which temporarily helped his character. But the marriage only lasted ten days and was purely formal; Miss Amelia threw her unlucky husband out of the house in shame, and he vowed to have his revenge; and in the end he achieves this cruel revenge with the help of cousin Lymon and some supernatural forces. The author unfolds this rather depressing Gothic* story like an ancient fairytale—epically, smoothly, harmoniously and somehow in an amazing musical fashion. But she is not talking about some never-never land in her strange fairytale about the fantastic whims of the human heart. This all occurs in a very realistic, briefly but well described town in the American South of our time, where the heroine sells whiskey, engages in petty but persistent lawsuits against the neighboring

---

*A term popular in American criticsm, an analogy with the old genre of the "novel of horrors" which originated in England. [Levidova's note.]

farmers, where:

> Yes, the town is dreary. On August afternoons the road is empty, white with dust, and the sky above is bright as glass. Nothing moves—there are no children's voices, only the hum of the mill . . . . There is absolutely nothing to do in the town. Walk around the millpond, stand kicking at a rotten stump, figure out what you can do with the old wagon wheel by the side of the road near the church. The soul rots with boredom. You might as well go down to the Forks Falls highway and listen to the chain gang.

If one goes on to Carson McCullers' last book as she did, through her previous ones, it reads differently. You recognize the familiar and notice what is new, you evaluate the discoveries and note the losses, and this last novel, in my opinion, has some of each.

Once when she was sending the first chapter of the novel and a detailed summary of the plot to the publisher, when the novel was still called *The Mute,* McCullers wrote: "The form is contrapuntal throughout. Like a voice in a fugue each one of the main characters is an entity in himself—but his personality takes on new richness when contrasted and woven in with the other characters in the book."

In *Clock without Hands*, as is correctly noted in M. Maretskaya's afterword, the story of each of the four heroes could have been told separately; but precisely in their interrelations and mutual rejections, "intertwined," they reveal and develop themselves—insofar as, let us add, the author allows them to do so. Again, as in all of McCullers' books, realistic features of the social environment, time (the novel is set in 1953), everyday life, subtle psychological configurations—all these serve as a basis for a moral fable. An old judge who is comical, but also dangerous in his militance, a relic of the confederacy, a reactionary and racist, loves his grandson Jester, loves him tenderly, pitifully and helplessly. Jester is devoured by turbulent feeling for Sherman Pugh, a "blue-eyed Negro," and Sherman—a foolish youth, an abandoned child, whose garrulity and childish bravado are only a smokescreen for his orphaned feeling and spiritual rootlessness—ridicules Jester and puts his whole heart into a hopeless search for his non-existent mother. The wife of the druggist Malone, who is dying of leukemia, is full of love and pity for him, but this feeling inspires revulsion in him; and when, only in the face of death, he does the sole humble moral and civic deed of his life—at a meeting of the town Klansmen he refuses to throw a bomb into Sherman's house—only then does he reestablish his long-lost closeness to his wife. All of these situations are organic for McCullers: human loneliness, lost and despairing love. Nor is music an accidental guest in this book. Jester and Sherman are closely tied by music in spite of their uninterrupted verbal (and not just verbal) duel. There is, however, something totally new (though not alien to the rest of the writer's work): for the first time the political, civic theme becomes the basis of the action, its dramatic mainspring. There is nothing unexpected in this. McCullers is an artist who has rare sensitivity to human suffering and debasement of its worth.

Even in her first book she depicted a self-sacrificing Negro doctor who gave life (in the most literal meaning of the word) to his people, and she depicted his daughter Portia with her amusingly solemn speech and intelligent heart. But it is not just sympathy which defines McCullers' position in these tragic events of historic proportions which have been shaking her native South and the whole country for several years. A sharp sense of justice and a clear, unprejudiced view of the future are innate qualities of McCullers—and in *Clock without Hands* she tried to tell a fable not just about the eternal strivings of the human heart, but also about those forces which now personify the state of affairs in the American South. The judge Klein is a symbol of naked but historically doomed reaction; the druggist Malone is flesh and flesh of the great multitude of ordinary "neutral" people, basically decent and peace-loving, but inert and not free of prejudice (we recall his latent anti-semitism), people who would like to stay on the side and who are nevertheless forced to act sooner or later. Sammy Lenk, Sherman's willing murderer, acts (it would be forcing things to add "and thinks") as a representation of the same ignorant, dull, poverty-embittered "white trash" should, as they vent their anger on "uppitty Niggers," the mob without which no raid on the Negroes can be made. And finally Jester and Sherman—the youth and future of the country. Sherman is drawn very curiously. In no way is he a stereotype of the "good Negro," to whom white liberals from the time of Harriet Beecher Stowe have turned. And not at all the stylizedly primitive, sensual creature drifting through many of the books of writers of the "Southern school." Sherman has characteristics of that American youth of the fifties which J. D. Salinger captured so perspicaciously. But in the "blue-eyed Negro" this confusion of feelings and cautious mistrust of the reason which is piercing through his shell is naturally burdened by something which he is fated to bear from birth and which multiplies tenfold his innate arrogant rebelliousness—the burden of race discrimination. And Jester? Jester again brings to mind Mick Kelly, and the young girls from McCullers' other work, although he is older, knows how to fly a plane, and he is a youth with a man's problems. His nature is seemingly frail, vulnerable, reflective, but its core is strong and healthy and his mind works in the right direction. The writer has big hopes for Jester and is confident about his future: he will follow not his grandfather but his father, a progressive lawyer who perished tragically in the thirties during an unequal clash with the laws of the racist South.

All of this is quite clear to the reader, clear from the very beginning, and as I see it, the sting of this new work of McCullers lies in this clarity. The work is conceived to be capacious, and one keeps expecting this conception to be overgrown with thick rustling foliage, to take on the depth and an epic quality which win one over in *The Heart is a Lonely Hunter.* But here the nakedness of the social conflicts, the sometimes almost sketchy brevity, the point by point report on the psychological life of the heroes create the impression of something externally "rounded off" and internally incomplete—it is rather the silhouette of the tree, a graphic intertwining of branches with barely forming buds. Perhaps the explanation is that it was physically painful for McCullers to write this book; when you learn how much she has had to bear in the last decade, you understand how heroically she worked. Her book is talented no matter how severely one judges it—every figure has its successful aspects and the intuitive illuminations in which her work is so rich. The Malone line of the novel is given with especial interest, subtlety, wholeness. In his process of "spiritual assimilation" of the idea of death and his late arrival at a reevaluation of the values of his interrupted life, one cannot but catch echoes of Tolstoi's "The Death of Ivan Ilych"—and of course Tolstoi and Dostoevsky played a great role in the formation of the writer's individuality. And it seems to me that there is something Chekhovian at least in the way she describes Malone as he learns the horrible truth about his illness from the doctor. ("As he sat stroking his scant, coarse hair, his long upper lip set carefully against the tremulous lower one, his eyes febrile and terrified, Malone had already the meek and neuter look of an incurable.") But none of the literary associations destroys the sense of artistic originality in McCullers; everything that happens to Malone touches one to the quick. It is all genuinely serious.

McCullers' tone, markedly original, maintained from beginning to end, is present in this book too. This tone is not always preserved in the translation, which, one must say, is uneven—alongside successful passages where the sense and the spirit and the rhythm are recreated, there is often a rough, free (in the negative sense) paraphrase of the sentence, imprecisely rendered nuances and even—what is surprising in such an experienced translator as E. M. Golysheva—sometimes mistakes, places in the original read incorrectly. But the main thing is the destruction of the tone, which is always even in the original, though each character has his own "compliment," even in the mixing of nuances. In the case of any writer like McCullers with her special musicality and polished lexical precision it is impossible to change "pronounced in a barely audible voice" to "barely muttered."

Maretskaya's afterword is pleasing in its obvious enthusiasm for the book and McCullers' work. She speaks justly of her humanism, attention to people, of the uprightness and uncompromising nature of her political views. But, as it strikes me, here McCullers' creative portrait is given traits which are not in reality characteristic of it: a kind of pantheistic major key ("Every line of hers is a hymn to life"), a beneficent sentimentality—when speaking of the enlightenment of the "coarse heart of the lonely Miss Amelia" who has fallen in love with the hunchback, Maretskaya says nothing about the cruel and grotesque finale of the story, and it is precisely this which sets the general tone of *The Ballad of the Sad Cafe*.

However that may be, it is very good that *Clock without Hands* has appeared in Russian translation. One hopes that our readers' acquaintance with Carson McCullers will continue to develop.

STARTSEV ON FITZGERALD

A. Startsev began writing reviews of American literature at least as early as 1931 in *On Literary Guard (Na literaturnom postu),* especially on Upton Sinclair. A book called *John Dos Passos* was published in Moscow in 1934; another book, *Mark Twain and America* (Moscow, 1963), gave rise to polemics with American scholars. Startsev has also provided extensive introductions for editions of the works of Bret Harte. He has written on John Reed. And most recently he supplied the introduction to the first Soviet publication of the poetry of T. S. Eliot (translated by Andrei Sergeev). The essay translated here is the first general article on Fitzgerald (published in *Foreign Literature,* No. 2, 1965). He also wrote the introduction to the Russian translation of *The Great Gatsby.* Before the Russian *Tender is the Night* was published in 1971, Startsev published an informative essay called "Fitzgerald and the 'Very Rich'," which appeared in *Foreign Literature* (No. 5, 1971).

A. Startsev

FITZGERALD'S BITTER FATE

There are many American writers who have suffered bitter fates and who have disappeared from the scene prematurely without fulfilling the promise of their gifts. Amid the noisy whirl of American life they have perished from loneliness, alcoholism, and hopeless despair, without any help or words of sympathy, as if they were in an uninhabited desert. Every such case again draws the attention of thinking people all over the world to the vices of American capitalistic culture and the "American way of life" with its stony coldness to the fates of men; the vices of bourgeois capitalistic civilization have not only become one with this way of life, they have reached extreme intensity.

In the period between the two wars the saddest drama of this type was the death of one of the foremost representatives of modern American prose, Scott Fitzgerald, author of *The Great Gatsby.*

The life, works, and melancholy fate of Fitzgerald are almost unknown in our country, and this is an obvious gap in our knowledge of twentieth-century American literature. Many people first learned Fitzgerald's name from Hemingway's book of reminiscences *A Moveable Feast.* But Scott Fitzgerald's basic works, especially *The Great Gatsby,* have become firmly established as "contemporary classics" in the West, and Fitzgerald's artistic innovations, repeated in the books of his pupils and imitators, have become the legacy of all.

In 1920 the twenty-four-year-old Fitzgerald published *This Side of Paradise,* a novel about American students, and thus became the first of his generation to win great acclaim—preceding the literary debuts of Hemingway and Faulkner which were still in preparation. The book earned him success and money. Only yesterday an unknown provincial, he became a wealthy man and took up residence in one of the most expensive New York hotels. Very soon the young Fitzgeralds, who knew nothing about money, who thoughtlessly burned the candle of life at both ends, became the "heroes" of the American society pages.

Fitzgerald was a writer who had striking and unquestionable gifts; on entering literature he had firm faith in his talent, and he had an optimistic picture of his writing future. However, initially he was not able to set up a strong line of defense which would separate his goals and ideals from the base goals of the American propertied classes. Not having done this, it was inevitable that he should fall victim to the destructive influences of bourgeois civilization.

If one begins with only one of the external facts of young Fitzgerald's life it might seem that without thinking about it much and even without resisting it, Fitzgerald came to the conclusion that the cheerful life of a wealthy man was in fact his ideal, an ideal quite compatible with his work as a writer, and that he was right to exploit his talent precisely as if it were invested capital or an oil well which he had acquired.

Actually it was a more complicated matter. From the very beginning there became clear a profound and tormenting contradiction on this very point, both in Fitzgerald's spiritual world and in his works. However, a complete realization of this came to the writer only much later.

After the success of his first book, Fitzgerald became a fashionable author, highly regarded in the American literary marketplace. When profits from his book were exhausted, he began to sell more or less hastily written short stories to the magazines at high prices. He wrote a great many of these stories during his life, and the majority of them are unworthy   of his talent. The popular weekly *The Saturday Evening Post* paid Fitzgerald the highest royalties, record sums for that time; its editor, Lorrimer ("big dog Lorrimer," as the American poet George Sterling called him with a curse) was notorious as a buyer and wrecker of young talents. It cannot be said that Fitzgerald wasn't warned about starting off on a dangerous road. Thus the well-known American novelist Charles Norris wrote him about the first stories which appeared in *The Saturday Evening Post:* "If you intend to go on contributing to his respectable magazine I advise you to rename it 'The Coffin Where Scott Fitzgerald's Talent is Buried.' Lorrimer will leave you nothing but your bones and throw them in the garbage heap..."[†] In the final analysis Norris's prediction came true.

The subsequent development of Fitzgerald's literary life took the following path: in 1922 he published the novel *The Beautiful and Damned*— about young people from the environment of New York's artistic Bohemia. Though Fitzgerald's love of life and emotional strength do not weaken in this book either, one can sense the author's growing uneasiness about the young hedonists whom he is singing. In 1924 Fitzgerald went with his wife to France, where at that time a colony of young American writers was gathered. Except for very short intervals, he lived in France until 1930. There, in 1925, Fitzgerald created *The Great Gatsby,* his most perfect work—in which (although he is still   not completely aware of it himself) he performs as an artist "voting" against American capitalism—which gets its ideal of beauty and morality from the esthetic and moral standards of the ruling classes. *The Great Gatsby* showed the power and profundity of Fitzgerald's talent, but the novel was not a commercial success in the   USA. People expected from Fitzgerald the "jazz rhapsodies" to which advertising had already tied his name.

After *The Great Gatsby* begins the tragedy of Fitzgerald; though there were still creative bursts, his talent was crushed. He turned from a gay reveler into a confirmed drunk and scandal-maker; he drowned his dissatisfaction with himself, his life and work in wine; he ruined his health and uprooted his faith in himself as an artist.

The bright spots in Fitzgerald's poisoned life were his friendship with Ring Lardner (the important American humorist and satirist who soon died of tuberculosis and alcoholism) and Ernest Hemingway—whom Fitzgerald helped get started in publishing. But though he was enraptured by Lardner's indifference to financial success and the iron writing discipline of Hemingway, Fitzgerald himself could not resolve to abandon the path he had taken. The *Saturday Evening Post* upped his payment to $4000 per story; Fitzgerald also made commercial deals with Hollywood and put off serious creative plans from one year to the next.

In *A Moveable Feast,* Hemingway's posthumously published memoirs of Paris in the twenties, Hemingway writes of his closeness to Fitzgerald, while simultaneously pitying him and rejecting his weakness. Hemingway's well-known observations in *The Green Hills of Africa* about the hard fate of the American writer, like analogous motifs in *The Snows of Kilimanjaro,* are suggestive of Fitzgerald's fate as a writer. Incidentally, one should note that for all Hemingway's indubitable sympathy for Fitzgerald he does not have sufficient depth either in his evaluation of his work or in his understanding of Fitzgerald's human tragedy.

In 1930 Fitzgerald's wife Zelda, who took part in all his revels and madnesses, fell ill with an incurable mental disorder, and this blow made the writer stop and think—as he was on the verge of physical and creative doom.

He began a battle with the three "devils"—alcoholism, the mental illness of his wife whom he loved so passionately, and finally with his attachment to the merry-go-round of material success which had been so disastrous for his talent. He fought this battle for ten years, and never winning a decisive victory, he died in 1940 at the age of forty-four.

The last ten years of Fitzgerald's life were very bitter, but at the same time they were important and full of significance for anyone who is concerned with the position of an artist in the world of capitalism.

Fitzgerald tried to make sense out of what had happened to him. Along with the bitter defeat (and he considered that as a man and as a writer he had suffered a defeat) he came to a deeper understanding of the social structure of the society in which he lived and the causes, both social and personal, which predetermined his failure. In 1934 he completed his new novel *Tender is the Night,* in which he depicted Americans—the rich fast livers and the intellectual Bohemians in Paris during the twenties. The book's internal theme (continuing the theme begun in *The Great Gatsby)*—is the inhumanity of rich people and the destructiveness of close contact with them for anyone who trusts them. As always using many personal elements in his novel, Fitzgerald describes the "spiritual bankruptcy" of the novel's main hero, Dick Diver—who has married a rich American girl and gradually lost sight of any moral basis in his life. In the character of the American composer Abe North (he is dying from alcoholism) Fitzgerald introduced his friend Ring Lardner, but there are autobiographical elements in this character as well.

However, Fitzgerald's painfully passionate desire to make total sense of his "bankruptcy" and draw from this lessons for himself and others was not satisfied by using the personal motifs which he introduced into the novel. In 1936 he published three short articles in the popular American magazine *Esquire*—"The Crack-Up," "Pasting It Together," and "Handle with Care" (in posthumous editions of Fitzgerald's works the three articles are united under the title *The Crack-Up*) in which, with exceptional candor, he examined his life and pronounced sentence on himself. These articles comprise one of the most tragic literary documents in all modern American literature.

The author informs his reader that he, the well-known writer Scott Fitzgerald, who from youth was full of love of life and optimism, has experienced the crack-up of everything he believed in, and for which he lived; he has lost his love of life and his will to live, he realizes that he has become a "moral bankrupt." This realization came to him too late, after the catastrophe had occurred.

Why, asks Fitzgerald, did this irreversible crack-up happen to him; why had his life "cracked" ("like an old plate")—allowing the vital and creative energy which had inspired him to evaporate and escape through this crack?

The necessary answer is that he, the writer Scott Fitzgerald, spent the whole sixteen years after the publication of his first novel without carrying out his intellectual and social responsibilities; he did not acknowledge his duty to himself and to society, he lived insanely and irresponsibly. Now he had to make an accounting of everything.

One of the most important questions which Fitzgerald tries to answer concerns his relation to the ruling class, to the rich people whom he could not find the strength to break away from when he began his writing career. "For sixteen years," he writes, "I lived . . . distrusting the rich, yet working for money with which to share their mobility and the grace that some of them brought into their lives." Fitzgerald considers it necessary to emphasize (and his words are confirmed by many concrete motifs in his works) that he had always felt hostility towards the exploiting classes. This was "not the conviction of a revolutionist but the smouldering hatred of the peasant. . . I have never been able to stop wondering where my friends' money came from, nor to stop thinking that at one time a sort of droit de seigneur might have been exercised to give one of them my girl."

Fitzgerald considers the passive attitude to reality which gradually possessed him a fatal symptom of his moral illness. "I only wanted absolute quiet to think out why I had developed a sad attitude toward sadness, a melancholy attitude toward melancholy and a tragic attitude toward tragedy—*why had I become identified with the objects of my compassion.*" He condemns this position, which borders on nonresistance to evil, and precludes any actively creative interference in life. "Lenin did not willingly endure the sufferings of his proletariat," he says, "nor Washington of his troops, nor Dickens his London poor." In these words obliquely outlining the position of a social activist and writer which he considers correct, Fitzgerald announces that for himself personally it is already too late to change anything in his life, to hope for anything, that he considers himself finished as a man and artist.

From now on he will remain a "writer only," a writer in the purely formal and technical sense of the word. He must say goodbye to the dream which had once inspired him—of being a writer in the tradition of Goethe, Byron, and Bernard Shaw. From now on he can love no one and be loved by no one; life will lose its charm for him and above the door of his house will be written *"Cave Canem!"* Fitzgerald concludes his jeremiad: "I will try to be a correct animal though, and if you throw me a bone with enough meat on it, I may even lick your hand."

The essays in *The Crack-Up* were in no way a pose. Fitzgerald really had suffered profound laceration and profound despair. A reporter from a New York evening newspaper, looking for a sensational piece, sought out Fitzgerald in the isolated Southern town where he was hiding from the public and the press; and the reporter recorded his interview with the sick writer: "Where are the people of my generation? They've become stockbrokers and committed suicide by jumping out of windows. Others became bankers and shot themselves in the head... And others became successful writers..." His face grew distorted. "O Lord! Successful writers!.."[†]

These words of Fitzgerald are as if an epitaph to the American "boom" of the twenties, a funeral dirge for the deep economic crisis of the thirties which embraced all areas of American life. And withth e last essay of *The Crack-Up* he connects his own bitter sobering up, the end of his self-deception, to the wave of despair which had swept across the country.

Having reached the conclusion that he could be a "writer only," Fitzgerald made a decision which fit the conclusion. He went to Hollywood and sold himself to Metro-Goldwyn-Mayer. In his contract he himself got a small sum for personal expenses; the rest of the money went to take care of his wife in the insane asylum and his daughter in a private school. Things went on this way for a time; Fitzgerald did not exist as a writer. When a young script-writer who came to Hollywood was told he would be working on a script with Scott Fitzgerald, he replied in surprise that he thought Fitzgerald was dead. "In that case I'm paying $1500 a month to a ghost," siad the producer with a smile.

However, Fitzgerald had buried himself and pronounced himself a lifetime slave of Hollywood prematurely. The very yoke of Hollywood helped him find himself as an individual and artist again. Even though he declared his creative death, he could not become a nameless cog in the machine of the American movie industry. He brought lively interest and creative individuality to his movie scripts. That is why when the well-known Hollywood producer Mankewicz used a dictatorial blue pencil to turn Fitzgerald's script (a screen version of Remarque's "Three Comrades") into a standard Hollywood pot-boiler, Fitzgerald suffered through another tragedy in his writing career.

Among other conditions the Hollywood firm which bought Fitzgerald's talent had made him take an oath of sobriety, but the offended author broke this clause in his contract. A new attack of alcoholism caused an irreparable break-down in his health, and ended his material security. Fitzgerald's contract was not renewed. Now Hollywood used him only from time to time for odd jobs. But the writer who had lived in the very center of the American film world for several years and was now mortally ill began to write his last work, a novel about Hollywood. Needing money, Fitzgerald bound himself to a cruel and unprofitable deadline; to get an advance from the publishers he had to give them a large part of the novel already finished. But it was not just this persistent need which drove him. He experienced a great creative surge, but his strength was leaving him with every page he wrote. Fitzgerald wrote the novel while lying in bed, then resorted to dictation, but he did not manage to finish his work, or get the money which he needed so much. This half-finished novel, *The Last Tycoon,* was posthumously published along with variants, notes, and outlines of unfinished chapters showing that in Fitzgerald American literature had lost a prose writer who was far from exhausting the power of his talent.

2.

The Great Gatsby is one of the high points of American literature and can rightly be considered one of the most brilliant accomplishments of the American twentieth-century social novel.

The Great Gatsby is unquestionably a social novel, though the action of this extraordinarily "densely" written book is limited to a six-month period and seems to be locked in a very narrow circle of events concerning the narrowly personal interrelations of five or six young people who met unexpectedly as a result of a capricious confluence of circumstances, and who soon part tragically forever. The social quality of Fitzgerald's book is determined by the fact that the events depicted in it, the characters and main conflict which determines the action, have a direct and vitally important relation to the fates of all of the people in the society which the artist is describing.

The book is about the destructiveness of a false civilization imposed on man, a civilization in which happiness is artifically equated with material success and all of man's spiritual and moral impulses are subordinated to the religion of wealth.

This theme—the theme of the "American way of life" as a trap for Western man—is such an important problem in all modern American literature that Fitzgerald's novel (which externally would seem to have little in common with Dreiser's epic social canvases) may be put side by side with *An American Tragedy* because of its inner pathos. Dreiser approaches this theme from the point of view of a sociologist who is documenting his observations; for the most part Fitzgerald uses moral and ethical criteria—but both have the same enemy, and both are disturbed and gripped by the same terrible anxiety.

Who is Gatsby, the hero of Fitzgerald's novel?

Jay Gatsby (alias James Gatz) is the son of a poor farmer from North America, and as befits an energetic young American, he goes in search of wealth and happiness when still a boy. When the United States enters World War One Gatsby is a young officer. For the time being his military uniform serves as his entree to higher levels of society. He falls in love with a girl from a well-to-do family, conceals his poverty, and wins her love. Daisy promises to wait until he comes home from the war, but does not wait—she marries a man "of her own circle," the very rich Tom Buchanan. Gatsby returns home wearing medals for bravery, but as before without a cent in his pockets. Inspired by the dream of winning Daisy back, he gets involved in that area of semi-legal activities which are an accepted part of the American system of capitalistic profit; and he acquires riches. He manages to meet Daisy and for a time to attract her by the strength of his faith and love. But Daisy and Tom represent the American ruling class, the country's caste of hereditary masters. Any attempt to contest their rights or disturb their peace must inevitably run into a solid wall—their internal solidarity. They do Gatsby in, throw him off his path, and kill him. And then they walk away, sated, cruel, indifferent.

But how is Gatsby great? What does the title of the novel mean?

Apparently this adjective is applied to Gatsby with a double meaning. Gatsby is falsely "great" in his role as a rich man with a mysterious reputation, the host of absurdly lavish parties which he gives in hope of getting Daisy's attention—parties about which the moralistic narrator is ironic. At the same time he is truly great in his depth of feeling, his devotion to his dream, in his rare "gift of hope," as is said of him in the novel, in his spiritual magnaminity—which in another environment and other circumstances might have made him a hero. The significance of all these characteristics in Gatsby is revealed by the fact that even though he is expert in the cruel art of "making money," from the moment when he realizes that Daisy (for whom he has done all this) is rejecting him, he loses all interest in his wealth and everything connected with it; Gatsby has a *de facto* parting with life even before the murderer's bullet strikes him.

In a certain sense, Fitzgerald's novel may also be viewed as a "novel of education." If you take it from this point of view, the narrator is at the center of the book—Nick Carraway, constant witness and commentator, and at times an active participant in the developing events. He emerges from them made wiser by the sad experience which leaves a mark on his whole subsequent life. It is not important that this school lasted only a few months or that the hero was already an adult when he entered it. It was equivalent to an entire moral university; and it crystallized many ideas which he had perhaps had earlier, but which had not been tested by decisive real-life experience.

Nick Carraway belongs to the so-called "lost generation" of young American intelligentsia; the first World War lay between the university and the practical life which they (and he) entered after a long delay. He is enriched by his experiences at the front; and he has a somewhat skeptical attitude toward postwar life in his homeland with its vaunted wealth, accumulated during the war.

During the summer and fall of 1922 his acquaintance with Gatsby and his part in the drama which unfolds induces a profound moral change in him. He enters the whirl of events still certain that he understands all "basic moral values" well enough. When he meets Gatsby he himself says that Gatsby embodies everything that he, Nick Carraway, "sincerely despised and despises."* On the other hand, much in the Buchanans is dear to him, pleases him, or at least attracts him. These likes and dislikes which have been inspired in him by habit and his environment are put to the sternest test and collapse in a way quite unexpected to him. "Gatsby justified himself..."† he ponders later, summing up what had happened. The shock which Carraway undergoes makes him reject the moral compromises which he had previously considered acceptable and in the "order of things." He looks ahead joylessly, seeing no salvation from the evil which governs life; and he considers it his duty to relate honestly that which he had chanced to see, paying the boldness of the human heart its due, but without disguising vice.

From beginning to end Fitzgerald refuses to idealize Gatsby; however, it is obvious that while on many key points the author's position is expressed in Nick Carraway's point of view and statements, the emotional bonds which tie Fitzgerald directly to Gatsby are also strong. Fitzgerald once called Gatsby his "older brother"; in a letter on the genesis of the novel he admits that though he set out to depict Gatsby with a certain other person whom he knew in mind, he later started using himself for the portrait. The problem of Gatsby, who was unable to separate his ideal of love from his ideal of wealth, eventually leads to his moral and ethical capitulation to the power of money. If we generalize this as it applies to the questions which the artist faces in a bourgeois society, we can speak of the intrusion, characteristic of that society, of a "fetishistic" (in Marx's well known definition) view of money and wealth into the essentially emotional sphere of human experience, including artistic perception and comprehension of the world. As has already been said, the whole series of questions which arises in this connection had prime (and in a way "fatal") significance for the young Fitzgerald.

In *The Great Gatsby* Fitzgerald draws readers' attention to that external sensual glitter which things and people acquire in the aura of wealth and material comfort. But he also shows how illusory this glitter is and how transient its charm is if one's eyes penetrate its blinding surface. As soon as genuine human emotions come into play and spiritually important interests and attachments are put under pressure, the props collapse.

Retranslated. In the original: "represented everything for which I have unaffected scorn."

Remarkable in this regard is the "decoding" of Daisy's voice, the description of Daisy's extraordinary and ineffable charm which is one of her main features. This decoding, however strange it may seem, is done not by Carraway but by Gatsby, whom love makes perspicacious almost to the point of "genius."

> "It's full of—" I hesitated. "It's full of money," he said suddenly. . . . That was it. I'd never understood before. It was full of money—that was the inexhaustible charm that rose and fell in it, the jingle of it, the cymbals' song of it . . . .

The lyrical density of Fitzgerald's prose in *The Great Gatsby* is sometimes close to that of poetry. Not only the hero's spiritual impulses, but every physical gesture is given intensifying emotional features. This applies both to the novel's central characters—Gatsby, the Buchanans, the Wilsons, Jordan Baker—and to the secondary and tertiary characters. The novel's emotional atmosphere is far from simple; it is always an "amalgam" of the inner voices of the heroes, and the voice of the narrator—which at first is indifferently sarcastic, and later sad and more austere.

A special role in the novel belongs to the moral-lyric digressions in which Fitzgerald wants to convey the basic mood of *The Great Gatsby*—an inner sense of instability, of the absence of social and moral foundation which is characteristic of this civilization built on a false principle, a premonition of its approaching material and spiritual crack-up. They are put in the mouth of the narrator Nick Carraway, but at the same time they belong to the author and serve as his condemnation of the world he is depicting. Especially important in this sense are the last pages of the novel—two moral and philosophical endings; the first concerns the noisy carnival of New York life, the show-window of American civilization, and the second deals with American history and life as a whole.

Having decided to return home to a dull, suffocating provincial life, which is nevertheless somehow dear to him because of his memories of childhood and boyhood, Nick Carraway takes with him that vision of New York which possesses him in the end:

> West Egg, especially, still figures in my more fantastic dreams. I see it as a night scene by El Greco: a hundred houses, at once conventional and grotesque, crouching under a sullen, overhanging sky and a lusterless moon. In the foreground four solemn men in dress suits are walking along the sidewalk with a stretcher on which lies a drunken woman in a white evening dress. Her hand, which dangles over the side, sparkles cold with jewels. Gravely the men turn in at a house—the wrong house. But no one knows the woman's name, and no one cares.

The symbolism of this picture conveys a sense of agonizing emptiness and anxiety; it is filled with a premonition of the inevitable crack-up of the "New Babylon."

On the eve of his departure, as he is lying on the sand on the beach in front of Gatsby's empty house, Nick Carraway again ponders the reasons for and circumstances of Gatsby's doom; and from these thoughts about his fate he shifts to thoughts about the life and fate of the American people. He compares the green light on the Buchanans' dock (it had attracted Gatsby and fed his dream) to the "fresh, green breast of the new world,"which had captured the minds of the people who had discovered the new continent and to the related American dream of salvation from any and all woes, of cloudless happiness forever. Like Gatsby, they believed in the attainment of this imagined happiness, and like Gatsby they were unable to understand that the dream was long ago left behind, that they were simply holding out their hands to a ghost of former illusions, and living on irretrievable memories: "So we beat on, boats against the current, borne back ceaselessly into the past." With these words the novel ends.

3.

For many personal reasons Fitzgerald did not take part in the social campaign of American writers like Dreiser and Hemingway which typified the thirties. He did not take part in writers' congresses; his signature is not on the declarations and manifestoes in which the active attitude, new for American literature, of men of the arts toward the political struggle of the proletariat was expressed. But the influence of the stormy events of the class struggle and Marxist ideas did not pass Fitzgerald by. This is shown by his works, his personal correspondence, and other materials published after his death.

Therefore the efforts of conservative American critics and historians of literature to present Fitzgerald as a writer who stood aside from the sociopolitical upheavals of the thirties are unfounded. Such efforts arise either from a superficial reading of Fitzgerald or an intentional falsification of the writer's ideological biography in order to offset his general trend toward the left, which is characteristic for American literature of the thirties. Even the bitterly exaggerated self-criticism which Fitzgerald develops in *The Crack-Up* is used in bad conscience toward these ends.

Anyone who wants to imagine Fitzgerald as a writer alien to politics should remember that in one of his earliest stories, "May Day" (1920), Fitzgerald outlined a tragic panorama of American life torn by social and political contradictions, and he was the first of the non-socialist writers to condemn New York's police and gangsters' mob laws directed against the foremost workers' organizations and socialist intelligentsia. In fact, in this boldly conceived, multi-levelled story he makes an outline for a social novel about American contemporary society.

Two years later Fitzgerald published his socio-fantastic fable "The Diamond as Big as the Ritz." There he depicts an American millionaire as alien to any humanity, an infinitely cruel maniac whom it is essential to harness and make harmless if society is to be safe. There he also ridicules the prestige of wealth and the universal cult of money in the United States of

America. "The richer a man is the more I like him," the story's hero, a young American brought up in an atmosphere of the total worship of the dollar admits naively. Subsequently the problem of the omnipotence of the dollar, as well as the moral insolvency of the propertied classes, which deprived them of any right to guide society, is never outside Fitzgerald's sphere of interest.

Tom Buchanan's agressive racism in *The Great Gatsby,* his dull confidence that he belongs to a race of lords, shows how accurately the writer had predicted the development of reactionary ideas in modern American society.

In his novel *Tender Is the Night,* Fitzgerald considered it necessary to show what a dazzling young millionairess costs people:

> Nicole was the product of much ingenuity and toil. For her sake trains began their run at Chicago and traversed the round belly of the continent to California; chicle factories fumed and link belts grew link by link in factories; men mixed toothpaste in vats and drew mouthwash out of copper hogsheads; girls canned tomatoes quickly in August or worked rudely at the Five-and-Tens on Christmas Eve; half-breed Indians toiled on Brazilian coffee plantations and dreamers were musculed out of patent rights in new tractors—these were some of the people who gave a tithe to Nicole . . .

One should not assume that Fitzgerald is introducing a socio-critical motif into the narration just to follow the general sociological tendency of American intellectual life and literature of the thirties, that he is following the dictates of current "fashion." As one can conclude from Fitzgerald's published correspondence, he became acquainted with Marx's *Das Kapital* in the thirties. "Someday," he wrote his student daughter (in the last years before his death he devoted great attention to her spiritual and moral education), "read the terrible chapter in *Das Kapital* on 'The Working Day,' and see if you are ever quite the same."

It is also interesting to note that in the first plan of *Tender Is the Night* Dick Diver, the novel's main hero, was conceived by Fitzgerald as a radical intellectual and communist sympathizer. After his breakup with his millionaire wife, he sends his young son to the Soviet Union to get a Soviet education. Fitzgerald did not carry out this plan; in the final text Diver is alien to politics, and the end of the novel is pessimistic and hopeless. However, one should not conclude from this that Fitzgerald "retreats" from his social interests. In the fragments of *The Last Tycoon,* there is an extremely interesting, completely finished episode where he depicts the clash of the film magnate Monroe Stahr with Brimmer, the communist leader of the workers, whom Stahr invites to his house in order to "study his opponent more closely."

In this episode, written in 1939 or 1940 when anti-Soviet, anti-communist propaganda in the United States was shaking many of the only recently left-inclined literary people, Fitzgerald openly and unambiguously emphasizes his respect for the workers' movement as a whole and for the American communists.

In the ensuing conversation Stahr assumes no political or intellectual superiority to his opponent. Though he himself is a gifted and strong-willed man, he cannot counter the quiet confidence of the communist with anything except cheap irony and jokes. Losing the moral duel, drunken Stahr tries to strike Brimmer; and forced to defend himself, the latter knocks the millionaire to the floor with a strong blow. " 'All right.' He stood looking down at Stahr as I came around the table. 'I always wanted to hit ten million dollars, but I didn't know it would be like this'."

In Fitzgerald's letters to his daughter there are numerous comments on American and world literature which characterize him as a writer who consistently defends the essentially social perception of life which typifies his central works.

He sees Dreiser's *Sister Carrie* as "almost the first piece of American realism..." Along with the classics he suggest his daughter read *Ten Days That Shook the World,* John Reed's great American book which bourgeois criticism has maliciously passed over in silence ever since its publication.

*

Against the background of the American social novel of the thirties *The Great Gatsby* stands out because of its emotional-lyric structure. However, it does not stand alone in the context of Western literary development...

The novel's atmosphere of romantic expectation, the artist's extraordinary graphicality, the sharp sense of hope for a happiness which ineffably attracts, slips away, and turns out to be false in reality, make *The Great Gatsby* similar to another successful work which stands at the threshold of modern Western literature and which was also written by a young writer—Alain-Fournier's *Le Grand Meaulnes.*

Alain-Fournier was before Fitzgerald, his book came out in 1913. The impulses of the young romantics of the West at the beginning of the century were limited by their still unbroken illusions about bourgeois democracy, but they were stifled on the bloody fields of World War One. However, these impulses were not pretended, and these young people made their loathing for the moral compromises of capitalistic reality a symbol of faith. The "moral maximalism" of *Le Grand Meaulnes* had a profound effect on a whole generation of French writers.

It is difficult to imagine how the romantic protest in Alain-Fournier's work would have developed—he died in one of the first Franco-German battles; but in Fitzgerald, who began ten years later, one should emphasize the ever-growing alienation from any concealment or masking of the class contradictions of the modern world.

Full of important social and political events, the decade which separates *Le Grand Meaulnes* from *The Great Gatsby* could not help having a decisive effect on the content of Fitzgerald's novel. In both cases one sees the unsatisfied desire of the poetic perception of the world clash with a stagnant and hostile reality; in both we see a hero meet defeat, suffer the crack-up of his illusions. In Fitzgerald, however, the struggle of the romantic fighting for his dream is "pushed" deeply into the modern world's hell of social and financial contradictions; and the hero himself, Gatsby, is spattered with the mud of dishonest gain.

If in the final analysis *Le Grand Meaulnes* is, as Louis Aragon says, "a terrible condemnation of society," in other words, its meaning is anti-capitalistic and its tendency is anti-capitalistic—we have even more reason and right to say the same of *The Great Gatsby.*

Fitzgerald's bitter fate and his works are an inseparable part of the basic rejection of the capitalistic world by the twentieth-century masters of Western culture.

LANDOR ON FITZGERALD

Apart from "May Day" which was anthologized in 1958, *The Great Gatsby*, published in Moscow in 1965 (50,000 copies), translated by E. Kalashnikova, was the first Fitzgerald to be translated into Russian. Until then Fitzgerald was known in Russia primarily from the translation of Hemingway's unflattering *A Moveable Feast. The Great Gatsby* was reviewed rather widely, and translations of "The Long Way Out," "The Diamond as Big as the Ritz," and four other stories followed in 1966-68. Landor edited several letters on *The Great Gatsby* and "The Crack-up" (in 1966). Finally, in 1971, *Tender Is the Night* was published; and the general Soviet attitude toward Fitzgerald seems positive.

M. Landor

GIFT OF HOPE

This novel has had a happy fate: both connoisseurs and uninitiated readers have been attracted to it. Literary scholars consider Gatsby among the most profound and complex characters in American prose. And disrespectful Holden Caulfield *(The Catcher in the Rye)* who seems to see "crap" everywhere, speaks of this novel almost with piety: "Yes, Gatsby. There's a man! Strength!" Many young Americans apparently share his open-hearted enthusiasm.

It is not difficult to explain this. At the basis of the novel's dynamic plot lies a romantic story which touches even those who do not appreciate all the complexities of the author's conception.

Fitzgerald's hero wants to return the past. The day before crossing the ocean to the First World War he met a girl with an "exciting voice"; the days when he first met her and fell in love were the best of his life. Even before he returns to America he learns that she has not waited for him but gotten married. But he is sure that the years which have passed don't count, that the romantic happiness which is possible for him only with her is attainable. It appears that this is indeed the case and that the hero's devotion will be rewarded. But on the threshold of happiness he perishes.

We perceive the beginning of the book as a pardox. The well-mannered and bashful nouveau riche has parties at his summer home near New York. There are many celebrities there, but chance guests are far more numerous; the bright lights attract everyone and no one is refused. The master of the house stays in the shadows, loses himself amid the general gaiety. Rumors circulate that he is the Kaiser's nephew, or perhaps, who knows, a successful murderer.

Who would guess there was a dreamer in this contemporary Trimalchio? A *nouveau riche* with an obscure reputation—and he is a romantic too? Perhaps Fitzgerald made the shadows too heavy? But when he learns Gatsby's story (and it is revealed near the end, before the denouement), the fabulously luxurious summer house does not strike one as irrelevant either to his character or his dream.

A boy from a farm in the sticks, he thirsted for a life unburdened by petty cares. A raucous pioneer of the Far West becomes the idol of his youth, a millionaire with a windblown face—as if he had stepped out of an ad for "American success." As he sails on the yatch of this bold and broad man of wealth, the son of a poor farmer discovers a life full of tinseled beauty which is irresistible to him.

In Gatsby's love, which is so poetic, there is also a purely American nuance.

Only the war gave him entree into society, into the cities of the South where he met the beauty Daisy. The poor fellow, who has an imagination, hesitates before acknowledging her the heroine of his dreams: "He knew all he had to do was kiss this girl, join her perishable breath to his . . . dreams, and goodbye forever the divine freedom of soaring thought."*

But precisely at this point, before leaving for the front, the glitter of wealth attracts him. In the rumbling, intertwining sounds of Daisy's voice he again hears the sound of money, and this does not upset him. The charm of luxury enhances the charm of the girl.

It is not easy for the hero to get Daisy back after the war; first of all he must return to her world himself. For this purpose he unhesitatingly takes the road of illegal profit. And fairly soon the penniless, demobilized soldier becomes the owner of a country home as dazzling as something out of Hollywood, one worthy of the Southern beauty.

Fitzgerald subtly shows that his romantic is an energetic Yankee; he belongs simultaneously to his dream and to the interests of business. During the long-awaited meeting with Daisy, when the hero feels both embarrassment and satisfied joy, the telephone rings; and business-like Gatsby complains to his slow-witted partner: "Well, he's no use to us if Detroit is his idea of a small town..." Romanticism—and at the same time habits which make delicacy impossible. The naturalness of the transition is striking; for Gatsby there is no contrast in this.

In his dream itself there is true beauty—and fake, tinsely beauty. His dream is an unnatural combination of love and money which doesn't smell. Before us is a romantic of the American type—one who has grown up in a country where wealth wears a halo.

But putting his hero in the very thick of American life, Fitzgerald shows his loneliness.

Gatsby has entree to various worlds, and he is alien to each of them. When the guests leave after his noisy parties he stands on the porch alone; these get-togethers were arranged only for Daisy, and she is not with him. He is also esteemed in the world of underground profits, but when he perishes no one there is concerned about it. Gatsby's patron, a big-time crook, does not even want to go to the funeral; business above all and one should not risk something for nothing.

What is to be said of the world of hereditary rich men which the hero wanted to enter in order to get Daisy back? There they view him as an upstart, a lower caste and even huge sums of money do not help. For Daisy's husband, dull-witted Tom, Gatsby, who has turned up from God knows where, is not simply a rival; no, he calls into question all traditional morality and family

---

*Retranslated. In the original: "He knew that when he kissed this girl, and forever wed his unutterable visions to her perishable breath, his mind would never romp again like the mind of God."

foundations. The infuriated Tom feels himself "on the last barricades of civilization." And to protect respectability he arranges the murder of the one who is disturbing the peace.

The story of the lonely and doomed dreamer turns into a novelistic plot quite naturally.

At the beginning of the book the narrator sees a trembling figure on the beach: Gatsby is looking intently into the distance. Later he calls his neighbor an artist who has created an ideal image of Daisy in his dreams. And he compares his hero, who is attracted by a green light on the dock at Daisy's summer house, to the first discoverers of a planet who see the untouched green bosom of the new world. Gatsby's romanticism, his rare "gift of hope" goes back to the great American tradition.

In the same figure we see national self-criticism and the poetry of the national character.

The depth of this figure was not immediately recognized. In any case, the literary people who sent Fitzgerald ecstatic letters about the novel were satisfied least of all by the main hero. The well known novelist Edith Wharton wrote: "In order to make Gatsby really great one would have to tell his pre-history in more detail; if the past were more fully illuminated, the reader would have a stronger sense of his tragedy."[†]   The poet John Bishop found that the figure of Gatsby seemed put together from scraps of different kinds of fabric. However, these rebukes did not take into account the dual levels of the novel: the hero exists in various dimensions, and he could not be depicted as the usual realistic character. An absurd modern Trimalchio—and a virtual symbol of the romantic dream. But this duality does not lead to the disintegration of the figure, and does not keep the book from finding a warm response, thanks to the masterfully drawn figure of the narrator.

The narrator, Nick Carraway, is Gatsby's complete opposite. By nature he is temperate and restrained; he studies the banking business carefully. His element is irony—the lavish parties at his neighbor's summer house annoy him; Gatsby himself strikes him as monstrously sentimental. Irony helps him to imperceptibly shift the narration from one level to another; in the most romantic passages devoted to Gatsby's love, poetry goes hand in hand with analysis.

But Gatsby and Nick do have something in common: they are both provincials, natives of the Midwest, who have not taken root in the East. The narrator, at first so far from Gatsby, will later shout after him that the people who surround him are "nonentity on nonentity, that's who they are . . . You're worth all of them put together." He compares the hero to the American people—who want to return what has been left behind and live on illusions. And at the same time he separates Gatsby, who is close to his American roots, from the pernicious and sham civilization of New York.

In his Paris sketches Hemingway said that Fitzgerald was a natural talent—like the pattern on a butterfly's wings. But he learned to think later, when the dust was rubbed off.

In speaking of natural talent, Hemingway apparently had in mind the freshness of romantic characters, something striking for a post-World War One writer. It is unlikely that any of the prose writers of the "lost generation" could have written about his hero's dream as Fitzgerald did—without fearing a skeptical reaction on the part of the readers: "A universe of ineffable gaudiness spun itself out in his brain while the clock ticked on the wash-stand and the moon soaked with wet light his tangled clothes upon the floor." Or as easily, as if by the way, sketch out the description of the same pink room lit first by the setting sun and later by a lamp. In general many of the descriptions in the book are saturated with lyricism and extraordinarily picturesque.

But combining opposites was part of Fitzgerald's talent. This aspect of his gift was pointed out after time itself helped evaluate the power of his poetic thought.

The narrator feels the enchantment of well-dressed and elemental gaiety at Gatsby's summer house; there is no regimentation here, no supervision—only great youth and love of life. He also feels the charm of New York "the racy, adventurous feeling of it at night." But on the way to the city is the valley of ashes—a gloomy dump over which the gigantic faded eyes of Doctor Eckleburg gaze from an old billboard advertising an oculist. This is a symbol of fate—alongside the carefree gaiety.

Fitzgerald was one of the most sensitive writers of the twenties—during the years of the boom he wrote novels and stories "with a touch of disaster," as he himself put it later—as if foreseeing (or rather, having a premonition of) the crash of 1929. The huge empty summer house with the extinguished lights and no guests—this was a prophetic picture.

The Great Gatsby is an accepted classic in America. For all the freshness of Fitzgerald's gift, one senses his high literary culture; beyond the narrator-moralist's tone one catches hints that the French and English have been read carefully. But Fitzgerald gave preference to the great Russian writer. "I always liked Dostoevsky with his wide appeal more than any other European," he wrote Hemingway. And defending *Gatsby* against the charge of being anecdotal, Fitzgerald observed that one could reduce *The Brothers Karamazov* to an anecdote too, but it was important to keep the second level in mind.

Kalashnikova's translation conveys the many levels of style in *Gatsby*—from parody of the society pages to dark visions in the spirit of El Greco. The Russian text preserves the novel's poetry, and this required inventiveness as well as imagination and great sensitivity to words.

In Western countries Fitzgerald is one of the most popular and respected writers of our century. It is well known that he wrote purely commercial things too; they have long been forgotten, but his best early stories are eagerly reprinted (such as the story "May Day" which has been translated into Russian). From this it is apparent that Fitzgerald had already learned to think in the very beginning of his career. In many countries his later novels have aroused great interest—*Tender Is the Night* and *The Last Tycoon.*These books, which contain his most penetrating analysis, show that his creativity was not exhausted even during the saddest years when he wrote apropos of his brief writing career: "There is no second act in the life of an American."[†]

It seems to me that Priestly was right when he noted in the preface to the London edition of Fitzgerald's work that what is striking is not that an American writer could not develop his talent (this caused him profound suffering), but that in difficult circumstances he could write so many first-rate things.

Those Russian readers who read Fitzgerald's best book will be waiting for new encounters with him—we hope they are not far in the future.

ORLOVA ON HEMINGWAY

Raisa Orlova (1918-) has been active as a critic of American literature for more than thirty years. She has written on virtually every major author of the twentieth century. Sometimes she co-authors articles with her husband, Lev Kopelev, a respected Germanist (who has also written on Hemingway and done introductions for the Soviet editions of Dorothy Parker); their 1958 essay on Faulkner was one of the first in Russian. Orlova's books include *The Descendants of Huckleberry Finn* (1964), *Jack London's* Martin Eden (1967), and *Harriet Beecher Stowe* (Moscow, 1971). The first book covers everything from Lincoln Steffens and Steinbeck to the most contemporary events, including one of her specialties—black literature and its relation to social movements. She has written widely on Martin Luther King and many of the black writers; currently she is working on a book about John Brown. A strong ideological tendency dominates her writing (according to the *Shorter Literary Encyclopedia* she has been a Party member since 1940), most of which is devoted to finding critical trends in American literature and society. However, when combined with her extremely broad information, ability to see historical lessons, and sensitivity—as in the Hemingway selection here—we see some of the best achievements of tendentious socialist criticism.

The Hemingway essay was published as a small book entitled *The Work of Ernest Hemingway* (Novosibirsk, 1968, 500 copies). It is translated in full except for a few pages which summarize American criticism of Hemingway. Hemingway, of course, is one of the darlings of the Russian reading public; indeed, he is probably the most popular foreign author. The bibliography of Russian editions and criticism fills an entire volume—with a political "recess" from 1939 to 1955 when absolutely nothing was written on him and only one story was published. This was broken with *The Old Man and the Sea* in 1955. However, because of its sensitive subject matter *For Whom the Bell Tolls* was not published until 1968—and then in a four-volume set of Hemingway along with heavy cuts in the text, particularly Chapter Eighteen.

R. Orlova

FOR WHOM THE BELL TOLLS

In May of 1937, on orders from the commanders of the Spanish Republican Army, an American named Robert Jordan crosses the front line to blow up a bridge in the Fascists' rear with the help of the partisans. He spends three days with the partisan band, carries out the order, and perishes.

If one had to do it in two sentences, the plot of Hemingway's *For Whom the Bell Tolls* could be summarized in this way.

One might retell the novel in detail, scene by scene, or tracing separate plot lines—Jordan, Maria, Pilar, the partisan band, the army staff. But this would inevitably break up that special artistically organized world outside of which there is no art, outside of which it is impossible to understand how a book could survive when it describes only a small episode in a distant and long-past war. Since that time many great, devastating wars and numberless battles have passed, oceans of blood have been spilled, and for us, the readers, *that* bridge, *that* band, *that* man, *that* hill—the last earthly retreat for Robert Jordan—have remained part of our own experience.

The novel's world is formed by a series of linkages peculiar to it; it is a world made dark by suffering, death, the tragedy of inescapable contradictions—but still it is a world of artistic harmony.

> But you, the artist, must firmly believe
> In ends and in beginnings. You know
> Where hell and paradise watch o'er us.
> It is your gift to measure all
> You see dispassionately.
> May your eyes be clear and hard;
> Expunge the accidental things.
> And you will see: the world is beautiful.

A retelling destroys the harmony of the artistic whole, cutting and simplifying these special linkages.

In order to avoid this, one must try, following the author, to enter this world in the same way an unprejudiced reader opening the first page of a new book would.

"No man is an *Iland,* intire of it selfe; every man is a peece of the *Continent,* a part of the *maine;* if a *Clod* bee washed away by the *Sea, Europe* is the lesse, as well as if a *Promontorie* were, as well as if a *Mannor* of thy *friends* or of *thine owne* were; any mans *death* diminishes *me,* because I am involved in

Mankinde; and therefore never send to know for whom the *bell* tolls; It tolls for *Thee."*

The epigraph gives the reader the key; definite conditions are established.

An excerpt from a sermon by the old English poet John Donne attunes us for the wave of poetry. Donne's poetry is full of magnetic power, and it returns many times during the novel: "No man is an island." It returns like a musical refrain, like the funereal tolling of the bell. It returns also because of its sense, its effects on reason—man is tied to humanity. Your acts are not only your acts, they concern others too. You do not live on an island—but on earth with other men.

The overture also attunes one to a philosophical strain—this will be a book about life and death, about the central problems of existence.

The first paragraphs after the epigraph give the reader other signals:

> He lay flat on the brown, pine-needled floor of the forest, his chin on his folded arms, and high overhead the wind blew in the tops of the pine trees. The mountain side sloped gently where he lay ; but below it was steep and he could see the dark of the oiled road winding through the pass. There was a stream alongside the road and far down the pass he saw a mill beside the stream and the falling water of the dam, white in the summer sunlight.
>
> "Is that the mill?" he asked.
>
> "Yes."
>
> "I do not remember it."
>
> "It was built since you were here. The old mill is further down; much below the pass."

This is a businesslike, realistic description; the details are as precise as possible, the location of the old and new mills is important. There is the tactical problem—the slightest imprecision could cost people their lives. Everything is important—both the steepness of the mountainside and the direction of the stream's current. This is not an impressionistic paysage, a capricious paysage based on mood—no, the author wants to assure the reader that this all happened precisely here, precisely at this time of year, precisely on this mountainside.

Twenty years later, in 1959, Hemingway went to Spain again. Mary Hemingway wrote in her diary: "By the road, to the right of the bridge, there was a river. It was the woods from *For Whom the Bell Tolls.* Through the trees you could make out the top of the hill where Papa had El Sordo fight, and on the bridge we saw where the explosion took place. Ernest murmured, 'I'm glad to see it; it's all just as I described it' . . ."*

The precision of realistic prose and the tension of elevated poetry intertwining throughout the whole book are not two separate qualities; they form a novellistic world which is as unified as the act of breathing.

------

*Retranslated.

The book begins with an objective third-person narrative: "He lay flat on the floor of the forest." This is the author's voice, the author describes the hero, his external appearance presents the old partisan Anselmo, the hero's guide. But already on page four, as soon as we learn that the young man's name is Robert Jordan, that he is hungry, and worried, we read:

> It was as simple to move behind them as it was to cross through them, if *you* had a good guide. It was only giving importance to what happened to *you if you* were caught that made it difficult; that and deciding whom to trust. *You* had to trust the people *you* worked with completely or not at all, and *you* had to make decisions about the trusting. He was not worried about any of that. *[My italics.]*

The objective epic narration is interrupted by a lyric monologue. The author's voice shifts over into the voice of a character—into disguised *erlebte Rede* or narrated monologue: "he" becomes "you." But this lyric monologue is not addressed to anyone, not any conversant—otherwise a constant "I" would be natural. Here Jordan is addressing Jordan, and a barely noticeable line separates the hero from the author who has just finished a sentence and broken off. There are no quotation marks, no introductory verbs ("thought Jordan"), not even a new paragraph. There is such unity of intonation that the shift from "he" to "you" may not even be noticed. At times "he" and "you" flow into each other ("And there is no 'I' which could judge 'you,' " he says elsewhere).

When he was beginning his literary career, Hemingway wrote to the well known critic Edmund Wilson, author of the first review of his first book *Three Stories and Ten Poems:*

> I've finished a book of fourteen stories with a short chapter from a book called *In Our Time* before each story—that's the way I conceived it—so as to give a picture of the whole before examining the details. It's like looking at an object passing by—and then looking at it through powerful binoculars. Or maybe looking, then going up close and living there, then going away again for another look from the distance again.†

For Whom the Bell Tolls is constructed this way too.

Jordan ponders the task before him:

> There was enough explosive and all equipment in the two packs to blow this bridge properly even if it were twice as big as Anselmo reported it, as he remembered it when he had walked over it on his way to La Granja on a walking trip in 1933, and as Golz had read him the description of it that night before last in that upstairs room in the house outside of the Escorial.

One more condition is set before the reader: the action unfolds in several time periods—in the present ("He lay flat on the...floor of the forest..."), the past (he was here in 1933, the not too-distant past), the day before he got the order from General Golz at army headquarters.

And there is a fourth dimension—the future, a conditional future.

Finally, there is an eternal category, beyond time, which is begun in the epigraph: "...every man is a peece of the Continent" yesterday, today, tomorrow—forever.

The transitions from one time to another are just as swift and un-noticeable as the transitions from the third person to the second. Jordan and Anselmo have just been talking, and all of a sudden Jordan and Golz are talking. Again the system of lenses changes.

The special, rapid tempo of the novel results from the instantaneousness of these transitions.

However, the tempo is not even, and toward the end of the book it gets markedly faster. But neither events nor people flash by fleetingly.

The narration is retarded by interpolated stories which are organically connected to the basic plot—such as Pilar's story about her lover, Phinito the matador, and the celebration dinner in his honor.

Enemy planes appear—a signal of inescapable danger—and immediately the tempo of the novel changes. When everything is ready for the bridge to be blown and the count gets down to seconds, the words and lines race head-long.

The "novelistic time" of three days is essentially a very short period. But during this time Jordan experiences curiosity, irritation, fear, bitterness, desperation, anger, rapture in battle, hope, tortured ruminations, love and separation from his beloved, the horror of inescapable death, and victory over this horror...

From the simplest experience everyone knows that not every hour is equal to every other hour, every day to every other day, each year to each year. In essence, because of their fullness, because of the intensive feelings, thoughts, and acts, these three days in Jordan's life are equal to a long lifetime.

The three days are inextricably tied to those which preceded them and to the whole history of his family and his country. Man is not an island—either in space or in time: men lived before you, and they will live after you. You are a link in an endless chain.

The past has grown organically into the present. Jordan's grandfather was a general during the American Civil War, and he determined important features of his grandson's moral character. A white American, he fought for the freedom of the Negroes. His grandson fights for the freedom of another people. There is reason for Jordan to address his grandfather so frequently at the end of the novel, asking his advice, trying to imagine how his grandfather would act in his place, to "look into" his grandfather to seek himself.

Jordan's father committed suicide. His memory of this has remained a recurrent feeling of sudden emptiness, a melancholy premonition of non-existence. This memory pursues Jordan even in his happiest moments with Maria. Because of this he feels shame and terror of acting as his father had; he fears egocentrism ("you have to be awfully occupied with yourself to do a thing like that," he thinks of his father—when he is quite sure that his own death is inescapable).

The novel is polyphonic; its ideological and its musical themes now occur separately, taking turns, now mix together, forming rich new variations.

Thus the theme of suicide comes up several times. It also comes up apropos of the fate of Kashkin the dynamiter.

Kashkin asks Jordan to shoot him if he is seriously wounded; he is afraid of falling into the hands of the Fascists and being tortured. He is seriously wounded, and Jordan fulfills his comrade's request. But then Jordan himself is seriously wounded. The same disturbing melody sounds. The Fascists are drawing near, and the partisan Augustin offers to shoot Jordan. But he refuses; he can still fight. A few minutes later, after Augustin leaves, when his consciousness is getting blurred, he does not allow himself suicide either:

> Oh, let them come, he said. I don't want to do that business that my father did. I will do it all right but I'd much prefer not to have to. I'm against that. Don't think about that. Don't think at all. I wish the bastards would come, he said.

The past cannot be thrown away and forgotten; it was and is; it breaks into the present and the future. But if necessary, one can surmount the past—it can be balanced against something else.

Future time occupies a lesser place in the novel. Military necessity obliges Jordan to think about the near future and the coming explosion, but he forbids himself to think about "afterward." However, still the distant, impossible future penetrates the narration. Pilar is teaching Maria how to be a wife. Robert asks how much time it will take for Maria's hair to grow out. They talk about their future children. He daydreams out loud about how Maria and he will go to Madrid, what hotel they will stay in, what they are going to do (however, even in his daydreams he flies across the ocean and introduces Maria to his college teachers only once).

Most often the future is a conditional future—what would happen if...

Pilar the gypsy reads Jordan's doom in his palm the first time they meet. True, in this situation no special prophetic gift is necessary. But only in the end, only when the near future has become a reality—the bridge has been blown, the partisans are retreating—only when Jordan is seriously wounded and knows with certainty that there are only a few minutes before his death, only then does he allow himself to dream about everything to his heart's content. About how he will destroy them—the Fascists—as many as possible, how he will hold them off for at least half an hour. And about other things—the whole army, the victorious general offensive, how the partisans need short-wave radios, and how "later on we will have these things much better organized."

The future is darkened first by the premonition and then by the certainty of his own doom. Darkened, but not blotted out entirely.

The intertwining of past and future time in the novel lends the book a quality of historicity, another kind of life.

Epic features which presuppose continuity and connection between the fate of humans and that of their nation are also part of this intensely lyrical novel.

As the novel progresses, the sense that the hours Jordan has left on earth are measured grows stronger. And this feeling is intensified by love:

> Well, so that is what happens and what has happened and you might as well admit it and now you will never have two whole nights with her. Not a lifetime, not to live together, not to have what people were always supposed to have, not at all. One night that is past, once one afternoon, one night to come; maybe. No, sir.
> Not time, not happiness, not fun, not children, not a house, not a bathroom, not a clean pair of pyjamas, not the morning paper, not to wake up together, not to wake and know she's there and that you're not alone. No. None of that. But why, when this is all you are going to get in life of what you want; when you have found it; why not just one night in the bed with sheets?

In our age Robert Jordan's life and death are both exceptional and ordinary. How many men there are since then—soldiers, prisoners, men locked up, evacuated, driven from their homes—who could repeat these bitter words. Bitter even in happiness. How many people there are who found their brief happiness in the dark and gave thanks for it. And here Jordan's experience has become universal experience.

Jordan's thoughts here echo one of the motifs from *The Fifth Column*. In the play Dorothy Bridges asks her beloved Philip, who fights in the ranks of the Republicans:

> Do you mean you wouldn't like to settle down someplace like St. Tropez, something like the old St. Tropez I mean, and live there for a long, long time, a peaceful and happy life, and have children and enjoy your happiness? I'm serious. Wouldn't you like for all of this to be over, the war and revolution and everything?[†]

And later the same words are repeated by Philip, the play's hero, during a very serious conversation with his friend. The tired, exhausted soldier dreams of peace. And these dreams are so natural, so humanly understandable

In Jordan's case, as in Philip's, the tragedy of unrealized dreams is intensified by the fact that they are completely realizable: of course, there, at home in America, he could have his own house, and clean pajamas, and a morning paper, and a bed with sheets. But then the life he had chosen would not exist, and that would mean Jordan himself would not exist.

II

For Whom the Bell Tolls is a book about Robert Jordan and a book about a partisan band, about the fighting Spanish people.

Hemingway's first book of stories, *In Our Time,* and his first novel, *Fiesta,* were books about himself and his generation, about his time, about eternity. But above all they are books about himself. Not just because they are in the first person. They are books not only about the lost generation, but, perhaps, *for* the lost generation as well. They are cut off from the other, larger world both by a way of life accessible only to a chosen few, and by their special jargon. Jake Barnes, the hero of *Fiesta,* says: "I don't care what the world is. All I want to know is how to live in it."[†]

Robert Jordan wants to know how to live in the world too. But he is no longer indifferent to what the world is.

A thousand threads tie Jordan to the heroes of Hemingway's first books. He is younger, and so he simply had no chance to participate in the first war which crippled their lives. But he speaks the same language, he read the same books, he went to the same kind of school, he said the same prayers, he ate the same apple pie. And he is very sorry about what he missed.

Robert takes a drink from a canteen in the partisans' cave, and one swallow like this:

> ...took the place of the evening papers, of all the old evenings in cafes, of all chestnut trees that would be in bloom now in this month, of the great slow horses of the outer boulevards, of book shops, of kiosques, and of galleries, of the Parc Montsouris, of the Stade Buffalo, and of the Butte Chaumont, of the Guaranty Trust Company and the Ile de la Cite, of Foyot's old hotel, and of being able to read and relax in the evening; of all the things he had enjoyed and forgotten.

This is what Robert Jordan thinks—but Jake Barnes could have thought the same thing. When the heroes of *Fiesta* go fishing in Burguete, an old man with a gristly grey head gets on the bus. He appears in the novel for only an instant—people like him are on the far periphery of Jake Barnes' (and the early Hemingway's) world. But for Jordan such men become much more real than customers in a Paris cafe, dearer and more real, his own.

Dozens of people are necessary in order for Jordan to carry out the order and blow up the bridge.

Unlike Hemingway's first books, the experience set down in *For Whom the Bell Tolls* is the heritage of many people, very many. Without the world of the common people this novel does not exist. It too is a continent of which every man is a part.

The first word uttered about Pilar is "barbarious," "very barbarious." However, for Hemingway it is not a swear-word. When Pilar's voice rings out, we hear pungent obscenities. And only then:

> Robert Jordan saw a woman of about fifty almost as big as Pablo, almost as wide as she was tall, in black peasant skirt and waist, with heavy wool socks on heavy legs, black rope-soled shoes and a brown face like a model for a granite monument.

Already in the physical description we have ordinariness, squatness and monumentality. Perhaps "granite" is the main word. Pilar is a mountain, a rock wall, the support of the small world into which Jordan walks.

The first words she addresses to Jordan are, "How are you and how is everything in the Republic?" The schematism of the sentence does not signify intellectual primitiveness. Pilar thinks clearly, she always strives to explain

124

the main thing without digressions. The Republic is the last and greatest love of this woman who has loved so much. When she dismisses Pablo, who runs off and takes away the explosives, she says to Jordan: "I have failed thee and I have failed the Republic."

She is the band's cook; her world is down-to-earth and sober. But she is a fortune-teller too; she is in contact with the world of incomprehensible, mysterious, black magic. She is a gypsy who has inherited an unquenchable thirst for freedom; who expects the Republic to give her freedom. And she is a Spaniard who is accustomed to submitting to her husband, but her husband Pablo is now losing his manliness and bravery—everything that made her fall in love with and marry him. But nevertheless he is her husband—and probably the last.

She has often seen death; she was the mistress of matadors; she is fearless and cruel, her heart has grown as hard as her overworked hands; but there is still female defenselessness under this armor. Pilar knows that she is very ugly—even so she is unaccustomed to this knowledge, she is hurt by her looks.

All of her inexhaustible tenderness has been concentrated on Maria. She protects and fosters Maria and Jordan's love, and she envies them in an older woman's way. She crudely interferes in their relations, but this is because she has a premonition—from wisdom and instinct—a premonition that their happiness will be shortlived, so she demands imperiously "hurry!" But she is truly delicate—she tries to cure Maria, to protect her from horror: Pilar orders her to leave when they are telling the story about the decapitated soldiers from El Sordo's band.

Jordan and Pilar quarrel about superstitions and whether one can foretell death. The naivete of self-satisfied reason is juxtaposed with a complex combination of the commonfolk's ignorance and profound wisdom. Pilar throws one sign of death after another at the stunned Jordan.*

You do not just read Hemingway's novels you see it, hear it, and touch it. Yury Olesha is right when he says that when one turns to Hemingway's novels "one cannot even be sure whether one is reading a book, watching a film, having a dream, or present at an event which is actually happening."

It is Pilar that Hemingway entrusts with the task of telling what is painful and important.

About the time that Jordan comes to the band, Pablo has become indifferent to whether the future is the Republic or Franco. He wants to live peacefully, eat his fill, and get drunk every day—only his own well-being interests him. "I can use dynamite," he says when he first meets Jordan. Pablo is a dangerous opponent. He is sober and practical, cruel and intelligent—and he is capable of anything. He knows how to hold back, even how

*Scott Fitzgerald had extremely high praise for this scene.

to withstand insults. He is the only one in the band who foresees the consequences of the explosion, precisely because he *cannot* believe as unconditionally as Pilar. He is a broad and dialectical figure; the cruel Pablo thinks about what is going to happen to the partisans after the explosion more than all of the good people do. Old horsetrader that he is, he is extraordinarily tender with horses; and it is only to horses that he walks like a human.

An anarchist, he has accepted the war of liberation primarily under the slogan "all is allowed." For him the revolution is an orgy of destructive instincts.

Pilar is the embodiment of reliabiltiy. Pablo betrays them twice in the course of the novel. He had opposed the explosion from the beginning: "I don't go for your bridge." "Thou wilt blow no bridge here." Then he walks off by himself, gathers up the blasting caps, and throws them in the river. He tries to act on the principle that "man is an island." But he feels so lonely that he returns to the band. Basically he repeats the words of Harry Morgan, the hero of *To Have and Have Not:* "A man alone can't make it." He comes to the same conclusion, but it is too late, very late.

A cynic, he is the last to believe in Jordan. The way his character develops is unexpected. Basically he is the one who saves the situation; the whole operation might have been aborted without him—and the men and horses he brings. But he remains himself to the end—the "extra" shots which the surprised Jordan hears (when the Fascists could no longer fire) meant that Pablo had killed the three new men whom he had brought. He killed them to take over their horses. Pablo is also capable of having pangs of conscience for the senseless and cruel murders of which he himself is guilty.

Pablo is a Spaniard to the marrow of his bones; he is proud of Spain, he mournfully complains that "a Spanish priest ought to die properly," and somewhere deep inside him there is a small hidden amount of Spanish chivalry. No, a woman like Pilar did not marry him just by chance.

Old Anselmo is a very kind man, a true Christian; for him the revolution is above all the triumph of good. He serves the Republic in faith and truth, but the soldiers' craft disgusts him:

> I don't like to kill, killing is a sin, we will all answer for it. Not all of our opponents are convinced Fascists. They are Christians like us. Why kill every one of them like Pablo and Augustin want; we should re-educate them, teach them with work. Otherwise we will never see the Republic.[†][*]

---

*"At this point the road crossed from south to north, and our group had to cut across this way. We were guided by an old Spaniard. He was seventy, his name was Batist, a man of the kindest nature. I told Hemingway that he was a confirmed opponent of killing people. For Spanish partisans, especially at first, this was to some extent characteristic; deciding to enter the Civil War was not so simple," recalls General Khadji Mamsurov. [*Zhurnalist,* No. 1, 1968.]

When the battle for the bridge is imminent, Anselmo fears not his own almost inevitable death, but the necessity of shooting at the sentry. He thinks of some form of civil repentance for the spilled blood. Pilar does the same.

There is a direct link between Anselmo and the fisherman Santiago, hero of *The Old Man and the Sea.*

Anselmo is just as reliable as Pilar. And Jordan's joy when he finds Anselmo at his post during the battle is quite natural—if in spite of snow, cold and fatigue one flank is holding, all is not yet lost.

Only when Anselmo is dead does Robert see how small, wizened, and old he is—sixty-eight.

The revolution has confused human lives, turned them upside down; each of the partisans has brought his past, his character and fate to the band— and here in the common pot everything is stewed. While retaining what is his own, each character is augmented and changed too; something which joins them all appears.

The characters in the band are inexhaustibly various—it is a model and a microcosm of human society in the twentieth century.

Fernando is a glutton and polite bureaucrat. An unintelligent, pompous bore, he seems to be cardboard. He likes to weave his sentences in dependent clauses.

The partisans discuss whether or not to leave Pablo alive. Fernando starts talking as if he were not in a partisan cave with seven people, but at the podium during a huge assembly:

> "Since it is impractical to hold Pablo as a prisoner," Fernando commenced, "and since it is repugnant to offer him—"
> "Finish," Pilar said. "For the love of God, finish."
> "In any class of negotiation," Fernando proceeded calmly, "I am agreed that it is perhaps best that he should be eliminated in order that the operations projected should be insured of the maximum possibility of success."
> Pilar looked at the little man, shook her head, bit her lips and said nothing.
> "That is my opinion," Fernando said. "I believe we are justified in believing that he constitutes a danger to the Republic—"
> "Mother of God," Pilar said. "Even here one man can make a bureaucracy with his mouth."

Addressing Jordan, Fernando calls him "Don Roberto"—he wants everyone to be polite and address each other this way. For him the revolution is above all order, a regimentation of words and relationships.

Fernando is mortally wounded by the explosion of the bridge; he asks his comrades to abandon him—he is doomed anyway, and they will still manage to save themselves.

Of Augustin Anselmo says from the beginning, "He is good." Very good. And coming from Anselmos this characterization is valuable.

Augustin is cruel. He expresses very different feelings (sometimes they are extremely complex and contradictory) in obscenities. (All of the members of the band swear except Fernando.)

Swearing is above all a defense against rhetoric, a form of lowering—the modern epos cannot be carried off completely in the solemn key of John Donne's stanzas.

Examining the meaning of swearing in ordinary life, M. Bakhtin writes (see his book *Francois Rabelais):*

> The downward direction is characteristic of all forms of carnival gaiety and grotesque realism among the commonfolk . . .
>
> Commonfolk carnival street language abuses as it praises, praises as it abuses . . . Every time conditions permit absolutely complete, non-official, vital interaction words begin to tend toward this kind of ambivalent fullness. As the ancient square comes to life when conditions such as one has in social contact in one small room hold, so intimacy begins to sound like the ancients' familiarity—destroying all social borders between people.

A non-official, complete, and whole vital interaction occurs in this partisan band—in social conditions which are not at all "indoor." This "ancient familiarity" is quite typical of these people.

Partisan life is primordial in everything including words.

Swearing which combines both abuse and praise directed downward is also an expression of relative immortality—the beginning of fecundity, the constant reproduction of the human race. Swearing is release—an almost physical release from tension.

After the bridge is blown Jordan begins to swear; he is not aping the others—the swearing is born of the circumstances.

The leader of the second partisan band is El Sordo—a neighbor, comrade, and friend—so says Pilar. El Sordo does not reveal himself to Jordan right away; he does not admit the reader into his inner world right away. He protects himself from outsiders—from the foreigner—by means of a special jargon which is elliptical. And only when El Sordo begins to speak normally does Jordan understand that he has been accepted as one of their own.

The hilltop which El Sordo defends is surrounded by the Fascists, who outnumber them many times and who have air support besides. The partisans are doomed. The legendarily epic hero is formed   while awaiting death in relation to death, in battle against death—this is the typical Hemingwayesque trial. The motif of suicide is repeated again, but here it is only as a stage-play to attract and destroy more Fascists.

In *For Whom the Bell Tolls* interior monolgues   reveal the spiritual worlds of the intellectual, Jordan, and the peasant, El Sordo.

El Sordo is seriously wounded. He is in great pain. He does not want to die. He does not accept death:

> Whether one has fear of it or not, one's death is difficult to accept....he looked at the sky and at the far mountains and he swallowed the wine and he did not want it. If one must die, he thought, and clearly one must, I can die. But I hate it.

Alone with himself El Sordo thinks, and grieves, and laughs, and he is ironical:

> It is shaped like a chancre. Or the breast of a young girl with no nipple. At the top cone of a volcano. You have never seen a volcano, he thought. Nor will you ever see one. And this hill is like a chancre. Let the volcanos alone. It's late now for the volcanos.

He plays no roles—he tells himself calmly and bitterly that the deaths of others in similar circumstances are no more consolation than it is for a widow to know that other beloved husbands have died too.

In Hemingway's universe people often perish, they talk frequently and at length about death. But for El Sordo:

> Dying was nothing and he had no picture of it nor fear of it in his mind. But living was a field of grain blowing in the wind on the side of a hill. Living was a hawk in the sky. Living was an earthen jar of water in the dust of the threshing with the grain flailed out and the chaff blowing. Living was a horse between your lets and a carbine under one leg and a hill and a valley and a stream with trees along it and the far side of the valley and the hills beyond.

It is characteristic for a peasant to perceive life this way. Formulating these sensations in words is characteristic above all of the intellectual, the writer—a man of highly developed spiritual culture. Narrated monologue unites the hero and the author—the epic and the lyric strains flow together.

For El Sordo the revolutionary war is the wealth of life.

The partisans are different kinds of people united by devotion to the Republic. The words "for the sake of the Republic" become a common expression of a just-acquired meaning to life. Even the furious swearer Augustin proudly says that he serves "the star of the Republic."

The end of El Sordo's band is described by Hemingway as a solemn requiem, as a poem in prose. But the pathos does not signify idealization. Before death the partisans recall various real and unreal insults, they slander and they swear, life is presented in its rich unpredictability.

When we first come to the cave with Jordan and see its inhabitants—who have already gotten unused to danger and are "starting to rot" (according to Pilar)—and we see laziness and irresponsibility, it is hard to imagine how they are all going to act (including Pablo) at the decisive moment, when the bridge is blown.

Hemingway knows how to make one feel the depth of the human sea and the many ways in which it may be measured. At the greatest depths there is the kinship of man with animal—there are also ancestral beliefs, wisdom accumulated during the centuries, the whole world of premonitions, prescience, and the irrational which is expressed especially obviously in Pilar.

The writer often relies on the method formulated in the letter to Wilson—to glance, then to look through binoculars, then to move closer and look from the inside out. When at dawn a Fascist unexpectedly appears near the partisans' cave on horseback, Jordan aims carefully at his chest. The man does not and should not exist in such circumstances—there is only a target. But several chapters later they bring the man's knapsack to Jordan and he reads his letters. The target turns into a man, a piece of another man's life comes into existence—the village of Tafale, the dead man's fiancee and sister...

Hemingway does not depict the people as god-bearers. Belonging to the oppressed classes is no guarantee against stupidity, cowardice or baseness.

The partisans see different things in the revolution. They are searching for different things in the revolution. Each fights for the Republic in his own way. But at decisive moments there is a transformation. At the explosion of the bridge and at the defense of the mountain, there is a mysterious leap, a miracle—and dissimilar, disunited, rugged beings become one—the revolutionary commonfolk.

III

Jordan is not a member of the oppressed classes. He is a college teacher and a writer—in a word, an intellectual. This revolution has not touched him personally; it is not even his own country that has been attacked. He has been drawn to the task of the Republic by conscience and conviction; he comes to the Spanish people's revolutionary struggle from "the skies of poetry."

Jordan's position in the band is that of a military specialist. He comes to the band as an emissary of the Republic, as the commander of the operation; but he still has to prove that his personal qualities match his position and that he is fit to lead. Initially, he makes a few mistakes. At the first council of war he should not have immediately started telling El Sordo and Pilar what to do, especially not with platitudes: "We have enough work and enough things that will be done without complicating it with chicken-crut. Fewer mysteries and more work."

But Jordan quickly corrects his errors. In three days he proves (proves with his life in the end) that he really deserves the right to lead.

In the beginning he tries to ignore the depth and contradictoriness of life. During the argument about superstitions he opposes Pilar using nothing but the calculations of abstract logic.

Besides lacking experience, besides the fact that Jordan's cultural background is different, his striving (which is not always acknowledged) to protect himself from future misfortune plays a role. Of course, he protects himself in order to fulfill his duty consistently. The more Pilar becomes attached to him, the more she wants to forget what she read in his hand—to hide it in the same unconscious depths from which her insight emerged. She does this not only because of her interest in Jordan, but also to protect the sacred cause of the Republic.

But Jordan's role in the book is much broader and more important than commanding the demolition of a bridge.

Several times he says (to himself and others) that his thoughts are on leave until the war ends. There is no truth in these words. Words such as these led to the widespread myth about the anti-intellectualism of Hemingway and his heroes. In reality, Jordan thinks intensely, frequently, and painfully. He searches for the truth: how can a man live a moral life during a revolutionary struggle? Jordan is not just an intellectual because of his untiring ability, his mental need to waver, doubt, and search for the truth, never stagnating and satisfied with a solution discovered previously.

Jordan gives himself a strict order: "You have no right to forget anything. You have no right to shut your eyes to any of it nor any right to forget any of it nor to soften it nor to change it."

Given the precious ability to think, one is obliged to think as fearlessly as one fights. One must face the truth, no matter how bitter it may be. And often this is no easier than fighting bravely.

Before the war Jordan had written a book about Spain, which in the opinion of the Soviet journalist Karkov possessed a rare virtue—absolute truthfulness. He dreams of another book too:

> He would write a book when he got through with this. But only about the things he knew. But I will have to be a much better writer than I am now to handle them, he thought. The things he had come to know in this war were not so simple.

In order to write this new book he had first of all to feel the struggle of the Spanish people as if it were his own personal affair. This did happen.

> ...you did the thing there was to do and knew that you were right. You learned the dry-mouthed, fear-purged, purging ecstasy of battle and you fought that summer and that fall for all the poor in the world, against all tyranny, for all the things that you believed and for the new world you had been educated into.

In *A Farewell to Arms* Hemingway excised high-sounding words which he felt had lost their value. But now ellipsis and allegory are supplanted by sublime words which contain a golden lode of truth and bravery; a sublime Bible lexicon and pathos are used together with the old English forms of address—"thee," and "thou." The intonation is solemn and religious.

Joseph Beach correctly noted that Hemingway was able "to combine in their effect on our feelings the mundane homeliness of the Republican cause and the poetry of religious feeling."[†] Another scholar, Edward Fenimore, in his work, "English and Spanish in *For Whom the Bell Tolls*" discusses the "Elizabethan tone of the language":

> ...and it is inevitable. His narration is epic in sweep because of the obvious fact that the characters he is describing stand for something bigger than themselves and the action in which they participate is the culmination of profoundly opposed national and international forces. Elizabethan language is the English epic language and Hemingway constantly uses the forms of precisely this language which corresponds to the world he is creating.[†]

The stanzas from John Donne put the reader in the correct mood; it is a sublime, tragic, purifying vein:

...you felt that you were taking part in a crusade. That was the only word for it although it was a word that had been so worn and abused that it no longer gave its true meaning. You felt, in spite of all bureaucracy and inefficiency and party strife something that was like the feeling you expected to and did not have when you made your first communion. It was a feeling of consecration to a duty toward all of the oppressed of the world which would be as difficult and embarrassing to speak about as religious experience and yet it was authentic as the feeling you had when you heard Bach, or stood in Chartres Cathedral or the Cathedral at Leon and saw the light coming through the great windows; or when you saw Mantegna and Greco and Brueghel in the Prado. It gave you a part in something that you could believe in wholly and completely and in which you felt an absolute brotherhood with the others who were engaged in it. It was something that you had never known before but that you had experienced now and you gave such importance to it and the reasons for it that your own death seemed of complete unimportance; only a thing to be avoided because it would interfere with the performance of your duty. But the best thing was that there was something you could do about this feeling and this necessity too. You could fight.

Though he is capable of rising to spiritual sublimity, Jordan still lives on a sinful earth. War is war, and in war his soul becomes coarser. If it is necessary for the living, he is capable of smashing his fist against a lifeless head in order to push a corpse out of an armored car.

Jordan would like to merge totally with the Republican struggle, and sometimes this does happen—but not always and not to the end. He gives his life to the battle unquestioningly, but "nobody owned his mind, nor his faculties for seeing and hearing."

Robert comes to the band, makes friends with the partisans, and they accept him. The first long, frank conversation he has is with Pilar. She tells him of her unqualified faith in the Republic.

"And do you have this same faith?"
"In the Republic?"
"Yes."
"Yes," he said, hoping it was true.

Another time, just before the explosion itself, Jordan writes a report to headquarters while Pablo interrupts him with questions:

"What did you say?" he asked Pablo.
"That I have confidence, Ingles," Pablo was still addressing the wine bowl.
Man, I wish I had, Robert Jordan thought.

Jordan is the very center of revolutionary events, but at the same time he can view it from above. The author gets across his ability to see things from above by means of a subtle stylistic "distancing."

One feels this distancing in many scenes where Jordan remembers the Gaylord Hotel. Jordan is not simply with the Republicans, he is with the Communists; he has accepted the discipline of the Communists during the war, but his mind, his anxiously searching mind accepts no discipline or limitations.

His predecessors in Hemingway's works had studied and learned how to insulate themselves from the bitter and difficult things. Nick Adams ("On the Big River") catches fish, and the monotonous repetition of identical movements dissipates the sadness of a man who has lost his illusions in an unjust war. But Jordan cannot do it like this. He walks to himself, reiterating bitter thoughts, trying to make sense out of what is happening. And thus he speaks not only as the leader of a military operation, but also as the memory and conscience of the revolutionary struggle. That is, he speaks as a member of the intelligentsia.

Let me cite the words of two members of the intelligentsia who stand at a maximum distance from politics, and therefore evaluate the battle in Spain using only the laws of morality. Albert Einstein wrote: "The only event which in the conditions typical of our age can support our hope for better times is the Spanish people's heroic struggle for the freedom of men and human values" (July, 1937).[†] William Faulkner answered the League of American Writers' question this way: "I want to state as frankly as possible that I am an unreserved opponent of Franco and Fascism in their violent acts against the legal government and all their violence against the people of Republican Spain" (1938).[†]

Among the childish diseases of "the left" in young revolutionary literatures is this: the role of the members of the intelligentsia in the revolution is measured by the extent to which he has managed to overcome the fact that he is an intellectual. Overcoming one's reflectiveness, overcoming the ability to doubt and vacillate, means in essence overcoming the ability to search for the truth. It means overcoming and rejecting the very thing which is always the main duty of the intellectual everywhere.

And perhaps in the light of historical experience it would be worth devoting some thought to this usual scheme: bourgeois intellectual (i.e. "limited"), plus the common people who are always right about everything— who are always superior to the bourgeois intellectual in everything. But can one really say that Jordan is inferior to Pilar, inferior to Anselmo or Pablo? His loyalty to the Republic is no less than theirs—he gives up everything for it. In the end, like El Sordo, he sells his life dearly. And his turbulent mind is not a selfish mind closed in itself; it is a mind which above all else protects the task of the Republic. It is a mind thinking about his comrades, their fate and future.

IV

Critics have often noted that Hemingway's novel is constructed in ever-widening concentric circles, with the bridge in the center. All threads of the plot lead to the bridge: Jordan has come here to blow up the bridge, in the end the bridge is blown up. On the philosophical level a bridge is a symbol of ties between people ("no man is an island").

Each chapter is strictly subordinated to the whole, but like a small dramatic scene, each chapter is complete in itself.

When a man gives himself completely to something it is characteristic that he consider this the main thing for other people too. Of course, such notions may not correspond to the truth (Pablo's partisans consider the blowing up of the train the main thing—Jordan does not agree with them); however, even in this case the abstraction itself might trick, entice, and infect. But if this thing could in reality be decisive and definitive—if it were true that "this bridge might turn out to be the axis around which the fate of humanity turns," then depicting this in its true proportions offers the writer a chance to create a work in which characters and actions reach far beyond the limits of the given, concretely-described event.

Operating with the category "if...then" is difficult in history. But if the Fascists had been defeated in this dress-rehearsal in Spain, if the United Front had not been broken, if there had been no tragicomedy of non-intervention, if everyone had fought like Jordan and El Sordo—then there might not have been a fall of Paris, nor the bombing of Coventry, nor Lidice, nor the swastikas at Kiev... Therefore Jordan's idea that "if we win here, we will win everywhere" is full of profound historical content.

The partisan band's battle is significant by itself, but it is also connected to a larger war, to other sections of the front, to headquarters—and the battle may extend beyond the boundaries of Spain.

This system of circles makes it possible for the author to do what he mentioned when he was still a young writer: to go up closely to something, examine it, then step back for a long distance look—this way there would be perspective.

As readers we transcend the small circle in the thoughts of Jordan or in Andres crossing the enemy lines with the report; then we find ourselves in different spheres, and it is as if the partisan detachment shrinks, becoming a visible but smaller and smaller point on the military map. It is a three-hour treck from the cave to headquarters. Only three hours. But how unbearably slow Andres moves.

The same event becomes a phenomenon which we perceive in completely different ways depending on our vantage-point—from inside, from outside, from various distances. The masterful structuring of the novel shifts the reader imperceptibly but constantly further and further from the frontline trench to the headquarters and then back again.

Then, in the Hotel Gaylord, the rumor that the Fascists have been firing on each other by mistake starts. Naturally everyone wants to believe it, but Karkov notices that Jordan is in the same partisan band "where this business they spoke of is supposed to happen." But we have just been there ourselves, and within a page we will return; we know what is actually happening there. The effect is stereoscopic; that fourth or fifth dimension of which Hemingway dreamed has been added to our vision.

Chapter 32 ends with Karkov lying down to get some sleep, "because at two o'clock he would be starting for the drive...to the front." And the next chapter begins with the words, "It was two o'clock in the morning when Pilar waked him." Grammatically, formally, "he" is Karkov, about whom we have just been told. But as a result of the higher structural logic to which the novel is subordinated, it is clear to the reader (who has already been prepared by what has come before) that "he" is Robert Jordan. We have again been shifted into the circle of central importance—the band.

Hemingway wrote his novel when the Spanish Republic had been defeated, when the Fascists were marching victoriously across Europe. This put a mournful cast on the tone of the whole book. Mournful, but not at all hopeless. It is by showing the conduct of his heroes that Hemingway asserts the necessity of fighting to the end in one's sector and considering one's machine-gun position the center of the world conflict with the Fascists and "the turning point in the history of mankind"—even though you will perhaps not see the end of this conflict. Most likely you will not.

Isn't this what the defenders of Brest felt and thought—the soldiers who fell, surrounded, near those for whom there was no land beyond the Volga? Didn't many of them think over and over, "if we win here, we will win everywhere?.."

The tragic dilemma is symbolized by the very structure of the novel—a system of concentric circles: what is man—an end or a means? It symbolizes the link between one small band, a tiny dot on the map, and the entire world, enveloped in war.

In war, in any war, man is a means. The basis of the novel's plot is the destruction of a bridge in order to protect the general offensive; i.e., the men who are blowing up the bridge are essentially means to an end which is located within them. But this is only one level of an artistic idea which has many layers.

Precisely at the moment when Jordan first meets Anselmo and thinks about the man who is going to help him and about other men, precisely then he imagines the bridge as "the point on which the future of the human race can turn."

Inside the partisan world we find a new circle of the plot: El Sordo's band perishes defending a hill, but the partisans of Pablo cannot come to their aid. It would be useless anyway, because the Fascists are infinitely more numerous; but in any case he cannot allow himself to do that, because then the bridge would not be blown. That is, the men of El Sordo's band serve as means to an end which is within them:

> You were fighting against exactly what you were doing and being forced into doing to have any chance of winning. So now he was compelled to use these people whom he liked as you should use troops toward whom you have no feeling at all if you were to be successful.

This is what Jordan thinks in his torment.

It is horrifying not to help El Sordo, more horrifying than helping him. To be so close, to hear the shots, understand exactly what is happening there.

And then, when the shots quiet down, and the last one... It is as if there, on the hill, which El Sordo is hopelessly defending, every Fascist shot is striking Jordan and Pilar and Anselmo—all of the participants in this tragical nonintervention.

It is terrifying for a man to be a means. Jordan forces himself to consider himself a cipher, a cog ("Neither you nor this old man is anything. You are instruments to do your duty"). That is the way military discipline is, that is the way revolutionary duty is.

True, in this respect too a partisan army differs from a regular army. A partisan band levels personality to a lesser degree; it is not chance that specifically partisan wars have produced so many colorful personalities—from Chapaev to Che Guevara.

But the heroes of a partisan band are also touched by the tragic and universal problem of the personal versus the general, the end versus the means.

If man is a means, then all is allowed for the attainment of the end—including the physical destruction of man.

In *To Have and Have Not* (finished in Spain in 1937) the following conversation takes place between the smuggler Harry Morgan and a young Cuban, a bankrobber:

> "We want to do away with all the old politicians, with all the American imperialism that strangles us, with the tyranny of the army. We want to start clean and give every man a chance. We want to end the slavery of the *guajiros,* you know, the peasants, and divide the big sugar   estates among the people that work them. But we are not Communists."
>
> Harry looked up from the compass card at him.
>
> "How you coming on?" he asked.
>
> "We just raise money now for the fight," the boy said. "To do that we have to use means that later we would never use. Also we have to use people we would not employ later. But the end is worth the means. They had to do the same thing in Russia . . . . I regret   the necessity for the present phase very much. I hate terrorism. I also feel very badly about the methods for raising the necessary money. But there is no choice . . . . I do things I hate. But I would do things I hate a thousand times more."

An interior monologue by Harry follows:

> To help the working man he robs a bank and kills a fellow works with him and then kills that poor damned Albert that never did any harm. That's a working man he kills. He never thinks of that. With a family.

In *For Whom the Bell Tolls* the theme of force, the right to force, arises during the very first episodes. Jordan says to Anselmo:

> "I do not like to kill animals."
>
> "With me it is the opposite," the old man said. "I do not like to kill men."
>
> "Nobody does except those who are disturbed in the head," Robert Jordan said. "But I feel nothing against it when it is necessary. When it is for the cause."

It is as if Jordan is reiterating what the young Cuban in *To Have and Have Not* said. The sentence and the feeling it represents are simplistic, almost sloganistic. There are many cliches in what Jordan says. This is the beginning of the theme. But as it develops it becomes far more profound, complex, and contradictory.

Without thinking about it, instinctively, Jordan does not kill Pablo—contrary to the partisans' expectations. Judging by calculation, by arithmetic, Pablo should be wiped away, "liquidated" as Fernando says. After all, not only does Pablo not wish to help, he is a hindrance—he could betray them. They are all in agreement about this, even Pilar.

Jordan is ready; physically he is ready to shoot, his hand is already unsnapping the holster. Jordan's reactions to the enemy are instantaneous; he shoots the Fascist horseman without a second's hesitation—because that shot is essential and justified. But in the cave he acts differently. Pablo is not an enemy. Pablo does not start the fight. And Pablo does not expect to be shot. Shooting him is against Hemingway's code. "I cannot act in that way. It is repugnant to me and it is not how one should act for the cause," he explains to the gypsy.

There is a complex interweaving of this theme, but the complexities are real, not contrived. Jordan acts according to the laws of the algebra of the feelings; he listens to his inner voice.

Not for a second does he doubt the final outcome: "[Why am I putting these good people in danger?] For what? So that, eventually, there should be no more danger and so that the country should be a good place to live in." But how is this to be achieved; what is the path, what is the means? The problem torments Jordan all through the novel. He cannot and does not want to run away from it; he does not dare forget it.

"How many is that you have killed?" he asked himself. "I don't know. Do you think you have a right to kill anyone? No, but I have to." This is no longer interior monologue. It is, rather, interior *dialogue,* a conversation, an argument between Jordan and his second "I," with his conscience. Different voices and convictions which are sometimes opposites clash; different shades of thought and feeling clash in one soul and one mind. Thus Jordan's sometimes corrosive doubts are planted in us too. Jordan searches for the truth:

> How many of those you have killed have been real Fascists? Very few. But they are all the enemy to whose forces we are opposing force.

These ruminations are definitely not scholastic abstractions, the exercises of an intellect at leisure. For Jordan action and idea are united. After all, these ideas arise precisely when the dead Fascist ceases to be his target and becomes a man, when Jordan reads the letters addressed to the man and simple peasant life appears before his eyes. The generalization is born of something concrete—personal feeling and observation. It is more difficult to forget the man you have just killed than the "thesis" of an argument.

> It is right, he told himself, not reassuringly, but proudly. I believe in the people and their right to govern themselves as they wish. But you mustn't believe in

killing, he told himself. You must do it as a necessity but you must not believe in it. If you believe in it the whole thing is wrong.

Critics have often reproached Hemingway for being "entranced by violence." André Maurois maintained that Hemingway "takes masochistic pleasure in suffering." Alvah Bessie wrote of his "pathological proclivity for blood and mutilation." But in reality the tragic necessity which became the personal and inescapable torment of the writer and his hero was the necessity of killing in order, at some later time, to not to have to kill anyone ever again.

Every sharp turning point, every lurch forward in the history of mankind has meant crossing rivers, or seas, of blood. Marx said that human progress is like the pagan idol which drank nectar only from the skulls of men who had been murdered.

The necessity of killing oppressors counters the abhorrence of violence which is deeply rooted in the normal heart and mind. The simplest and holiest commandment "Thou shalt not kill" is contradicted by the impossibility of obeying this commandment in a world of war and Fascism. And therefore Jordan is forced to expunge his doubts sternly:

> I have to keep you straight in your head. Because if you are not absolutely straight in your head you have no right to do the things you do for all of them are crimes and no man has a right to take another man's life unless it is to prevent something worse happening to other people.

It was not "all straight" to Hemingway himself. And to whom was it straight?

The numerous scenes of Fascist violence make one catch one's breath over and over, from pain and anger; over and over one understands why it was impossible to stand on the sidelines, impossible not to shoot.

The novel also contains a scene of violence directed against the Fascists—Pilar's story about how in a small village during the first days of the war the Falangists were subjected to painful (and senseless) execution. It is bitter and painful to read this scene, more bitter and painful than reading about the Fascist atrocities, because it is about one's own comrades.

As Hemingway emphasizes, it is true to historical reality for the anarchists to behave like wild animals. Still and all, these *were* men and women from the masses, the people.

At the start of this chapter Pilar talks about herself and her ugliness; but the word "ugliness" becomes crucial in a different sense—a moral one: her story about human hearts which have been mutilated and made ugly.

Different sorts of people—among them kind, merciful, and quite ordinary men—turn into the many-limbed, many-headed beast known as the mob. The English word "mob" means not just "crowd," i.e., not just a simple collection, a multitude, but specifically a crowd of people in a psychotic state, people turning to violence.

The natural man (the hunter, fisherman, matador, or peasant) about whom Hemingway wrote so often is definitely not the noble savage from

Utopian novels. He too can act like this.

Hemingway is just as terrified and repulsed as Pilar is by everything he sees, and like her, he cannot turn away. He has to see everything; he follows his own precept that one should not close one's eyes.

Pilar also brings up this terrible recollection because she believes sacred-ly in the Republic, and her harmonious character demands exorcising every-thing that does not match its ideals.

Centuries of oppression cannot but be expressed in the very character of a revolution. Pablo's concept that the revolution is an orgy of destructive instincts is not simply his personal misconception. That was the way it was in the Movement, and it could not have been otherwise: the human material was too heterogeneous and too maimed.

Unfortunately, the thirty years which have passed since the publication of the novel present many proofs of the accuracy and the power of what he foresaw.

Jordan returns to this circle of thought over and over; the night before the explosion, recalling Pilar's story, he says to himself sadly:"I know that we did dreadful things to them too. But it was because we were uneducated and knew no better." The grief and shame of the Republic are his own per-sonal grief and shame—not "they," but "we."

The peasant Anselmo thinks of the same thing: "If we no longer have religion after the war then I think there must be some form of civic penance organized that all may be cleansed from the killing or else we will never have a true and human basis for living." Truly, the simple people's morality dic-tates such thoughts: "That we should win this war and shoot nobody," An-selmo said. "That we should govern justly and that all should participate in the benefits according as they have striven for them."

I do not know whether Hemingway ever read Babel, but Anselmo repeats almost exactly the ideas of another dreamer, the witness of another civil war. Gedali, the owner of a shop in Zhitomir, says: "I want an Inter-national of good people, I want one that would take care of every soul and give it a top priority ration."*

Anselmo concludes: "That we should shoot none. Not even the leaders. That they should be reformed by work."

Almost everyone would like it to be this way. So far in history it has not been this way. And can it ever be?

But in these naive Utopian dreams we find the embodiment of that future for which people are willing to fight, for which they agree to lay down their lives.

And it is not primarily enemy lives which Anselmo is protecting here; he is protecting his comrades, it is them he wants to save from participation in the executions—and even from the sight of the executions, something

---

*Babel and Hemingway are compared—on totally different grounds—

which always corrupts.

Of course, the problem of ends and means, the problem of violence is not a new one. It arose if not with the first killing on earth, at least with the first awakening of conscience.

Ivan Karamazov returns his ticket to the future, rejecting the crystal palace if that palace is built on one tear of a tortured child.

Of course, Hemingway did not solve these problems, no more than Dostoevsky did. But writers do not have to solve problems.

By embodying in words a part of the moral experience of his contemporaries, Hemingway fulfills the writer's obligation. This experience teaches: when one man is humiliated, tortured, and killed—these humiliations, tortures, and killings touch me too, "for I am Part of all Humanity."

V

Each man is tied to other people, and therefore it is a necessity created by circumstances to subordinate one life to others. But at the same time each human life is valuable in itself. "If a cliff is swept into the sea by a wave, Europe becomes smaller." Andrei Platonov's hero expressed the same idea this way: "Without me the nation of people is not whole." This is one of the main contradictions which moves Hemingway's novel.

The system of images in the novel asserts that man cannot be a means to any end, however noble it may be. Man is not a cog; each man is unique and irreplaceable.

It is precisely fullness of life which is so attractive in El Sordo and Jordan. Hemingway's polemic with the soulless concept that "man is a cog, man is a means," is revealed by the way characters are depicted—each has his own special world.

The singularity, the uniqueness of each personality is most significantly expressed in the love of Jordan and Maria("He himself was nothing—he knew that, and death was nothing too . . . It was true that in the last few days he came to realize that together with another human being he could be anything").[†]

Jordan enjoys food, drinking, the sun. And most of all—love.

For Whom the Bell Tolls is a book about love. Love sudden and profound, love from the first glance to the last gasp, chaste and sensual.

At first it seems that Jordan and Maria's relation is just one of the many brief liasons that are formed in the fire of war when every kill and every embrace may be the last. And if that's the way it is, does it make any difference whom one kisses or caresses?

But no, Jordan and Maria's relation is different. It is a meaningful,

---

by Frank O'Connor, the well-known Irish story writer and student of the short story genre. He asserts that they both "romanticize violence."

unique, tempestuous relation characterized by the features of a great and singular passion. No, it does make a difference whom one caresses. Love is selective. The loved one is unique and irreplaceable. And neither Jordan nor Maria had anything before they met—both of their lives begin on their first night together. The fullness and uniqueness of love stand in opposition to violence:

> Then there was the smell of heather crushed and the roughness of the bent stalks under her head and the sun bright on her closed eyes and all his life he would remember the curve of her throat with her head pushed back into the heather roots and her lips that moved smally and by themselves and the fluttering of the lashes on the eyes tight closed against the sun and against everything, and for her everything was red, orange, gold-red from the sun on the closed eyes, and it all was that color, all of it, the filling, the possessing, the having, all of that color, all in a blindness of that color. For him it was a dark passage which led to nowhere, then to nowhere, then again to nowhere, once again to nowhere, always and forever to nowhere, heavy on the elbows in the earth to nowhere, dark, never any end to the nowhere, hung on all time always to unknowing nowhere, this time and again for always to nowhere, now not to be born once again always and to nowhere, now beyond all bearing up, up, up and into nowhere, suddenly, scaldingly, holdingly all nowhere gone and time absolutely still and they were both there, time having stopped and he felt the earth move out and away from under them.

Many motifs from Hemingway's earlier works come together in *For Whom the Bell Tolls.* The Spanish *nada* (nothing) is a much more frightening word than the English "nothing," and for Hemingway it was a symbol of death and the road to death (for example, in "A Clean, Quiet Place"). The nearness of death is always with and in Jordan. But in this case the black tunnel leads to his loved one, to her sunny orange-red world, to her body and to her heart.

Many good books have been written about love, and Hemingway devoted many fine pages to the subject; but none of his other works is so full of love as *For Whom the Bell Tolls.* Nowhere do we see the limitation imposed by the tie of this most sacred island of human relations with the continent of humanity.

For Maria there is only Jordan. For Jordan only Maria. Each has become bigger than he was before. And neither exists separately any more. (This motif is played out tragically at the end of the novel: only by reminding her, by repeating over and over like an incantation, "we don't exist separately, I am thee; thee art I, wherever one of us is, both of us are," does Jordan manage to make Maria go away and leave him).

Maria and Jordan's love is not the only life-preserver, as it is in the case of Catherine Barclay and Frederick Henry. Their love is not a mirror which cuts them off from the world, a mirror in which there are only two faces; it is, rather, a magic glass through which the entire world shines all the more brightly.

They are self-sacrificing people in the full meaning of the word. After all, crossing the front line was not particularly complicated; Andreas had crossed and theoretically Jordan could head for Madrid taking Maria with him. Pilar mentions this at the very beginning of the novel. But they do not do this or even think of doing it. They are ready, without pondering it, to give up the most important and finest thing that has happened to them so that others can have love and happiness. Can one call their love a means? No! It is an end in itself—the feeling keeps strengthening and giving wings to their self-sacrifice.

On the last night of their love, and the last of his life, Jordan says to Maria:

> "I have worked much and now I love thee," he said it now in a complete embracing of all that would not be, "I love thee as I love all that we have fought for. I love thee as I love liberty and dignity and the rights of men to work and not be hungry. I love thee as I love Madrid that we have defended and as I love all my comrades that have died. And many have died. Many. Many. Thou canst not think how many. But I love thee as I love what I love most in the world and I love thee more.

This is a passionate confession of love intended for only one person, but then it merges with a confession of love for Madrid, one's comrades, and the Republic—a confession which can be made aloud to everyone. The island joins the continent. And again Hemingway uses the resonance of the old English pronoun "thee" and the "elevated Elizabethan language."

Jordan's feat is profoundly human. The feat is the result of struggle and victory, victory over weakness, doubt, and the natural desire to live—especially when one has found a woman one loves.

Hemingway's hero keeps depreciating his feat; he tells himself that he does not want any Thermopylae. But then who knows if the hero of Sparta wanted it? Maybe he too wanted to be with his Maria? He didn't want to go, but he had to—so he went.

The night of love turns out to be quite brief. The Fascist appears and Jordan fires at him. Now decisions must be made immediately, and love gives way to war. Jordan orders Maria to leave with Pilar. This is still not the last farewell; it is a rehearsal, a false ending, a preparation, a structuring of the readers' and heroes' mood.

Maria tries to protest, she naturally wants to be beside her beloved; then she calms down and asks for him to tell her that he loves her:

> "Say that you love me."
> "No. Not now."
> "Not love me now?"
> "*Dejamos..* Get thee back. One does not do that and love all at the same moment."

One cannot simultaneously be a part of a machine of destruction, terrible even in a just war, be a cog, a soldier, give and take orders—and love. That is, one cannot do these things and be irreplaceable and unique like what Robert who has never and will never exist in the world for anyone else...

The American critic Mark Shorer says that in *For Whom the Bell Tolls,* contrary to the epigraph, Hemingway asserts the "insignificance of the individual and the absolute significance of the political whole." One can say this only by completely ignoring the artistic fabric of the novel, its polyphony, those finished artistic "sum totals" which remain in the reader's heart, even though they are not subject to simple measurement.

VI

"I came here voluntarily and if necessary I will give every last drop of my blood to save freedom in Spain and freedom all over the world."—This was the oath which every International Brigade volunteer had to take. Precisely Fascism, with its zoological racism, arrogantly threw down the gauntlet to people joined by the brotherhood, by bonds more elevated than nationalistic ones, because they were freely chosen by the hearts of men. When Hemingway was in Spain he felt this himself. He alwasy had friends from varied countries, of varied nationalities; in Spain they were the Dutchman Ivens, the German Jew Halibrun, and a Hungarian living in Russia, Mate Zalka.

The International Brigades are not directly shown in *For Whom the Bell Tolls,* but the whole book is filled with the same spirit which engendered that movement. It is no accident that the most elevated tones in Jordan's monologues ("It was a Crusade...") occur precisely when he recalls 63 Velasquez St., the International Brigade Headquarters. The novel is about an American fighting for the freedom of Spain.

Sometimes Jordan repeats one word in different languages—"now," *maintenant, ahora, heute;* "dead," *mort, muerte, todt;* "war"—and he thinks the German *Krieg* is most expressive. He tests the word out loud, feeling his way, as if trying to take off its national "shell" and to discover, like our Khlebnikov, a kind of abstract, supranational, higher, ancient, general sense.

In the International Brigade movement as in all earlier cases of Internationalism conceived under the banner of world revolution, one can see humanity's future, as well as the naivete of proselytes and the utopian desire to get away from a single nation. Men so inclined formed a minority in every country. Of course, one reaction to Fascism's condemnation of whole peoples to doom was an unprecedented intensification of all forms and varieties of nationalistic feeling.

Another peculiarity of the historical situation in Spain was that the civil war was also a war against invading foreigners, against Hitler and Mussolini. (Three hundred thousand foreign soldiers fought for France; thirty-five thousand for the Republic.)

It was natural for Hemingway to show nationalistic strains when depicting the reality of the war in Spain. The hero himself is a true American who is almost totally free of the cosmopolitan characteristics of the voluntary expatriates, characteristics which were always found in the heroes of Hemingway's early stories, the ones who lived for the most part on the Left Bank in Paris.

Imminent doom intensified home-sickness. One see it in instinctive, primal sensations:

> This is the smell I love. This and fresh-cut clover, the crushed sage as you ride after cattle, wood-smoke, and the burning leaves of autumn. That must be the odour of nostalgia, the smell of the smoke from the piles of raked leaves burning in the streets in the fall in Missoula. Which would you rather smell? Sweet grass the Indians used in their baskets? Smoked leather? The odour of the ground in the spring after rain? The smell of the sea as you walk through the gorse on a headland in Galicia? Or the wind from the land as you come in toward Cuba in the dark? That was the odour of the cactus flowers, mimosa, and the sea-grape shrubs. Or would you rather smell frying bacon in the morning when you are hungry? Or coffee in the morning? Or a Jonathan apple as you bit into it? Or a cider mill in the grinding, or bread fresh from the oven?

When Hemingway decided that his hero would be from Missoula, he made a special trip there while he was working on the novel to walk the ground there again, hear its voice, and smell its smells. How else could this be conveyed to the readers with maximum precision of detail?

Jordan expresses his feelings for his homeland in various ways. When he hears Pilar's story about the execution of the Fascists, he recalls seeing a Negro lynched when he was seven years old. The closer to the end we get, the more frequently scenes of childhood appear.

When Jordan feels very bad, he talks to himself in English simply to hear the sounds of his native tongue.

Jordan's attitudes reveal his homeland's influence. He is one of those idealists, typical of the best part of American intelligentsia, to whom the spirit of competition, greed, and money-grubbing is abhorrent. These men counterbalance all kinds of mass psychosis. Though isolated, like Henry Thoreau, Clarence Darrow, or John Reed, they stand their ground. If justice demands it, they support "lost" causes, participate in "unpopular movements," and protect persecuted, "unpopular" people.

Many contemporaries perceived the Spanish civil war as a battle of natural against unnatural forces, of people who were inseparable from the soil against people from a mechanized civilization.

Criticism of bourgeois society from Rousseauistic positions is an important tradition in the history of American thought and literature. Some of the landmarks in this tradition were set by Cooper, Thoreau, Emerson, Melville, Whitman, and London's "Northern stories." This tradition stands behind Robert Jordan. When he repeats the slogans of two revolutions as symbols of his faith—"life, liberty and the pursuit of happiness"; "liberty, equality, and fraternity"—the naturalness of man not separated from the soil is part of this complex of ideas.

This inherently American tradition is simultaneously akin to the Spanish one.

It was not Jordan or his country which were attacked. The injustice was done somewhere far away. But that makes no difference—when anyone in the world is having a bad time, you are too. Never ask for whom the bell tolls...

In spite of the profound respect and even esteem for the national, the particular and unique which we find in Hemingway's novel, there is not a trace of chauvinism, exclusivity, or the tendency to elevate one people at the expense of another.

. . . .

VII
. . . . *

I first heard an excerpt from *For Whom the Bell Tolls* in August of 1942. The Germans were approaching Stalingrad. A kind of conference on Anglo-American theater was arranged by the All-Russian Theatrical Association. In the audience were many military personnel who had come to Moscow for a day or two.

Among those present was Ilya Ehrenburg. And he read the scene which ends the novel, describing the last moments of Jordan's life. In his reading Ehrenburg conveyed both his long-standing love for Hemingway and his enthrallment by his art. But he also conveyed what he himself had seen in our country, not Spain.

I had no doubt at the time that Hemingway's book was not about that war which ended in defeat, but about our men, our friends, those who at that very moment were fighting in their sectors. Within a few days after this first encounter with the novel, my husband perished at the front. And I always remembered that one should not ask for whom the bell tolls, it tolls for thee...

I have returned to the book often over the long years. The first time I opened it I identified with Maria. And now I am older than Pilar. A whole lifetime has passed.

There are books that one reads as a child, and then if one happens to return to them again, it is like returning to one's childhood room, to other dimensions—and one feels awkward, unnatural, like an adult among toys.

And there are books up to which one may grow for a whole life—and with every new reading one still discovers that they contain new facets; pages you have long known by heart are illuminated by new life experience.

Sometimes when I turned to *For Whom the Bell Tolls* love seemed to

---

*Four pages are omitted here; they deal primarily with Western critics on Hemingway and this novel. *[Editor's note.]*

be the most important thing. There were other times when it was as if *I myself participated* in the battle on El Sordo's hill. There were times, however ashamed I am to admit it today, when I was very offended by Hemingway because of Marty. After the Twentieth Party Congress I read the novel again in a completely different way.*

Other times I would open the book and when I was rereading the ending—knowing that in a second they would cross the highway and knowing what would happen then—still I would think hopefully, "What if the bullet misses?" "What would happen if Jordan remained alive?" Thus one sits by the bed of close, beloved friends, praying for a miracle even though one knows that miracles are impossible.

The first version of the novel's title was *Undiscovered Country.* The novel became that undiscovered country to which everyone can return again and again. I believe that my children and the children of my children will find things in this book which I will never see in it now, never discover...

VIII

In spite of the concreteness of its detail, in spite of the complete illusion that this is one detachment in Segovia in May of 1937, *For Whom the Bell Tolls* is a book which goes beyond the bounds of this place and time.

The novel is naked lyricism, a confession, a diary, a seismograph of the mental vacillations characteristic of the American intellectual in the first third of the twentieth century, and intellectual who was participating in a revolutionary war, and for all this uniqueness and singularity the vacillation has been familiar to and understood by people of many different countries and different times.

However, the novel does not fix in one's mind just the hero's and author's lyrical self-expression. For Hemingway the concept of "epic" was synonymous with bad literature ("all bad writers adore epics"). *For Whom the Bell Tolls* belongs not among the pseudoepics, those fat volumes of problem novels which try to reflect everything; it belongs among the true epics.

Barea called his thunderous essay "Not Spain but Hemingway." No, that's not true. *Both* Spain and Hemingway, and all humanity in the twentieth century.

For Whom the Bell Tolls is also an epic work because life is presented in its basic, root forms: man and death, food, drink; man and nature; man and woman; the striving for freedom. That is, universal problems common to all ages, all countries, and all peoples.

---

*That is, after the official denunciation of Stalin's crimes. *[Editor's note.]*

The great epics of antiquity, such as the Bible or the *Iliad,* depict society at a stage when human individuality has scarcely developed. The "I" is hardly separated from the "not I."

Since then, centuries have passed—centuries of enrichment and change in the development of individuality in art and in reality itself.

Jordan's inner world is the contradictory, fluid world of contemporary individuality. It can be no other way. Therefore the ties between the "I" and "not I," the ties of the island to the continent, are complex, contradictory, dialectic ties.

Jordan's fate is inseparable from the fate of the fighting people of Spain. It is not a chip thrown into the torrent by someone's hand; his life (significant as it is in itself, filled to the brim by itself) is simultaneously a link between the past and the future.

Unlike the heroes of the ancient epic, Hemingway's hero has been given the possibility of choice. At every turn of the plot, at every turn of fate.

Jordan could have *not* been a soldier in Spain—he freely chose to take part. He could have refused the dangerous assignment; after all, Golz suggested he should think it over—but he chose to lead the blowing of the bridge. He could have gone to headquarters himself, instead of Anselmo, to try to explain that conditions had changed; and in an obvious way this would have been more reasonable. —However, he chose another fate—to remain with the band.

Jordan even continues to choose when it would seem that everything is foreordained. The partisan Augustin offers to shoot Jordan; death is inevitable anyway, and this way he would avoid possible torture by the Fascists. After all, in his time Jordan had acceded to the request of a seriously wounded comrade and shot him. But he decides to continue the fight. When he is left alone, he rejects suicide too; at the last moment he chooses the path of most resistance—to die fighting...

Stephen Spender recalls this about the intellectuals who died for the Republicans: "Men like Cornford, Cadwell, Ralph Fox, Julian Bell and the young American James Lardner were all killed in Spain. In the combination of life and death they fit the classical idea of tragedy in its purest form: the ideal for which the hero fights is revealed to the world at the moment of the hero's death—precisely by this death."[†]

In ancient epics the death of the hero is often the embodiment of the tragically irresolvable contradictions of existence.

The death of Robert Jordan stands not only for the end of the Republic in Spain, but for the tragic inevitability of death itself—the fate of all men:

> And the abyss opens up before us
> With all its terrors and darkness,
> And there is no boundary between it and us;
> That is why the night terrifies us!

Terror before the dark, the night, the hopeless, is stamped on many of Hemingway's works. One finds it in *The Bell* too, the ominous road to black Nothingness.

If death is inevitable anyway, the writer seems to say, then it is more worthy to meet it face to face, in the heat of battle, in the youth of love.

Hemingway uses words from "Ecclesiastes" as the epigraph fo his first novel *Fiesta:*

One generation passeth away, and another generation cometh; but the earth abideth for ever.

The heroes of that book, members of the lost generation, are still completely alienated from the common people, from the eternal earth. It is sufficient to recall how alien the fiesta itself is to them, the folk holiday which all they can do is spoil (as Brett Ashley spoils the triumph of Romero the matador).

As always in Hemingway, the motif of earth can be felt physically. The journalist Olga Carlisle-Andreeva reported one of her conversations with Pasternak: "The greatness of a writer has nothing to do with the content of his work—only with how much this content *got to* the author. This is shown in the corporeality, in the density of his style. In Hemingway's style one can feel the material itself—iron, wood."[†] We can carry the idea further and add "and earth."

The epicality of the novel is revealed in the relation of man to earth— an ancient, truly epic theme.

Jordan makes his bed on the earth, and he makes it with meticulous attention to detail, just as carefully and slowly as Nick Adams does. Robert and Maria's bed of love is on the earth, on crushed heather. The machine-gun is set up on the earth. The hero accepts death on the same earth, strewn with pine needles.

In his Spanish works the motif of eternal earth is transformed; in this one can see the profundity of the Spanish war's effect on Hemingway's work.

In the solemn requiem "To Americans Who Fell in Spain," he glorifies the men who became "part of the Spanish earth": "And the earth cannot be turned into slavery. For the earth abideth forever. It outlasts all the tyrants."[†]

There is not the abyss between the people as a whole and the individual units which there was in *Fiesta.* Thus the epic motif changes—the hero perishes, but the people are immortal. Here we find the historical optimism of the epic. The earth and the people who "are not abstract concepts, separated from real, grieving people by millions of light years." They are not just the Biblical "ashes to ashes" we find in the epigraph from "Ecclesiastes" and the plot of *Fiesta* itself.

Fernando and Anselmo, Robert Jordan and El Sordo become parts of the Spanish earth. It is they who perish, unique, unforgettable people whom we have come to know in the most contradictory traits of their characters; and as they perish the quiet, dignified majesty of the epic reigns. It begins: "He lay flat on the brown, pine-needled floor of the forest, his chin on his folded arms, and high overhead the wind blew in the tops of the pine trees." It ends: "He could feel his heart beating against the pine needle floor of the forest." The harmonious structural symmetry symbolizes the immortality of humanity. The immortality of humanity's striving for freedom and happiness. The years wash away the tip of a promontory. An island may vanish. But the human continent is eternal.

PALIEVSKY ON FAULKNER

Pyotr V. Palievsky (1932-) began a meteoric career in publishing
before graduating from Moscow State University in 1955. He has written
much on the theory of literature and criticism, and is currently associated
with the Union of Soviet Writers' Gorky Institute of Literature. Though
of strict Party orientation, he was one of the first to have students read
widely in Rozanov and other Russian conservative critics and philosophers
from the end of the last century. He is also, reportedly, one of the theore-
ticians of the recent Slavophile, or nationalist, movement. But he has written
both on Russian writers (Tolstoy, Bulgakov) and Anglo-American ones
(Graham Greene, Aldous Huxley). Along with V. Lakshin, Palievsky is often
said to be among the foremost critics in the Soviet Union.

Palievsky has done several things on Faulkner and is one of Faulkner's
strongest supporters in the Soviet Union—and he holds an important post
on the editorial board of *Foreign Literature,* so one may assume that the
translation of *The Sound and the Fury* and the three-volume collection of
Faulkner's works soon to be published owe something to him. Faulkner's
acceptance in the Soviet Union was slow (see Landor's survey in Section
Two below for part of the history). A few stories were published in the
thirties, including "Victory." In 1958 a book of seven stories appeared, and
a smattering of other items followed. Finally longer works were printed:
The Mansion (1960), *The Hamlet* (1964), *The Town* (1965), all in editions
of 100,000, and *Intruder in the Dust* (1968). Orlova and Kopelev's 1958
article "Myths and Truth about the American South" was the first important
critical appraisal of Faulkner; the dean of Russian critics of American literature, Ivan Kashkin, introduced the first collection of stories, but he was
essentially a Hemingway man. A variety of reviews and critical essays
followed, of which Palievsky's is easily the best.

P. V. Palievsky

FAULKNER'S ROAD TO REALISM

In the violent arguments about modernism, one simple but decisive fact remains unnoticed: in its leading works and names contemporary literature remains realistic. Of course, this applies to Western literature too, where modernistic trends are best known. It is sufficient to recall briefly the names of recent writers: Hemingway, Martin du Gard, Mauriac, Greene, Amado, Laxness, Moravia, Böll, and many others are all realists—and compared to the twenties the influence of modernism on literature has on the whole weakened considerably. This has created obvious consternation even among many of its constant observers. Thus, for example, English critics have long been discussing Graham Greene's return to the "traditional" form, his lost ties with Freudianism, Joyce, etc.

One should also note that in its essentially experimental form (Robbe-Grillet is most characteristic), modernism is not basically literature. It is literature about how to make literature—in essence it is professional, experimental criticism, which, incidentally, is why the place where it is discussed and read is precisely in criticism. Apart from whether one agrees with what these writers say or not, one must begin by conceding that they speak for the most part not as writers—about life—but as critics—about literature. This mix-up could already be seen in twenties' literature under the sway of modernistic influences, for example Andre Gide's *Les Faux-monnayeurs* (1926) and Aldous Huxley's *Point Counter Point* (1928) where significant parts of the novels are composed of discourses by the novelist-heroes about how one should write; and their very structure was subordinated to these discourses. Current modernism has gone completely over to literature of "experimental example" or "exemplary experiment."

This whole history of self-containment also makes extremely dubious the so-called "right to experiment" which contemporary modernists defend so vigorously. One should not forget that the classics did not have this right; in any case, they did not make public use of it. Either they wrote literature of good quality, or they did not write at all—or, finally, if they began as Chekhov did, they wrote somewhat worse at first than they did later—but still not for "the elucidation of technique," but for the reader; and that was the way the reader took it.

When they did invent something new in technique, it was never a blueprint or construct, but a living creation which—even though it generated and used this construct—used it only to achieve something immeasurably more important with its help. Thus, when in doubt about his calling, hiding behind initials, Tolstoy sent his first radically innovative work, *Childhood,* to be judged by Nekrasov, the latter replied "this is precisely what Russian society needs now—the truth"—and only later did Chernyshevsky note and point out (without trying to separate it and announce a technically accessible mechanism) the method by which this truth was attained, Tolstoy's "dialectic of the soul."*

However, because of fashion, the literary convictions accepted in their circles, editorial queries, and many other reasons, the relation of many contemporary realists—writers of the twentieth century—to the problem of "technique" and construction has formed in quite a different way. Their road to realism—which is the end they achieved—was made difficult even in what would seem to be a purely professional regard.

William Faulkner is perhaps the most important and characteristic artist of this type. He was a mighty talent who went along his own road almost hidden from the outside by different aims and a different disguise.

William Faulkner possessed a colossal power for growth, not only in relation to the environment he chose and his own literary system, but also in relation to all of the reality of his time. In this sense he stood out among many of his colleagues—the writers of the West in the twentieth century—who knew very well, perhaps too well, what it means to look at things realistically—i.e., they had gotten used to measuring the possibilities of their humanism exclusively in relation to conditions which had come about and without any special faith in the ability of man to change these conditions. In this sense William Faulkner went much further. He rejected the power of circumstances. He declined to accept them, he announced in Stockholm in 1950, "simply because man will nevertheless overcome them."**

This testimony might seem strange, but Faulkner was completely satisfied with it. For him man's striving to bend circumstances to his own benefit was always more real than the circumstances themselves. Because of this his realism was full of "sound and fury," hollow, terrible blows as if someone were smashing a dungeon from the inside.

At the same time Faulkner never evaded the gloomy refutations of his view; on the contrary, he met it head-on, challengingly. There was no dirt

---

*Tolstoy sent his first work, *Childhood,* to the poet and editor Nekrasov in the early 1850s. A few years later the critic Chernyshevsky became the first critic in any nation to name and discuss the device of "interior monologue," which he also called "dialectic of the soul," using Tolstoy's works as examples. *Editor's note.*

**Retranslated. Nothing exactly like what Palievsky quotes is in the speech, though the gist of things is the same. *Editor's note.*

which could upset him, even though it made his critics' flesh creep; they did not hold back and started saying that Faulkner was a sadist who gloried in seeing how men act when at a dead-end. However, it is precisely the pertinacity and irreconcilability of a man who does not want to admit what seems to have been proven to him—and who is managing to get out of a dead-end—that were for Faulkner the most reliable evidence and source for his own imperturbable certainty.

> I decline to accept the end of man . . . Even when the bell of fate tolls for the last time, predicting doom, and its last useless echo flies by and fades somewhere in the last red evening at the edge of the darkness, and dead silence falls, even then there will still be one more sound: the weak but inexhaustible voice of man, still talking. I refuse to accept this. I believe that man will not merely endure: he will prevail.*

In the pertinacity and crushing power of his talent Faulkner recalls Balzac. He too had to fight his way to acceptance, catching onto what was considered new and attractive in literature, and even enticing the crowd with a description of terrifying passions (the novel *Sanctuary,* 1931). Like Balzac, he then discovered his own world where unforgettable characters began to meet each other and move from novel to novel; and life opened up before the readers as a whole city—true, Jefferson, not Paris, but it was impossible not to believe in it. This life went on by itself, and like Balzac, Faulkner even settled two virtuous raisonneurs in his town—Stevens and Ratliff** whom he started calling on when he had to illuminate some dark turn of events.

It is not impossible that such parallels suggest a general similarity in the state of the literatures of the West during the twenties of the nineteenth century and the twenties of the twentieth. There are other features as well which help us to understand things better today.*** But one thing is certain—Faulkner had to discover realism for himself. But this discovery happened for a second time, anew—as if realism had never before existed.

---

*Quoted in retranslation, to show the liberties that are taken in the Russian version. To quote the speech in the original:

> I decline to accept the end of man. It is easy enough to say that man is immortal simply because he will endure; that when the last ding-dong of fate has clanged and faded from the last worthless rock hanging tideless in the last red and dying evening, that even then there will still be one more sound: that of his puny, inexhaustible voice, still talking. I refuse to accept this, I believe that man will not merely endure: he will prevail.

**Just like Blondier and Bianchon—knights of good in Balzac's *Human Comedy.* [Palievsky's note.]

***For example, similar problems of man vs. machine, poetry vs. prose, etc. [Palievsky's note.]

* * *

In this discovery of the already discovered we see his peculiarity and originality with respect to the literary currents surrounding and accompanying his progress. One should not forget that not only for him, but for many other Western writers who began their careers in the twenties, realism in fact did not exist. For them a senseless war had smashed realism and relegated it to the past as the embodiment of calm, confidence, and knowledge of the world—things which now seemed simply ridiculous. And its tradition was completely overwhelmed (on the surface, at least) by the vociferous declarations of various avant-garde schools.

T. S. Eliot, the "grand master" of the avant-garde hailed the appearance of Joyce's *Ulysses* (1922) and explained the book's meaning to the bitter youth of the day: "Mr. Joyce has created a method which other writers should take up . . . I do not think we can use the term 'novel' in regard to *Ulysses,* nor does it explain much if you call it an epic. *Ulysses* is not a novel for the simple reason that the novel has outlived itself." Joyce, said Eliot, had invented a different form which was remarkably suited to the time—"simply the ability to control, to establish order, to give outline and sense to the grandiose panorama of hopelessness which is modern history. We can now use the mythic method instead of the narrative method."[†]

Eliot was clear and seemingly convincing. There was only one item in his program which one had to accept on faith—the black chaos of life—but few young writers doubted that after a war which had been so cheerfully started by pleasure-loving "oldsters." All the rest followed point by point with logic which quickly began to win over groups of like-minded persons.

Their reasoning went something like this:

Life is senseless, or at least unworthy of trust; the realist who attempts to draw his form out of it is at best naive. But the truly contemporary artist does not throw down his brush or abandon his pen. He answers chaos with his own iron organization. He puts sense into the world, he gives everything outlines, and this is his accomplishment. Joyce had already managed such an accomplishment; he fettered the hostile elements with the help of myth, i.e., onto the chaos of contemporary Dublin life he superimposed Homer's world of mythological relations (the story of Odysseus); he created an allegory, a "parabola."

The crowd and myopic critics consider *Ulysses* an uncontrolled stenographic record of all human rubbish—whatever the eyes happen to see and whatever flashes through the mind. But Eliot pointed out—he really did do this—that *Ulysses* is precisely calculated and controlled. Even in a nobody like Bloom, Joyce captured a special meaning, albeit ironical, by enclosing all of his humble "departures" in the mythic category of Odysseus's wanderings. The outlines were made with graphic precision. Now other real artists are going to do the same thing. Of course, it is not obligatory for the *Odyssey* to be the mythic scheme. The choice is rich: for example, there are Freudian myths—and others—that is not the point. What is important is to understand

154

the unlimited possibilities of the new technique.

Thus, avant-gardism made its debut as a new esthetic order ready to wear various "badges," but on the condition that those who turned to it should share the general fascination and confidence: art can *make,* it can *fabricate* from forms which the boldest, most successful innovators are going to find. Then large bands of enthusiasts and hopeful, excited mediocrities went to work looking for these forms in various countries of Europe and in the United States.

The words "too much a litterateur" precisely convey the direction of the threat which avant-gardism made to literature. Soon after this, Blok openly and indignantly spoke of it in his essay on the Guild of Poets—"Without Divinity, without Inspiration."* Important writers of many nations were moved by this essay; for example, Herbert Wells wrote about it in a well known letter to Joyce apropos of *Ulysses.*

However, correctly naming the danger did not mean stopping it. The idea of synthetic literature was too seductive. The artificial paints which the avant-garde began manufacturing for writers had great practical virtues: they were garish, they could forcibly attract attention like advertisements, they could be put readily into any combination. But the main thing was that in an interesting and even somehow mysterious way, combining them helped the writer manage the straight-forward idea which he had thought up for himself.

Besides, anyone could use them. If before it had been considered tasteless and inartistic to repeat the forms of one's predecessor, the avant-garde reversed the rule and proclaimed that after such and such an innovator, one cannot "write as before" without shame ("Mr. Joyce has created a method which other writers should take up..."); if you have not taken this technique into consideration you cannot even think of being contemporary. Formerly they taught how to read and understand literature; now they had started teaching how to write and spread it. Special schools opened, authoritative teachers appeared. Gertrude Stein instructed the young American writers; T. S. Eliot and Pound the English and in general the international avant-garde; Andre Gide the French; and in our literature it was LEF**with its first command: "Every flea of a rhyme must be taken into account," etc. This

*Alexander Blok's essay on the Russian Acmeists (their Guild of Poets emphasized craft, technique, and concreteness) takes its title from a romantic lyric by Pushkin. *Editor's note.*

**Left Front of Literature—a group, and literary journal, organized by Vladimir Mayakovsky, the revolutionary poet. *Editor's note.*

created the impression that a really new age was beginning, an age in which a "savage" talent who did not want to study the "innovators" would first have to retreat like an Indian and then languish on a reservation until qualified professors extracted every last "technical secret."

* * *

Faulkner was such a savage talent. But he did not retreat and submit—although he frequently got enmeshed in the nets of his craftsmanship and had to tear them apart as he moved further on. It was his lot to try almost every avant-garde innovation on himself—and there is nothing surprising about this, because he was a genuine provincial looking to the capital for truth.

"Faulkner," said Sherwood Anderson, the most independent figure in American literature at the time, "you are a country boy. All you know is that little piece of land that you came from there in Mississippi. But then that's enough."[†]

Faulkner realized what this meant many years later. In the meantime he listened attentively to the problematic noise of the literature contemporary to him, and he too tried to choose for himself a problem which was a bit more novel and a bit more widely known—one of the so-called problems of the generation. He quickly wrote two such novels. The first, *A Soldier's Pay* (1926), was told by a crippled soldier about returning to his home town where no one needed him. The other, *Mosquitoes* (1927), was a book about intellectual disillusionments—it could have been written jointly by Huxley and Eliot—about how "hollow men" gather on the yacht of a well-to-do widow, talk and go home. These novels did not get rave notices from anyone.

Then Faulkner decided to try his luck with the "stream of consciousness." His plan was to enter the world of one family, to analyze the reasons for its human fall, using the technique developed by Joyce and lauded by T. S. Eliot.

There were few events in the whole story; but as he conceived it, it had internal meaning which he wanted to convey to the reader. The daughter of a lawyer named Compson, the family favorite Caddy has to marry a respectable young man named Herbert Head. But they soon part—Caddy has been having a liaison with another man and she gives birth to an illegitimate child. What was secret becomes known; the family falls apart and declines. Her brother Benjy vainly strives to understand the meaning of what is happening; in his dim mind the drama is fractured—he is an idiot whose development stopped when he was three. His brother Quentin is a man who has deeply rooted convictions about honor, a secret romantic; he decides to commit suicide to revenge himself on the world. Finally, the third brother Jason, a greedy creature of limited abilities, conceives furious malice because he has not managed to get the position in the bank which had been promised him by Caddy's husband. He hides the money left for the care of Miss Caddy's illegitimate daughter, Miss Quentin, in a box; but she later steals the money (knowing nothing of its source) and runs away from home. This is all that happens in the course of approximately thirty years.

But we repeat—Faulkner was interested in the internal motives and actions, the only things which could make this external canvas sensible and coherent. He still had to understand why this small society had fallen apart, a society which in the beginning was held together by certain unquestionable human values (the father and the mother and the children, including even Benjy, had these values) and to examine whether it would have been possible to replay the entire story, to see if there were not any possibility of maintaining and preserving these values. The "stream of consciousness" discovered by Joyce, offered a way to fill in this tragic story, to give it outlines; so Faulkner took it and boldly set out into unknown depths.

But this is precisely where the real esthetic battle took place. Faulkner encountered unforseen obstacles, and he started overcoming them with the cold indomitability which at this point appeared for the first time, and which then distinguished him all during his life. This is what he himself said about it:

> I had already begun to tell the story through the eyes of the idiot child, since I felt that it would be more effective as told by someone capable only of knowing what happened, but not why. I saw that I had not told the story that time. I tried to tell it again, the same story through the eyes of another brother. That was still not it. I told it for the third time through the eyes of the third brother. That still was not it. I tried to gather the pieces together and fill in the gaps by making myself the spokesman. It was still not complete, not until fifteen years after the book was published, when I wrote as an appendix to another book the final effort to get the story told and off my mind, so that I myself could have some peace from it.

Probably no one since has described so graphically the spectacle of a talent and writer struggling with the stream of consciousness method after voluntarily deciding to use it. It is a classic example, and the title *The Sound and the Fury** which Faulkner gave the novel would also seem to say something about the mood which possessed him when he was writing it.

It did not even occur to him to doubt what the newly famed innovators were proclaiming all around. The chaos of life is given outline, they said, and the sense of consciousness *inside* is conveyed. Very well—so he takes *one* consciousness. Not only that—he does it more decisively and more experimentally than anyone before him; he takes it in its simplest elements, a consciousness which to the observer seems to have fallen apart, the consciousness of an

---

*As if reminding the modern epoch of Shakespeare, which in general twentieth-century Anglo-American writers like to do in their titles. Compare Greene *(The Power and the Glory, The End of the Affair),* Huxley *(Brave New World),* and many others. Here from *Macbeth,* V, 5.

idiot (Benjy does not even distinguish time—only odors, colors, and tastes—which are either pleasant or repulsive).

One who has not read the novel can scarcely imagine what resulted instead of the proposed story. The sound and the fury really does emerge from these pages, a clash of separate "earthly entities" which is all the more terrifying in that something vaguely human can be perceived in it, though distantly; the connection between these particles is a different kind—not exactly chemical, not exactly clinical—and it is only a faint glimmer of that which the author wanted to achieve.

However, Faulkner does not stop there: "I tried to tell the story again."

The fact that Faulkner was forced to take other "points of view," first Quentin, then Jason, is very important. In a practical way it signifies the destruction of the method itself—since it becomes clear that the "stream" still does not work without explanations from the outside (even though they are streams of *other* consciousnesses). These explanations begin to unify anew a world which has been split and disintegrated into infinitely small "points of view." This is the first step toward reconstitution, and one should note that Joyce himself did this. A feeling of incompleteness made him introduce, in addition to Bloom, the "streams" of Stephen Daedalus and Molly, Bloom's wife.

Faulkner too would have stayed on that level if he had stopped with these unsatisfactory features which bothered Joyce. But as usual he had a desire to make the next "hopeless" step as well. He made it, and he went beyond the limits of the avant-garde. In essence this was a return to forgotten realism.

"I introduced one other narrator, myself." Note how he puts it: "one other narrator." Faulkner does not say that he decided to write as people had written before him, from his own point of view. He returns from avant-gardism in circles, like someone coming out of a forest, completely convinced that he is going forward. For him all the author is is one of the possible "narrators." But this has completely different significance for the reader. Because now he is told the story not by the idiot Benjy, and not by the gloomy misanthrope Jason, but by a talented man who knows how to touch the quiddity of life and understand Jason and Benjy and Quentin and anyone else he wants to from a single root.

Of course, "points of view" do not disappear even seen this way. However, their meaning becomes completely different. Without the author, without their creator, the union can only be external and artificial; they just collide and limit each other—they are blind to each other, impenetrable and mosaic. But in the case of a writer who is a realist, every such "ray of vision" (Alexei Tolstoy's expression) illuminates the whole; with his unified view the writer connects them into a living and dynamic world which is like the real world. In a word, he gives the needed center to this entire artistic "cosmos," and failing this, it is no more than chaos.

That is why Faulkner wrote the entire fourth part of the novel in freedom, filling in, as he said, "the gaps." As if at sunrise, powerful transformations began to change the landscape: the mysterious shadows disappeared, objects became more rounded and distinct. Instead of just the creations of inner terror, even hope appeared—as Faulkner begins to reveal for the reader that which the Compsons had not managed to save was preserved in their servant, the Negress Dilsey. But basically it is already too late; the novel is ending, the story has been told—new "streams," one feels, will add little to it, or they will form another novel.

Thus this strange book remains, composed of several pieces, a monument to the hybrid art of the 1920s. Faulkner said later that he had worked harder on it than anything else, and therefore he loved it more than the other novels, "as a mother loves her deformed child." Of course, a writer of the old pre-war (1914) stamp would not have allowed himself to publish anything like this. In good conscience he would have written variants, as Chekhov and Tolstoy did, until that single and final version which leaves a feeling of satisfaction appeared.

But in the first place there could be no single one here; uncertainty and searching were rooted in the very structure of artistic thought. The question was whether this idea should be acknowledged as the new law or overcome; Faulkner answered with his firm decision to create the whole.

In the second place, the well-advertised new moods which, as has already been said, drastically changed the life of literature during the twenties, had not passed Faulkner by either; like other of his contemporaries, he was of the opinion that one could no longer hope to be noticed in the backwoods by some all-seeing literary "authority" and thus brought to glory. The naively provincial Chekhovian rule about writers had long been forgotten: "There are big dogs and little dogs, but little ones should not be embarrassed by the existence of big ones—all are obliged to bark, and to bark in the voice which God gave them." Without risking carrying this comparison further, one must admit that the case was different with the innovators of the twenties: in their circles not being a genius was considered repulsive. In this respect Faulkner did not remain on the sidelines; sometimes one can see a shade of purely American businessman's contempt in the way he behaved. "The unquestionable genius of his artistic gift," wrote the critic L. Thompson in 1963, i.e., summing up, "was overshadowed from beginning to end by an amazingly arrogant and conceited contempt not only for the reader, but also for self-discipline and changing of views."[†]

Unfortunately, this is true. These traits were revealed quite openly in *The Sound and the Fury,* the novel which the essential Faulkner began with, and the reader of any of his other novels should know about them in advance. But perhaps without this self-assurance and contempt, it would have been difficult for Faulkner to discover what he was constantly discovering: the impossible, even the unknown, amid generally accepted ideas. As we have seen, it was precisely this way, floating in the "stream of consciousness," that he again discovered realism.*

Naturally this discovery did not immediately illuminate him and turn him into a realist. Like many other discoveries it was made in the guise of something non-existent: "I introduced one other narrator, myself." More than that, Faulkner rejected realism many times, experimenting further with avant-garde innovations, experimenting with and destroying them to the end of his days.** Thus, less than a year after *The Sound and the Fury,* as if again appearing at the wall of a fortress which he had not taken, he storms the "stream of consciousness" trying ten times harder; now he uses sixty interior monologues for one story (the novel *As I Lay Dying,* 1930). But in the interval, he made a new discovery, perhaps the most important one of his whole life: not realism in general—he found the road to his own personal, Faulknerian realism. This road was pointed out to him by *Sartoris* (1929) in which Faulkner used several family legends and incidents from the life of the small American town where he had grown up.

> With *Soldier's Pay* I found out writing was fun. But I found out afterward that not only each book had to have a design but the whole output or sum of an artist's work had to have a design. With *Soldier's Pay* and *Mosquitoes* I wrote for the sake of writing because it was fun. Beginning with *Sartoris* I discovered that my own little postage stamp of native soil was worth writing about and that I would never live long enough to exhaust it, and that by sublimating the actual into the apocryphal I would have complete liberty to use whatever talent I might have to its absolute top. It opened up a gold mine of other people, so I created a cosmos of my own. I can move these people around like God, not only in space but in time too. The fact that I have moved my characters around in time successfully, at least in my own estimation, proves to me my own theory that time is a fluid condition which has no existence except in the momentary avatars of individual people. There is no such thing as *was*—only *is.* If *was* existed, there would be no grief or sorrow. I like to think of the world I created as being a kind of keystone in the universe; that, small as that keystone is, if it were ever taken away the universe itself would collapse.***

---

*In America *The Sound and the Fury* is often proudly called "the best American stream of consciousness novel," but the qualifications which are made while saying this are quite revealing. For example, that Faulkner has "unity of action . . . in other words, he has a basic plot, something which is absent in all the other stream of consciousness novels."†R. Humphrey, *Stream of Consciousness in the Modern Novel* (Berkeley, 1954).

**Faulkner considered Joyce and Thomas Mann the most important twentieth-century writers; apparently he was always stunned by their bibliographic culture and virtuoso ability to use any style, something towards which he could only aspire.

***From an interview in Jeanne Stein in 1956.

These words should be printed in place of an introduction to every novel Faulkner wrote. The point is not whether each of the separate ideas here
is correct or incorrect (for example, what he says about time, where one
senses Bergson, etc.); they cannot be correct because they are in fact directed
as if from a cosmos, from a single center, each straight in its own direction;
but these ideas do contain the spirit of Faulkner's talent.

For Faulkner, this "vein of gold" turned out to be a small imaged area
of the American South which he called Yoknapatawpha. Later Faulkner drew
a map of it, as Stevenson had done for *Treasure Island.* In the north flowed
the Tallahatchie River, along the shores of which the descendents of Indian
chiefs Ikkemotubbe and Mokotubbe had settled. In the south was the settle-
ment of Frenchmen's Bend, from which the Snopes family emerged; at one
time old man Varner lived there with his beautiful daughter Eula and venge-
ful little Mink. And in the center is the town of Jefferson with its railroad
and later its airport, where all of the interests of the big and little families
come together, the Snopeses, Thompsons, Sutpens, Sartorises and others.
All of these people, as well as the farmers, the Negroes, the lawyers, etc., etc.,
began to meet each other, clashing, quarreling, multiplying, becoming mortal
enemies or friends and together changing the face of the city. Each new person immediately entered this special world, his past undecided, his connections to the others distant and confused; therefore what Faulkner intended
to tell about him could not be something separate—a story, a novella, a novel—
and its definition as a genre was lost.

Everything that he began to write now turned into a saga: stories could
be put together in a novel (for example, *The Unvanquished,* 1938, *Go Down
Moses,* 1942); if necessary, novels could easily have stories separated from
them (for example, "Percy Grimm" from *Light in August,* 1932). It was a
narrative about events which were common to the whole small cosmos of
Yoknapatawpha, whether past events or events which were only developing—
as yet unresolved, but already full of human interest.

At the same time Faulkner began to return more often to one and the
same event—whenever he found that he had, so to speak, new "facts"—say,
opinions, or reminiscences of other participants. For example, *The Mansion*
(1959) retells the whole history of the Snopes family from the two preceding
books of the trilogy—*The Village* (1940), *The Hamlet* (1954). However, in the
same book dozens of other names and events are mentioned, or worse still,
they are not mentioned, but do influence that which happened in *The Mansion.* They work silently, offstage; although their main life is in another novel,
one cannot get along without them here either. For example, Chick Mallison
and his relations to Linda will be poorly understood by anyone who has not
read *Intruder in the Dust* (1948).

Faulkner's high-handed treatment of his readers is involuntary here, but
it causes great difficulties. The story by which we are usually engulfed when
we open a book with Faulkner's name on the cover, has neither beginning nor
ending; he simply leaves us on some street of Jefferson or as a guest of one of

these dark families and proposes that without a common language or preliminary introduction we start living among them and understanding them. But they talk and think about things which we can only guess at. Quite often the denouement does not satisfy them just as it does not satisfy us. Thus it remains only to replay all of this together with them (or with their friends or relatives) in another novel.

Perhaps American literary scholars should publish a "Guide to Jefferson" with the family tree of each family and a dry list of events, citing which novels and stories they occur in. This would be something like the history of myths for the reader of Greek tragedies.

But when you get used to it this constantly irritating "unknownness," begins little by little to attract and absorb you. You feel that this is a kind of truth which contemporary writers—overly schooled, overly well-read, ironically evasive—are no longer used to, writers to whom one may apply Tieck's words: "They would be ashamed if there were even one riddle in the human soul hidden from them which they could not solve." It is not that Faulkner is a mystic—that is not so at all. He does not look for riddles, nor does he avoid them. But in each of his stories, wherever and whatever happens, we see that the unknown plays a role too: man is a product of a distant and infinite life without beginning—but everything that has ever been in it is now present and has an influence, providing unforeseen possibilities. And choice is a kind of enlightenment of one's fate.

Basically, his "theory of time" tells us nothing more than this. Of course, it is not a theory at all. It only shows how Faulkner sees man: in one continuous plane from the past and the present, which means that he also has a future which cannot be stopped. Sartre, who has always been more attracted by philosophy than art can express, refused to see this in Faulkner. In his essay "Time in Faulkner" he wrote of the future, saying, "since it does not exist" Faulkner draws it (supposedly) in the following way: "One present rising up out of the unknown draws after itself another present. This is like the increase of a sum which we keep adding to and adding to: '...and...and... and after that'."

But this fragmentary world is not Faulkner's world; it could appear perhaps only in the works of Robbe-Grillet. The future *does* exist in Faulkner; it does effect man and it plays a role in what already is. This is how it appears on the very first page of *Light in August* (1932), without a shade of mysticism, in the midst of everyday life:

> The wagon mounts the hill toward her. She passed it about a mile back down the road. It was standing beside the road, the mules asleep in the traces and their heads pointed in the direction in which she walked. She saw and she saw the two men squatting beside a barn beyond the fence. She looked at the wagon and the men once: a single glance all-embracing, swift, innocent and profound. She did not stop; very likely the men beyond the fence had not seen her even look at the wagon or them. Neither did she look back. She went on out of sight, walking slowly, the shoes unlaced about her ankles, until she reached the top of the hill a mile

beyond. Then she sat down on the ditchbank, with her feet in the shallow ditch, and removed the shoes. After a while she began to hear the wagon. She heard it for some time. Then it came into sight, mounting the hill.

The sharp and brittle crack and clatter of its weathered and ungreased wood and metal is slow and terrific: a series of dry sluggish reports carrying for a half mile across the hot still pinewiney silence of the August afternoon. Though the mules plod in a steady and unflagging hypnosis, the vehicle does not seem to progress. It seems to hang suspended in the middle distance forever and forever, so infinitesimal is its progress . . . so that at last as though out of some trivial and unimportant region beyond even distance, the sound of it seems to come slow and terrific and without meaning, as though it were a ghost travelling a half mile ahead of his own shape.'That far within my hearing before my seeing,' Lena thinks. She thinks of herself as already moving, riding again, thinking *then it will be as if I were riding for a half mile before I even got into the wagon, before the wagon even got to where I was waiting, and that when the wagon is empty of me again it will go on for a half mile with me still in it* she waits.

This is a short excerpt; here the past and the future are little removed from the present, "a half mile away" as Faulkner says. But in other cases they can be separated from each other by vast distances—backward through one's forebears, and forward through one's descendents. And still man holds them in himself, as this woman does the image of a squeaky wagon, the wagon of time. He may not know this, he may only vaguely sense it, but when such a connection does play a role, he has the power to understand it with all his being. Therefore in Faulkner man is seen as part of a kind of vertiginous whole reminiscent of a concept of fate.

But never did any of the people whom Faulkner called to life acknowledge predestination or submit to that which was against him, no matter how strong it was. The chain of fate is dead, but man is alive; only he sets it into motion, and therefore he is obliged to be independent and prove his worth—that is the main thing which Faulkner saw, understood, and was able to embody in his work. .'I have no main theme," he told a journalist in 1956, "Or, maybe there is—you could consider it a definite faith in man, in his ability to prevail and triumph over circumstances and his own fate."[†]

We just read the beginning of *Light in August* with the mules, wagon, and woman resting on top of a hill. The woman's name is Lena Grove. She goes to look for the father of her child. She knows only the man's first name—and that, as it turns out later, has been changed; she has no idea where to look for him. But one night she crawls out a window (even though no one is holding her—this is stunning psychological truth—precisely going against fate), and she sets off on a journey with unshakeable conviction that it could be no other way, and that everything will be according to the worth which exists. And in the end—in general the novel is perhaps the best in terms of purely Faulknerian characters—she does find the man.

Or Chick Mallison, the nephew of the lawyer Stevens. We meet him in *The Mansion,* but another novel, *Intruder in the Dust* (1948) is devoted especially to him. There Chick is a little boy. He is saved from drowning by a

Negro; and Chick, as a young but noble and well-educated white southerner, offers him some money. But the hand hangs in the air; the Negro contemptuously refuses the reward. And this smashes the foundation which Chick, without thinking about it, had stood on so firmly. The whole story of the novel becomes an intense, stubborn striving by Chick to reestablish the human worth which he himself has destroyed. With the help of improbable adventures which made one reader recall Huckleberry Finn, he does attain his goal; he proves to the whole town which has been upset by a typical crime that the murderer was not the Negro who had been suspected by everyone, but a white just like the other proper citizens.

Faulkner is a realist, so of course not every man in his novels fights openly for the human values which Lena Grove or Chick Mallison defend. But everyone, or almost everyone, overcomes the circumstances which as he understands it, stands in the way of his truth. These men are ignorant and trapped by all kinds of prejudices and inclinations and roots from the land out of which they have grown; but their fierce strength and violence in surmounting all obstacles do not submit to description. Their collective image could be rather an animal than a man.

But even in the most ignorant of them we can still see the man, not the animal. The point is that the furious attack which such Faulkner characters mount against circumstances develops from inside, albeit with horrifying errors, with a quite special goal. Their passion is *justice*.

Take Thomas Sutpen from the novel *Absalom, Absalom!* * (1936). His father, a sharecropper, has sent him to the manor house with a message—until this time Sutpen has never left his village or seen such houses. (The story begins in 1817 in the mountains of Virginia.) But when he gets to this house, the Negro butler in luxurious livery does not even let him across the threshold. He is told that he should never again dare to come close to this door. This enfuriates Sutpen. He makes a vow to himself to get a house just like that, a Negro just like that, and to throw anybody he wants to across his threshold.

From this moment his life is gripped and enslaved by one passion for the sake of which he sacrifices everything. Because he has committed many crimes Sutpen is doomed as a human; but even when both of his families, which have been created with painful efforts, are perishing, and the house he has built must remain empty, even then he makes one more dark effort—the daughter of his old cohort Jones bears him a new baby. Sutpen is murdered. He is like a Faulknerian Macbeth; but after him, as after Macbeth, the idea of unsatisfied, undecided justice remains.

We discern this idea more clearly in the fate of Mink in *The Mansion*. To an insult which has been committed against him, trampling into the dirt everything by which he has lived, this small human spring answers with a terrible blow, first one then another, which he has been storing up for twenty years. Mink's stay in jail, his trip to Memphis for a revolver, all of this steel anticipation, his trusting conversations with fate ("he" or "they" who get in his way torment him, but then nevertheless fail to lead him there)—this is real

Faulkneriana. It is from this that we can confidently learn the most valuable thing that there is in Faulkner: the idea of man's indomitable movement upward out of any pit, no matter how deep.

Sometimes this movement begins in such a black environment that one stops involuntarily; we are seeing something like a prehistoric swamp where the most ancient of instincts rise up and enter into battle with furious roars. The story "Red Leaves," for example, about ritual killings among the Indians, or the story about the love of the rustic fool Isaac Snopes for a cow in the novel *The Hamlet* (1940), are carried off in such states, as if testing the strength of the idea. At such moments even the idea's best-informed defenders, people of broad intellectual horizons such as Stevens and Ratliff, stop believing in it. In the words of the critic Longly: "They understand very well that they will manage to survive, only because the world does not consider them important enough to be worth destruction."[*] Here the reader feels that he may boldly act on the formula "he who has borne it out to the end will be saved." Because Faulkner, the "master of the cosmos," never loses his presence of spirit; his positive hero is not Stevens and not Ratliff, but the indestructible ability of man to overcome, or as he expressed it, to become "the captain of his soul."

Here, incidentally, we also see what a deep contradiction separates Faulkner from that other famous American from the literature of the twentieth century, Ernest Hemingway. Hemingway is stoic waiting and defense; Faulkner is fierce attack, convinced of its superiority. In Hemingway man decides that his situation is hopeless, but he acts because his human duty orders him to do so. None of "Faulkner's people" would move a finger if he thought anything like that. All of them are convinced that in some degree they are equal to all the forces of the world, and with effrontery which is incomprehensible to these forces, they begin to crush them; very often they are victorious. Hemingway says "when the bell tolls the bell tolls for thee." Faulkner replies contemptuously, "Even when the bell of fate tolls for the last time . . . even then there will be still one more sound: the weak but inexhaustible voice of man."

Only in one instance is Faulkner's hero like a giant struck by Hemingway's idea—the test pilot Bayard Sartoris *(Sartoris,*1929). His life has been made senseless by his awareness that during the war his brother died instead of him, and perhaps it was his fault. But neither does he want to accept sentence from the hands of fate; and he stubbornly searches for his own doom until he does perish, as if having left all circumstances in confusion: circumstances could ask of him the question "why?"—not he of circumstances.

---

[*] Retranslated. Palievsky's footnote reads: " Faulkner himself said of Stevens: 'He was a good man, but he didn't know how to live by his ideals. But I think his nephew, that boy [Chick Mallison] , could grow up to be a better man than his uncle. I think he'll learn how to be a man'." Retranslated.

Generally when Faulkner takes someone from the twenties or a former soldier, the critics vainly rush to connect them to the "lost generation"; basically they have nothing to do with that group. For example, it is said of the story "Victory" that "it differs little in manner from Aldington's stories on the same themes."* But it is truly the difference between the heavens and the earth; Faulkner's Gray is not only not a victim of the war, on the contrary, he rises up out of it like a wild beast from a ravine; it is a tale of satanic pride which despises simple humanity.

Aldington, Remarque, Dos Passos, and others—and even Hemingway himself—were writers of the generation, or several generations, writers for the time when each of them passed through his page of disillusionment and discovered with amazement that grinding, mightily impersonal "contemporary life" which was indifferent to him.

At this time Faulkner was busy with something different. He sought in the contemporary something that linked it to the past, an unbroken chain of human values; and he found that its source was his own native soil—that "little piece of land there in Mississippi" about which Sherwood Anderson had once told him. Here he uncovered a "cosmos," a connecting thread which was indivisible and did not run out in hopelessness. And he spent the rest of his days uncoiling this thread. That is why it turned out that Hemingway, Aldington, and others became internationally known writers who quickly spread the waves of contemporary problems out from themselves—while Faulkner—indisputably a national, or even a local artist—became, rather, *universal* as he slowly and painfully showed the alienated world his kinship to it and the importance of humanity's foundations.

Truly, in Faulkner one can see, hear, and touch the American national character as one of the new branches of the human tree. The spirit of his works and the characters he calls into being immediately refute the primitive conception one still runs across of the American nation as a chaotic jumble of other nations and a neutrally-technological "multi-national" people. In his heroes we feel that the people who arrived on the deck of the Mayflower and then on other ships in order to move to the New World, even though they came there from different places and different peoples, came *not by chance;* each of them was already in some way American; and all of them, one might say, came together as Americans because they had something in common which even simple people who choose a single profession, say pilots, have.

Dividing the "merged" traits of these people into virtues and vices is difficult; and it is also difficult to name them, because each such name inevitably draws us into value-judgments, which are especially dangerous to apply to entire peoples. For example, if we say that these new arrivals had a proclivity for adventure, absolute independence, that they relied only on themselves

---

*I. A. Kashkin's afterword to W. Faulkner, *Sem' rasskazov [Seven Stories]*. On the whole this is the best essay on Faulkner in Russian. *[Palievsky's note.]*

and their own strength, etc., then all such traits will be only isolated and distorted features of an entire branch of the human family, traits which one could see in the independence of many American writers: Cooper, Twain, London, and perhaps nowhere as strongly as in Faulkner.

This location of the "branch" in Faulkner also leads to this: as we travel inward, moving with him back in the direction of the main trunk, we unexpectedly are able to discover his literary forebears (in terms of types of writer) not at all where it would seem easiest to find them (in the similarity of burning questions of the day), but somewhere in another corner of the earth, which is far-removed from "mainstreams of contemporaneity" and seemingly excessively self-sufficient.

For example, there is an unquestionable similarity between his world and the artistic world of Sholokhov. Begin with the fact that Yoknapatawpha is an Indian word meaning "quiet flows the water across a plain." This is the epic idea of a large river, the flow of life, which is also embodied in the title *The Quiet Don;* besides this, the word "quiet" in both cases masks the opposite which it contains. The American South portrayed in Faulkner's Yoknapatawpha plays a role similar to Sholokhov's Don; here it is taken as a special patriarchal society which has been preserved, but simultaneously as a reactionary portion of a larger whole which is confronted by the necessity for drastic changes. The idea of Mother Earth, so strong in Sholokhov, is very noticeable here too. And the transition, the disruption of its norms is accompanied by gains and by irrevocable losses. The movement is toward change and sharp contradictions which demand for their expression special devices: characteristic of both Faulkner and Sholokhov are completely uncapricious transitions from humor to tragedy and back, wherein one feels not contrast, but on the contrary, the natural "polarity" of life. They also have much in common in style, in maintaining the individuality of each character, and so forth.

The Faulknerian hero who tenaciously asserts his own rights, who is fiercely independent even when things are hopeless, who stubbornly gets confused and is incapable of understanding and accepting real conditions, is indubitably similar to such people as Melekhov or Aksinya.* Like Sholokhov, Faulkner views them simultaneously with sympathy and sobriety which seems to border on "cruelty" (precisely this word has been used by critics to define the first impression created by the novels of the two writers).

However, there is of course a dividing line between them here too; in Sholokhov the changes in the life he is depicting move in the direction of revolutionary reconstruction; in Faulkner—toward capitalism's predatory destruction of all human values. Therefore the general view of the modern world and the place of humanism in it was naturally different in Faulkner. Speaking to a graduating class in his home town shortly after receiving the Nobel prize,

---

*The hero and heroine of *The Quiet Don. [Editor's note.]*

Faulkner described it thus:

> What threatens us today is fear. Not the atom bomb, nor even fear of it, because if the bomb fell on Oxford tonight, all it could do would be to kill us, which is nothing, since in doing that, it will have robbed itself of its only power over us: which is fear of it, the being afraid of it. Our danger is not that. Our danger is the forces in the world today which are trying to use man's fear to rob him of his individuality, his soul, trying to reduce him to an unthinking mass by fear and bribery—giving him free food which he has not earned, easy and valueless money which he has not worked for;—the economies or ideologies or political systems, . . .* who would reduce man to one obedient mass for their own aggrandisement and power, or because they themselves are baffled and afraid, afraid of, or incapable of, believing in man's capacity for courage and endurance and sacrifice.
>
> . . . . So, never be afraid. Never be afraid to raise your voice for honesty and truth and compassion, against injustice and lying and greed. If you, not just you in this room tonight, but in all the thousands of other rooms like this one about the world today and tomorrow and next week, will do this . . .** you will change the earth. In one generation all the Napoleons and Hitlers and Caesars and other assorted tyrants*** who want power and aggrandisement, and the simple politicians and time-servers who themselves are merely baffled or ignorant or afraid, who have used, or are using, or hope to use, man's fear and greed for man's enslavement, will have vanished from the face of it.

Faulkner offered no more than he could offer—the old human values But profoundly significant remains the fact that the two biggest writers of the modern world articulated and constantly defended the same idea: "Man does not merely endure, he prevails," or as Sholokhov said in his story "Man's Fate" (and as it would perhaps be most accurate to translate Faulkner), he will "predominate": "A man of unbending will . . . will predominate, and at the side of the father will grow up the son, who when he is mature will be able to bear all burdens and overcome all obstacles which lie in his path."

* * * *

The independent discovery of realism which Faulkner made in the middle of the twentieth century was an extremely difficult task for him; the best efforts of his vast talent were expended on a dismantling and re-examination of the bases of his art. And it seems unlikely that one would be correct to assert that this work was futile, and that it would have been better for him not to "discover what had already been discovered." The point is precisely that as a result of this bold and independent analysis and testing of accepted truths (and for each person this testing is done on the basis of models which his life presents), the artist moves ahead to the new truth, his own truth; only

---

*Palievsky omits the words: "communist or socialist or democratic, whatever they wish to call themselves, the tyrants and the politicians, American or European or Asiatic, whatever they call themselves." *Ed.*

**Palievsky omits: "not as a class or classes, but as individuals, men and women." *Ed.*

***Palievsky fails to note this omission here: "and Mussolinis and Stalins." The address was made in Oxford on May 28, 1951. *Ed.*

then do such things happen as a Columbus setting out to discover a known India and discovering an unknown America.

True, the latest studies say that Columbus already had maps made by someone else and that he knew the way to the New World. But of Faulkner we can say with confidence that the avant-garde maps he had pointed anywhere you like—but not at the "Big Country." And then it was all the more alive when he found it. He did not know, or did not want to know, that legendary Vikings had been here before him, that perhaps a man mightier than he had won fame here. Leif Erikson, and not just Erikson.

He made his discovery. Amid "carelessness" and indefiniteness he sought wholeness and definition; the shores of the continent he had caught sight of kept getting outlined more and more clearly, as did the inexhaustible riches on it. His realism was formed not by the accomplishments of the past and present, no matter how brilliant—it was recreated from the beginning. And this had a special, vital significance for literature. If we mentally, arbitrarily try to put him beside the other great Western realists of the twentieth century, men like Thomas Mann or Anatole France, we realize that in his "regrowth" and development Faulkner achieved special proofs (ones which cannot be erased by anyone, ones important for the twentieth century) of the power of art and the power of realism.

There is every reason to believe that Faulkner will remain more than a writer for our time. Because of his independence, and therefore the vividness of his discoveries, he will be read not for specific information, but because of that profound human interest which has always stood at the center of any knowledge and which in the final analysis (at least until now) has defined the directions this knowledge takes. This central position of Faulkner in relation to the various possible "questions" is evidence that he was a real artist and that although his books have already been written, published, and discussed, there is still much that is new to be expected from them.

PART TWO

ENGLISH-LANGUAGE ARTICLES PUBLISHED IN THE SOVIET UNION

This section is composed of essays published in English in Moscow. All but Orlova's review of Shirley Ann Grau (from *Soviet Woman,* No. 11, 1969) were printed in a magazine called *Soviet Literature* by Progress Publishers, Moscow. *Soviet Literature* is published in several major languages as an official organ presenting fiction, poetry, and criticism—usually that which for one reason or another translators in other countries have not taken up. Thus all of these articles were translated by Soviet translators (generally not named).

THE AUTHORS

Ivan Kashkin (sometimes spelled "Kashkeen"), 1899-1963, was the dean of Russian critics of American literature. He wrote widely over many years, especially on Hemingway—who is on record praising Kashkin among all his critics. He was responsible for pushing through the publication of many works of American literature, sponsoring translations, encouraging students and young scholars. With M. Zenkevich he edited the only pre-war anthology of American poetry published in the Soviet Union. His last big book *For the Modern Reader* (Moscow, 1968) contains essays on everyone from Chaucer to Robert Frost, both of whom he introduced to Russian readers.

Alexei Zverev has written a number of reviews of American novels, including John Killens, William Burroughs, John O'Hara, and John Hersey. His survey covers only a few major Soviet works on American literary criticism. Zverev is among the younger generation of Soviet literary critics whose work shows more sophistication than many of the older literary scholars.

M. Landor

FAULKNER IN THE SOVIET UNION

It cannot be said that people in the Soviet Union were too late in discovering Faulkner. An anthology of 20th-century American short stories was published back in 1934, in which Faulkner was represented by a powerful and very typical story "When Night Falls," excellently translated by Olga Kholmskaya. A little later Valentin Stenich, who had brought Dos Passos' best novels, *The 42nd Parallel* and *1919,* to the attention of the Soviet readers, translated Faulkner's interesting, though not so original short story "Artist at Home."

But unfortunately, that was as far as matters went then. Faulkner enjoyed far less popularity in the Soviet Union than some other American writers of his own generation. This was not, of course, entirely by accident: both critics and readers were at that time under the spell of newly discovered Hemingway, of the classic clarity of this acutely contemporary writer. However, there was no logical inevitability in this. In the 1930's new American prose was published widely in the Soviet Union, even such grotesque works as Caldwell's *Tobacco Road,* were translated and such painfully psychological novels as Wright's *Native Son.*

In the first postwar decade not many works of American prose were published. In 1955 *Foreign Literature* magazine, which has done a great deal to acquaint Soviet readers with this great American novelist, began publication. It started by publishing Elena Romanova's article "Anti-War Themes in the Work of William Faulkner" (No. 6, 1955).

The article focused on an analysis of his then recently published novel *A Fable* which provoked controversial reactions in the West. Some of Faulkner's admirers regarded it as a failure. Elena Romanova wrote that it was an event in world literature. In this complex novel she saw the result of Faulkner's deliberations on war and peace; she showed how it combined contemporary analogies to the Bible stories with acute social criticism and a passionate appeal against war.

A Fable, the critic pointed out, did not stand alone in Faulkner's work. What is new here is a clear view of the causes of wars and an active moral standpoint of the author. But Faulkner even in his early works was a trenchant anti-militarist—for instance, in his novel *Soldier's Pay* and the short story "Victory" (the Russian translation of this story soon appeared in *Foreign Literature*).

While duly noting the great qualities of *A Fable,* Elena Romanova did not share the laudatory attitude shown to the book by some of the Western critics. The novel's literary form gave rise to mixed feelings on her part. "So oddly are mediocre and crude elements in the novel interwoven with brilliant, delicate and magnificent prose, so suddenly is mature thought interrupted for the sake of largely incomprehensible mystical outbursts, that the reader's feeling of joyful amazement more than once involuntarily changes to one of perplexity and annoyance." But it is not these lapses and complexities (which Faulkner's opponents so exaggerate) that are stressed in the article, but his lofty and passionate humanism.

In March 1958 *Foreign Literature* published a second article on Faulkner. At about that time the magazine published Faulkner's detective short story "Smoke," in which Soviet readers first met that noble intellectual, Gavin Stevens, upholding justice in Jefferson. By that time the novel *The Town* had been published in the United States. The article by Raisa Orlova and Lev Kopelev set itself the aim of describing the first two novels about the Snopes family and of giving readers a general orientation in Faulkner's densely populated Yoknapatawpha county. The title of the article was "Myths and Truth About America's South."

In the story of the Snopes—their invasion of Frenchman's Bend (*The Hamlet*) and their settling in Jefferson (*The Town*)—the Soviet critics saw a deep social significance. Flem Snopes and his insatiable relations embody the bourgeois principle in pure form—a chase after dollars, unrestrained by any morality, usurps their hearts. We are face to face not with a Gobseck, the philosopher of money, nor with a Soames Forsyte, the lover of painting. The invasion of this patriarchal backwater by capitalism is crude and naked.

Faulkner damns the Snopes, in whom he sees the world of bourgeois inhumanity, write the authors of the article. And in his search for a moral prop he turns to the past: in his novels he sets a poetically transformed Old South against the triumph of stupid and pitiless bourgeois. Sometimes Faulkner recalls with regret the time of the aristocracy's glory, but more often he is talking of something else: of the patriarchal community uniting independent farmers. Gavin Stevens, the supreme Don Quixote of Yoknapatawpha, idealizes and tries to uphold the pre-bourgeois way of life.

The article did not overlook the writer's prejudices and illusions which linked him with the milieu of "Southern gentlemen." But the emphasis is on something else: Faulkner was not only an enemy of racial discrimination, he was organically bound to the Negroes and their culture. This kinship is felt in everything—in his manner of constructing images, in the musical composition of his language and, lastly, in the fact that he embodies his moral ideal in portraits of Negroes (from *The Sound and the Fury* to *Intruder in the Dust*).

Orlova and Kopelev dispute the view that Faulkner is a decadent: they quote his Nobel Prize speech, but find the main proof in the novels written long before it. "Even in his bitterest and most tragic works Faulkner preserves a sense of the indestructibility of life, even though at times it is only a vague feeling, somewhere deep in the general background." In support of this view they quote the endings of two of his sombre novels—*Light in August* and *Absalom, Absalom!* In their opinion, even if Faulkner would not have named Cervantes, Dickens and the Russian classics among his favorite writers, a close study of his novels would have led one to these literary sources.

The two articles in *Foreign Literature* had above all an informative aim.

They dispelled the existing prejudice against Faulkner: it was natural that his work was examined predominantly in the social and moral aspects, an analysis of artistic from was yet to come. These articles were only a "first step" in dealing with certain questions. Nevertheless, they display some features of the attitude to Faulkner in the Soviet Union.

In America among Faulkner's enthusiastic supporters as well as among his opponents there are some who think there is a gulf between his later humanist declarations and the "black" novels of the thirties. It would be simplifying matters to overlook the writer's changes and contradictions. Nevertheless, the *Foreign Literature* critics regarded Faulkner's work as a unity, they perceived a moral basis in his early works, too. Some literary scholars of the "new criticism" school recognize only Faulkner among all twentieth-century American prose writers. In the Soviet Union we do not isolate the creator of Yoknapatawpha from his predecessors and contemporaries—from Sherwood Anderson to Steinbeck. This is in full accordance with his own views and it strengthens the reader's conception of the great variety of American prose writing.

Faulkner owes his world fame largely to France. It was there that this apparently "local" writer was taken up as one of the most profoundly tragic artists of the century. But for French critics Faulkner has frequently been an object of conjecture and literary speculation; after the war an attempt was made to use his name to bolster up the theory of "the death of character." Faulkner impresses us by the reality and full-bloodedness of the world he portrays; as distinct from certain anaemic French writers he creates an increasing number of live new characters; his novels are marked by an impetuous and at times cruel humor, deriving from a folk tradition. His novels are sufficient to show the baselessness of talk about the crisis of the novel, so much the vogue in certain literary circles in the West.

There are, of course, plenty of serious studies of Faulkner by American and European critics; some of them (for instance, Malcolm Cowley's well-known article) have received favorable comment in the Soviet Union. The study of Faulkner in the Soviet Union is only beginning; special studies of how the writer is received in his own country and in Europe will no doubt appear in due course.

Faulkner's first volume—*Seven Stories*—was published in Moscow in 1958. It was compiled, edited, and equipped with an afterword by the late Ivan Kashkin, an outstanding Soviet expert on new Western prose and a very sensitive critic and translator. He translated the first two stories himself—"Barn Burning" and "A Justice;" the book also included "Red Leaves," "When Night Falls," "Smoke," "Percy Grimm" and "Victory."

Kashkin's article is devoted to Faulkner as a story writer, but he also gives a general estimation of the writer's work. He regards as untrue the widespread myths about Faulkner in the West: according to one version he is an oracle and a classic, according to another—an unpleasant, harmful, modernist. The truth, thinks Kashkin, lies somewhere in between. He finds contrived horrors and unwarranted formal innovations is such novels as *The Sound and the Fury* and *Sanctuary.* But he recognizes the rare artistic power behind the "epic of many planes and patches," which most of Faulkner's novels appear to be. Kashkin defines the social significance of the writer's work as follows:

"In his epic of the South he shows the Southern states in their full complexity: not through the eyes of a Northern observer nor of oppressed Negroes, but from the viewpoint of those who have enjoyed all the benefits of the South and now see the collapse and end of the old plantation-owning society. This gives all the greater significance to the recognition of the tragic impasse to which the curse of slave-ownership has brought the South."

It is no accident that Kashkin pays attention to Faulkner's stories. Hemingway's style with its surprising simplicity was close to Kashkin's artistic ideal. And in Faulkner he valued the tension and understatement, and condemned his verbosity, heaviness and bombast. This is noticeable when he says:

"Faulkner is an uneven and capricious writer to a high degree. He can write laconic, gripping and fast-moving stories and at the same time permits himself to compile fragmentary novels from puffy and long-winded short stories which he also prints separately."

However that may be, Kashkin has given a very precise description of Faulkner's literary technique as a story writer. In his story "Barn Burning" he notes the filigree-fine rendering of the stream of consciousness with masterly changes of tempo; this does not exclude traditional methods as well: the father's portrait is drawn in a Tolstoyan manner by an accumulation of particular traits. His remarks on the short story, "A Justice," are of particular interest: Kashkin calls our attention to the interweaving of time (the beginning and end of the nineteenth century), to the leaps in the action, the combination of lyrical moods with harsh and laconic humor. Concluding his observations on Faulkner's stories, the Soviet critic refers to his poetics of contrast.

Following upon the first volume of stories, another volume of somewhat different contents was published in the *Ogonyok Library* series, and then a third book in the same series: this included the short stories "Turnabout" and "Delta Autumn." All these books were published in mass editions of up to 150,000 copies each. The interest of readers was aroused and his stories began to be published in the Soviet literary magazines *Moskva, Znamya* and *Druzhba Narodov.* One of the biggest mass circulation magazines, *Ogonyok,* published his story "Dry September." Translator O. Soroka, a Faulkner enthusiast, came forward to acquaint Soviet readers with his hunting stories: first "A Bear Hunt" and later "The Bear" (the version from the novel *The Big Woods*).

At the end of 1961 *Foreign Literature* published Rita Rait-Kovaleva's translation of the last novel in the trilogy about the Snopes—*The Mansion.* Due tribute should be paid to the translator who had undertaken the task of rendering Faulkner's style as a novelist in the Russian. His style is apparently lacking form: clumsy, with repetitions, pauses and amplifications; with digressions into history amid an endless period; the surges with which the narrative proceeds; the combination of simple folk speech with a highflown style which calls the Old Testament, or Ancient literature, or the Gothic novel to mind. Not all the readers of *Foreign Literature* liked *The Mansion,* of course; probably some did not read it to the end. But the story of Mink and the episode of his death made an impression on many readers that modern literature very rarely makes—the impression of art of classic power.

Novy Mir wrote of the translator's skill: "Her work is distinguished not only by technical virtuosity, but—and this is the main thing—by a very exact and careful sense of atmosphere, of shades of emotion and, lastly, of the novel's rhythm. We are face to face with the genuine Faulkner and can judge him without making any allowances for the translation."

This estimate was given in an article, "Saga of a Gloomy Dynasty" (*Novy Mir,* No. 7, 1962), by Inna Levidova. The Snopeses prompted a natural association with the Forsytes, but Inna Levidova pointed out how different the author is from traditional realists of the Galsworthy type.

"Faulkner is an artist of truly gigantic imagination, turned inwards, and everything he has learned and felt in his long life as man and writer has always been just raw material for the seething cauldron of his own inner hurricanes, antagonisms and conflicts." Perhaps what distinguishes Faulkner from past realists is here expressed too sharply, especially since the narrative of the Snopeses often reminds one of Balzac's novels, especially his *Les Paysans.* But Inna Levidova herself explains that "Faulkner's imagined world is bound by a thousand threads to American reality—not to humdrum everyday reality, but to its quintessence."

She has a fine sense of the form of Faulkner novels, of the poetic power lurking beneath the ostensible disorder. The incidental stories (these are often examples of "savage" humor) are not at all foreign to this genuinely American novel, which does not heed the classic sense of moderation and proportion. But she finds artistic unity above all in the first two parts of the trilogy.

The Village, she writes, "was integral and genuine, like a raised and overturned layer of soil with its torn, hardened and crooked roots, with its scent of rot and human sweat. *The Town* was an intensely developing novel of characters with characters socially illumined, of course, by Faulkner's poetic-grotesque view." Passing on to *The Mansion,* she notes that it has compositional weaknesses and that "the whole magnificent story about Mink could exist quite separately."

But in this part of the trilogy Inna Levidova and other Soviet critics are amazed by Faulkner's strength of spirit, by the continual movement of his thought. The boundaries of Yoknapatawpha recede: contemporary history enters the novel. Faulkner passes frank and independent judgement upon reaction—including the "witch-hunters;" he writes with profound respect of the Spanish and American anti-fascists. Among the fine characters in *The Mansion* is the Communist Linda: in her the writer sees a person of lofty ideals, although he does not find action for her in commercial-ridden Jefferson.

At the beginning of 1965 the Khudozhestvennaya Literatura Publishing House issued the complete trilogy about the Snopeses in an edition of 100,000 copies. It was quickly sold out. Many people have already been able to enter Faulkner's poetic world and to obtain pleasure from his difficult art.

Intense work by translators preceded the publication of the trilogy. Rita Rait-Kovaleva directed it; after *The Mansion* she translated half of the novel *The Town.* She found inspired and skillful colleagues in the young translators Victor Hinkis and Simon Markish.

Both already have a literary reputation: Markish, a student of Ancient literature by his education, is well-known for his translations of Plutarch and Ulrich von Gutten, and he has translated short stories by Edgar Allen Poe. Hinkis has attracted attention by his translations from English, although he translates from other languages: he has introduced to Soviet readers Steinbeck's *Of Mice and Men* and Updike's *The Centaur.* The most highly qualified translators have been engaged on "mastering" Faulkner's exceptionally complex style.

They emerged triumphant. Many passages in *The Village,* in which simple peasant speech is combined with Ciceronian rhetoric and bookish metaphors with boisterous folk humor, are translated with virtuosity: I must mention at least the symbolical episode of Flem's conversation with Satan.

Soviet critics are taking an even deeper interest in Faulkner. Among recent studies let me mention two articles. One is by Abel Startsev, a veteran scholar of American literature, and the other is by a young critic, Pyotr Palievsky.

In his article "William Faulkner's Trilogy," published as a foreword to *The Village,* Startsev concentrates attention on the profound changes in the writer's work. In the novels from *The Sound and the Fury* to *Absalom, Absalom!* he finds oppressive gloom and formalistic quests, although he adds: "One can hardly name a single novel of Faulkner's where sincere alarm and pain for suffering mankind does not break through the black pessimism." He regards *The Village* as a turning point: in it realist principles triumphed and American reality was presented in a socially significant form.

Startsev analyzes the novel's poetry and humor, he sees it in the peasant, farmer basis of the whole trilogy. But he has a particular liking for later Faulkner—for the author of *The Town* and *The Mansion.* Having particularly in view the transformation of the portrait of Eula in these books, he writes of the advance in Faulkner's artistic thought—he "rejects accentuated attention to the primitive and instinctive element in man in favor of intellect, will and the socially conditioned motives of human activity."

Startsev also sees the writer's progress in the abolition of Yoknapatawpha's "autarchy." He has in view not only Linda and the political deliberations in *The Mansion.* The boundaries of Faulkner's province expand and the inroad of "Russian motifs" into these novels of extremely American substance and spirit is no accident.

Abel Startsev has made a serious study of 18th-century cultural links between Russia and America. Naturally he was particularly interested in deciphering the name of V. K. Ratcliff, one of the characters dearest to the author. Towards the end of the trilogy he turns out to be an American of Russian descent: his initials stand for Vladimir Kirillovich.

This "Russian fantasy" of the novelist is no fantasy, the critic remarks: "Documents have recently been found in our archives which show that Russian people were actually present in the United States during the period of the American War of Independence. Here, as usual, Faulkner displays his excellent acquaintance with the oral traditions of his native parts, which evidently also preserved the memory of a Russian settler."

Pyotr Palievsky starts his article, "The Discoveries of William Faulkner" (*Znamya* No. 3, 1965), by saying that the Nobel Prize speech expresses the very essence of the writer's work. "Man's endeavor to bend circumstances to his own use was for him always more real than the circumstances themselves." Palievsky was the first critic in the Soviet Union to write of the obsession and fierce stubbornness which are distinctive features of Faulkner's characters; and he offered his own interpretation of Faulkner's early and most agonizing books.

According to Palievsky, "Faulkner never shunned the gloomy refutations of his own outlook; on the contrary, he accepted their challenge. No filth could embarrass him in this respect, though it made his critic's flesh creep, who could not bear it and began to say that Faulkner was a sadist revelling in the way people behaved in an ultimate impasse. But it was precisely the stubbornness and irreconcilability of people refusing to recognize what had apparently been proved and extricating themselves from the impasse, which were for Faulkner the most reliable evidence and source of his own imperturbable resolve."

In the character of Mink Palievsky notes what he considers most valuable in the writer's work: the idea of man's rise from any pit no matter how deep.

Palievsky also speaks of an affirmation of realism in Faulkner's novel. But he thinks it could be already detected in *The Sound and the Fury,* which, in his view, marks Faulkner's beginning as an independent artist. Responsive to avant-garde innovations, Faulkner had intended to tell the story of a family's disintegration in the manner of the "stream of consciousness;" but the thrice told story seemed to him incomplete until he had introduced yet another narrator—himself. In Palievsky's view this was a fresh discovery of realism—at a time when young writers had forgotten this trend in favor of avant-garde allurements.

The critic considers that the crucial novel for Faulkner was not *The Village*, but the earlier novel *Sartoris:* the writer realized that he could write all his life about the tiny postage stamp of his native country. The idea of a cycle about Yoknapatawpha formed in his mind. The writer, who might have seemed parochial, became universal, slowly and painfully proving to the disjointed world his own kinship with it and the importance of human foundations.

Many Western critics have compared Faulkner with Dostoevsky (no one in the Soviet Union has yet made such a comparison in detail, although it suggests itself). Palievsky offers what is at first sight a parodoxical comparison—with Sholokhov, but upon close examination there is an undoubted affinity between *And Quiet Flows the Don* and the world of Yoknapatawpha.

"The idea of mother earth, so strong in Sholokhov, is very noticeable here, too. Moreover, a change and a severance from its norms bring a number of gains and unrequited losses; advance is by series a of sharp contradictions, whose expression requires special devices: typical is the transition, which is quite involuntary both for Faulkner and for Sholokhov, from humor to tragedy and vice versa, and it is not the contrast which is sensed but, on the contrary, the natural polarity of life."

Far from everything carries conviction in Palievsky's article, which is acute, penetrating and excellently written. He speaks rather sharply of Hemingway: he exaggerates the dependence of early Faulkner on the recipes of the avant-gardists (he was quite independent even in his daring experiments). His essay is, of course, not the last word of Soviet critics on Faulkner: thorough critical studies of him will no doubt appear. But no one can say that a Soviet view of Faulkner has not been formed. He is unequivocally one of the greatest writers of this century, a powerful and original epic writer, a man who has gone through hell with his characters and so has all the more ground for saying to us: "I believe that man will not merely endure: he will prevail."

Ivan Kashkin

WHAT IS HEMINGWAY'S STYLE?

Everyone thinks much of Hemingway's style though for different reasons. But what is it, this style of his? Is it the journalistic compression, or the understatement, the subtext of his early books, or the broader breath of *For Whom the Bell Tolls,* the convulsive restraint or the lively unforced dialogue, the accuracy of laconic descriptions (or the boundless periods of other descriptions) and the lyrical haze of the inner monologues, the emphasized dryness of the "objective" tone or the agitated pathos of his articles and speeches? It is none of these things in isolation. It is all these things together. As a craftsman Hemingway was versatile and comprehensive.

The fact is that he was a master of many forms of writing and at different times used them separately and sometimes together, depending on what he was aiming at, the artistic problems to be solved, and the given circumstances.

The fact is that there is no such thing as an abstract, stable, once-for-all "Hemingway style"—clipped or diffuse, restrained or patiently ironic—but there is the gradual evolution of an intelligent approach by a great master to the different forms of the artistic essence that he wished to express in a given work.

The clearest example of this may perhaps be found in the tale *Big Two-Hearted River.* At first sight it seems to be an all but overwhelmingly scrupulous fixation of every detail of Nick Adams' fishing trip. If so, then at the end of the day, after wandering with Nick along all those creeks and channels, we are as worn out as the fisherman himself and in that sense the author has achieved his purpose of making us spend the day with Nick.

But why does the author insist on listing in detail all those mechanical actions of Nick's: he picks up a box of matches, removes a match from it, strikes the match on the box, applies it to the brushwood, kindles the fire, etc. And what is the reason for the haunting rhythm of those clipped phrases— he picked up, he lighted, he put down and so on? It is as though Nick is trying not to leave a chink in the chain of successive acts, into which an obtrusive thought could slip. And that is the truth. The fact is that *Big Two-Hearted River* is not an isolated episode of catching fish, it is the last tale in a book about Nick Adams and his experiences in our "peaceful" times. *In Our Time* is a book about the way life assails the immature mind of young Nick from all sides, and in all ways. There is in it an unbroken series of blows: social, family, professional, personal. Physical, psychological, moral, emotional, blows. This tension persists throughout the whole book and reaches its culmination in *Big Two-Hearted River.* Here the author shows the result of those shocks at a time when they are already stored away in Nick's mind, yet still oppress him like a time bomb, even here, on the peaceful Big River. That is why Nick does not give rein to his thoughts which might lead him God only knows where, making him "a way you'll never be." He forces himself to think only of what he is doing at the moment. This is an act of instinctive self-preservation.

The author does not say a word about this overtly. But every word refers to it indirectly—by the very form of expression. As to the reader, he is free either to gather all this from the twelve tales about Nick Adams, or else to be content with the dullish story of a fishing trip.

It is characteristic that when some action is sufficiently dramatic or tense to hold Nick in its grip (for instance, when he sees his first big trout or catches and frees a small one)and thus helps to keep out the intrusive thoughts, the monotonous rhythm of a mechanical action that he no longer needs is broken and for a while the author's phrases flow more broadly and freely.

In the following evolution of Hemingway's writing you see how the careless haste of the telegraphic language soon changes into a highly-finished laconism, the unintentional clumsiness into an elaborate angularity when that is required to show the way a person speaks. The master no longer flaunts his crude clumsiness of style but when necessary he lends it to his characters, if they happen to be genuinely crude.

Much has been said about a special, Hemingway "iceberg theory." Admittedly, this is a highly successful way of putting things and the important fact is not only that Hemingway formulated it but that in practicing it in his work he gave substance to one of the ever-fresh requirements of the art of realism—a strict, conscious selectiveness, this guiding principle of realism. Hemingway learned from his great teachers Stendhal, Tolstoy and Flaubert. Out of the mass of painstakingly mastered material, the pile of sketches, the "thousands of tons of verbal ore" the genuine realist selects only that which is most characteristic and important, not even one-eighth of the iceberg but perhaps a thousandth part. It is the naturalist who writes exhaustingly about what is important and unimportant alike. From this aspect Hemingway's style is marked by his unique, painfully acquired application of the method of realistic selection. And it is the depth of perspective, the mass of the submerged seven-eighths of the iceberg which determines and provides the precious pithy simplicity that has nothing in common with a cheap and superficial simple-mindedness.

In his short stories Hemingway usually takes the bull by the horns, singling out the particular situation and usually limiting himself in time to the immediate present. For years and years Hemingway walked beside his characters but in his works people appear from unknown places as if out of the shadows and disappear into the night under the rain or into death. In that exclusion from time, both calendar and historical, in the hero's absorption in what is happening to him at the moment lurks the danger of weakened links with society and of self-isolation. But Hemingway, when he forgets his own statements, is too true a brother-in-arms, he values too highly action and the possibility of exerting his strength in helping others, to yield entirely to this danger. A few crucial moments are caught as in the short flash of a search-light aimed at the ring or on "no man's land." but the author shows his characters in moments of the highest tension, struggle or experience, when everything is revealed—the best and the worst in them. And from the creative side it is by this condensing of time that the narrative attains depth and full-ness.

The precision of detail of Chekhov's prose, the analytical depth of Tolstoy, the understatement of the Chekhovian drama, all these Hemingway converts in such a way that he forces us to accept the result as something that belongs only to himself. At the same time his theory of the iceberg is in no way dogmatic. When necessary, he reinforces the story of what is happening here and now with the reminiscences of the writer Harry or of Jordan. And this theory is in no way undermined by the introduction of a usual, common-place background, which only serves to emphasize by contrast the tension of the principal action.

Hemingway often said that one should write only about things no one has written about before. Or if the subject has been handled by others then one should write about it better than one's predecessors. We may take as an example the novel *The Sun Also Rises* (Fiesta). Hemingway was not the first to tackle the subject of the "lost generation." Fitzgerald and Michael Arlen had done so before him but it was only in *The Sun Also Rises* that the thoughts and speech of the people of the lost generation stood out as clear as crystal. Hemingway believed in writing about what he saw with his own eyes and experienced himself and in communicating what he saw and felt ac-cording to the way he understood it. He spurned the conventional way of seeing things and the conventional manner of describing them. This principle governed both his choice of themes—war, hunting, sport—and of character—the soldier, the journalist, the sportsman, the hunter—in short, men of action, and, finally, the very manner of his descriptions and narratives—direct, com-pressed, forceful. While striving at direct vision Hemingway sought to write without any prejudice and as concretely as possible about what he actually felt; to write by holding firmly to the facts, things and events from which his feelings originated. It was his view that the writer should not formulate or describe but stimulate the reader's perception and imagination by showing him things as he himself sees and feels them.

This too is something he inherited from the great realists, a tradition handed down to our days. The reader ought to feel and experience what the author wishes to express. And Hemingway has told us that he wishes to ex-press the truth of life and reality in such a way that it should enter the mind of the reader as part of his own experience—and to do so with a minimum of importunity on the author's part, with the rejection of all explanatory ad-jectives and metaphors.

Hemingway rejected all that was fortuitous, superficial and trivial, but the main images that arose out of his experience of life stood out all the sharper and were for ever engraved in his memory. Why should a room be crammed with the unnecessary furniture of similes? Things should be shown as they are, irrespective of other things and happenings. Similes are permissible either when they are indisputably apt or when direct illustration is insufficiently clear. There should be no explanations by the author, no intrusion of sentiment or rhetoric, nothing but plain objectivity. All these features were typical of Hemingway at a certain period. Later he revised this all too uncompromising attitude. All the same when, in *Across the River and Into the Trees,* he resorts to author's definitions, it strikes one as a departure from his own credo.

A graphic example of Hemingway's compressed and seemingly dispassionate manner is provided by the short story "A Clean, Well-Lighted Place." It consists of three pages in all. The whole tale is hard, void of all poetical adornments, yet it is constructed like a poem in prose in the way it contrasts the feelings of horror and compassion, light and darkness.

If these three pages are read by those "who never felt it," such readers will not linger on them. Anyway the story is not meant for them. But those whose feelings are attuned to the right level of perceptiveness, will respond to the mordant irony of the incongruity between the title and the subject of the story. A writer of a different stamp might have shown here the confusion of anxious philosophical thought but Hemingway simply gives us a concrete sensation of emptiness personified, as it were, in the half-dead old man; the sense of Nothingness both in the outer material world and in the inner world of man. And he does all this with imagery alone.

Hemingway is aware of the danger of excessive verisimilitude. He searches for a truth that is deeper than empirical facts. What he got from his own experience is usually told in the language of images.

He was not interested in trivial factual verisimilitude but in that authenticity which is sometimes more convincing, closer to the truth than the half-truth of an eyewitness. And that is an indication of an art reflecting the great truth of life.

Hemingway's dialogue has amazing authenticity. But it is not a tape recording of a conversation he once heard, but a strictly controlled *montage* of hundreds of such conversations heard by the author and moreover passed through the filter of his creative mind.

Perhaps it comes out slightly different from the original but we see here the truth of art which makes art the sublime expression of reality. That is what you feel when reading *The Sun Also Rises, A Farewell to Arms* and *For Whom the Bell Tolls.*

When Hemingway speaks about the fourth and fifth dimension of his work I think he has in mind mainly the time dimension, the concentration on *now,* on direct influence. And then the next dimension is the completeness of influence, that utmost convincingness of realistic art which he instills into the mind of the reader by using the whole battery of the artistic and ideological means at his disposal which forces the reader to accept, to absorb what he is reading as his own experience. Among these means Hemingway names not only talent but self-discipline, intelligence, disinterestedness, independence (getting free from outside influences), clarity of aim ("the conception of what it can be"), that is, the possibility of carrying out one's conceptions not in declarations but in deeds; and also, constant work and "an absolute conscience as unchanging as the standard meter in Paris." Thus did Hemingway himself understand the many items out of which the style of a real artist is formed.

Hemingway wrote about concrete things, he wrote about events, but the more he wrote the more he became convinced that his main task was to write about man. Like his writer Harry, he felt an ever growing desire to write "not just the events.... He had seen the subtler change and he could remember how the people were at different times" under the influence of events. Take two of his "undefeated," separated by a thirty-year interval: Manolo Garcia and old Santiago. The former is shown more on the professional plane; Santiago's psychology is revealed from within. In the miniature "Minarets of Adrianople" an almost impersonal stream of human beings is shown; in "The Old Man at the Bridge" Hemingway concentrates on one man and through him draws a general picture of a whole nation.

I have referred above to some features of style at which Hemingway deliberately aimed; but in addition he had some stylistic peculiarities arising from his choice of characters. These children of his pen wish to speak and think and behave for themselves. And willy-nilly the author has to pay heed to their demands and emendations. The style which is characteristic of Hemingway's counterparts and of the characters with whom they come into contact, in particular, their verbal characteristics, reflect their social environment and their time, their spiritual formation and structure. Together with Hemingway they endured the moral shocks and physical mutilations of war and the unrealized hopes of great changes. Unstable, bruised by life, the best of these characters try to find support in strict self-control, in work, physical or intellectual. Hence their search for a well-regulated precision of language and for an equally precise conception of the outer world. If they happen to be writers, then by putting down on paper their vague thoughts and feelings they hope to free themselves both from their burden and from the duty of understanding them. They want to free themselves as quickly and as thoroughly as possible. Is that not the reason for the meaningful laconicism of their dialogue and descriptions?

The tense atmosphere of frustrated expectations and shattered hopes makes their behavior and speech equally strained. They seem fettered, convulsively halting. The more ravaged of them remind one of marionettes and their speech, so abstract and colorless, is like the dialogue in a Berlitz manual. In Hemingway's short stories nearly all the people we meet belong to the same circle, they are as it were seething in the same cauldron, they have common interests or rather what they have in common is a lack of interest in anything, which is why they understand each other in half-spoken phrases. Hence the many hints and reservations and silences in their talk. Each of them seems to be speaking with himself, replying to his own thoughts, conducting a sort of inner dialogue to which his interlocutor replies by an inner dialogue of his own. And yet they understand one another. That is the origin of the famed poetics of the subtext.

Hemingway tried, elaborated, and later rejected the technique and the very manner of the unspoken subtext in his short stories. It was noticeable as early as in his "Cat in the Rain" and perhaps was apparent most fully in "The Killers." Aware of the possibly diversified meaning or ambiguity of subtext Hemingway in his larger works had recourse to the context essential for understanding his hints, or provided the key to them. In works of that nature he constantly puts questions before the reader. What, for instance, is the meaning of "The Cat in the Rain," "Cross-Country Snow," "Hills Like White Elephants," "Homage to Switzerland," "A Way You'll Never Be?" And later he asked the reader—what is the meaning of *The Old Man and the Sea?*

In all these cases, the help of the context is needed really (and in the last instance the reader has to make up his mind whether the book is complete, or a fragment, or part of a suite). The context helps in various ways. "Hills Like White Elephants," for example, becomes at once comprehensible against the background of the many other tales about expatriates and of *The Sun Also Rises.* It is possible to interpret "Cat in the Rain" in an abstract way— as boredom, langor, inaction. But remembering the context of the tales "Cross-Country Snow," "Soldier's Home," "Homage to Switzerland," *The Snows of Kilimanjaro,* "Macomber," or *The Fifth Column* and even *Across the River and Into the Trees,* you begin to get a different view of "Cat in the Rain." In this context the first short story acquires a deeper significance. "Cat in the Rain" turns out to mean not merely boredom but the first signs of nostalgia, of the woman's longing for a home which frightens and antagonizes the man.

What is the meaning of "A Way You'll Never Be?" A psychological sketch of a mind injured by shell shock? Yes, but more than that. And only in the context of *A Farewell to Arms* and "Now I Lay Me" does it become clear why an insane man in American uniform is allowed to stroll about a battlefield. We understand not only Nick's state of mind but his attitude to the "big lie" in which he is taking part and from which he soon tries to escape into a "separate peace," whether he is shell-shocked or not, shot as a deserter or decorated with medals. Words like "sacred," "glorious," "sacrifice" ring as falsely in his ears as they will do to Frederic Henry.

Knowledge of the context helps to understand the individual stories. This is specially the case in the psychological studies while in his long works such as *The Sun Also Rises* the separate hints and understatements are clarified by the context of the whole novel.

In these psychological sketches Hemingway keeps posing problems both to himself and to the reader. To himself, the problem is how to leave a number of questions unanswered and yet by using his writer's skill to make the story convincing and impressive, stirring to the reader's mind and at the same time comprehensible even without the support of the additional context. And for the most part he succeeds without either any inner commentary or unexpected endings in the spirit of O. Henry.

As for the reader, Hemingway's psychological sketches pose a problem that requires only attentive, active reading and then is easily solved, not at all the kind of problems found in many of the tales of Edgar Allan Poe, Ambrose Bierce or Conan Doyle, which only the author or someone in his confidence—Sherlock Holmes or others—is capable of solving by sooner or later revealing the cards in their hands to the reader.

This is a really new feature contributed by Hemingway to the genre of the psychological sketch.

Hemingway's characters are weighed down by the complexities of life. There is much that they cannot understand, but neither can they accept it. They are quite helpless. They do not believe that they can change anything. They try not even to think of anything complicated. However, it would be wrong to transfer this mechanically on to the author whose main asset is not reason but a wise heart and who could have said of himself in the words of Frederic Henry: "I never think and yet when I begin to talk I say things I have found out in my mind without thinking." And many of his characters try to speak not about the things that worry them but about all sorts of trivialities. Hence the mass of apparently unnecessary digressions which in fact creates the natural background of an existence in which people eat and drink while in the meantime their lives go to ruin. They artificially limit their horizons and their interests which are trivial enough anyway. But vaguely they are aware of many things and although they cannot explain to themselves what it is all about, nevertheless in their chaotic inner monologues they at least try to comprehend why they are worried.

Some critics reproach Hemingway for the narrowness of his horizon and for escapism. True, in his youth Hemingway went through the school of American reporting when he was expected to give an account of what had happened and strictly forbidden to pose the question why it had happened. True, in Paris the masters of the avant garde taught him in every possible way to concentrate on *how* to write and not of *what* and to forget the accursed word "why." That influenced Hemingway at a certain period and in certain works but it cannot and should not be said of all his work. The more thoughtful of his critics—Young and Levin—have every ground for disagreeing with that view. True, Hemingway sometimes escaped from the responsibilities of saving the world by turning to bull-fighting or to fishing. But after all at the responsible moments he forgot his anarchistic and individualistic declarations, he flung himself into the very thick of the struggle and escaped, if anywhere, into war itself. It was a pity, of course, that after Spain and World War II he did not embrace the "horizon of all," a pity he did not live long enough to achieve a universally broad world view. But if we are to appreciate and judge him we must take into account all the circumstances. We must not ask of a man more than the much he managed to give to his readers and to world literature. Not many managed that much.

In this general examination of Hemingway's style it will not be amiss to dwell on some other special features of his manner of writing, on some of his stylistic devices. We will now turn to a few of them.

The structure of Hemingway's books is unusual and changes according to the intention. In the collection of short stories *In Our Time,* Hemingway, preceding Dos Passos' *Manhattan Transfer,* interspersed the narrative with contrasting miniatures.

In *The Sun Also Rises* the structure is simple and harmonious. In *A Farewell to Arms* Hemingway successfully blended two planes, war and love, the epic and the lyrical. The chaotic medley of styles of *Death in the After-noon* and *The Green Hills of Africa* reflects a period of inner vacillation but also of stubborn thinking about art and the writer's trade. The broken structure and a picture as viewed by different persons in "To Have and Have Not" and the shifting of time in *Snows of Kilimanjaro* are echoes of the deep distress of the author who had come to an impasse. In his novel *For Whom the Bell Tolls* we find again a broad structure on several planes. *The Old Man and the Sea* is a tour de force in which for one hundred pages the author keeps the reader's attention riveted to the single figure of the old man and his simple actions and thoughts.

Hemingway, like Chekhov, is fond of the "gun that is fired in the last act": the cushion tossed into the ring, on which Manolo Garcia trips, in his ruin; an untimely fall of snow destroys the camouflage of El Sordo's guerillas and serves to bring about their death.

Hemingway sees the outer world, objects and actions with the clear, sharp eyes of a hunter and a soldier and he brings them down in flight with short direct impetuous blows as accurate as those inflicted by his beloved bullfighters. He has a purely physical sense of the world which he feels like the weight of a trout pulling at the line. Both he and his characters are aware of themselves as inseparable particles of that world.

For his imagery Hemingway mostly borrows from nature: the crowd crawls slowly from the entrance fo the circus slowly like a glacier; sinister rain forms the background of the whole of *A Farewell to Arms.* The image of invincible stubbornness in achieving one's aims is the leopard reaching the summit of Kilimanjaro to die; the image of the end is the hyena, or the birds, or the writer Harry himself like a snake with a broken backbone, or people in general, like ants shaken off a log into the camp-fire.

Grasping on to this feature some critics belonging to the Symbolist school now fashionable in the United States, in particular Carlos Baker, give a disproportionate and unjustified significance to Hemingway's imagery which they proclaim to be allegory and symbols. Thus Baker conceives of *A Farewell to Arms* simply as the unfolding of the image of the mountain—the symbol of all things lofty—and the plain, symbolizing all things low. Similarly in *Across the River and Into the Trees* he attributes phallic significance to the quay-side posts on the canals. In *The Old Man and the Sea* such critics seek for Christian symbols. Hemingway, however, always keeps within the limits of the real, straightforward image and all these interpretations may be left on the conscience of the interpreters. But when Hemingway considers it necessary he makes the landscape to serve his aims by giving it a psychological part to play, as, for instance, in "An Alpine Idyll."

Hemingway's language is changeable. Now it is the spare laconicism of an artist, now the rather careless tittle-tattle of the feuilletonist or the fact-collector of *The Green Hills of Africa* or simply the celebrity being interviewed. Now it is the dry, colorless language of the hollow people of his generation, and now the characteristic speech of those whom he wants to single out—the brilliant, swift retorts of Karkov, the bombastic ruminations of Fernando, the swearing of Augustin, the conventional officer's language in the miniatures of *In Our Times* and *The Snows of Kilimanjaro.*

Hemingway resorts to characteristic speech the more readily when he wishes to poke fun or laugh at people. He insists on his right to play the fool, to act the schoolboy, to jest.

Irony is the inseparable companion of nearly all of Hemingway's books. Leaving alone tales which specially aim at irony, such as "The Torrents of Spring," we find echoes of it nearly everywhere in his works. As the years passed we found out that the title *In Our Time* was a part of the phrase in *The Book of Common Prayer,* "Give peace in our time, O Lord." This title was conceived as an ironic contrast with the terrible contents of this far from peaceful book.

Quite often we find an ironic tail piece which by its bitter irony underlines the significance of what has happened.

But the stress is gradually shifted, the skeptical mockery gives way to pity and sympathy, the defensive irony in relation to the existing order changes to active sympathy and compassion and later to rendering active help to the victims of that order. From the combination of a fading irony with a growing sense of human compassion springs Hemingway's humanistic humor whose echoes we hear down to his last works like the story "Get a Seeing-eye Dog."

Translated by Ralph Parker

Inna Levidova

JOHN UPDIKE'S "THE CENTAUR" IN RUSSIAN

Visiting the Soviet Union in 1964 John Updike was inevitably asked at the meetings with Moscow critics and translators: "What led you to introduce a strand of mythology into your novel *The Centaur?*" "What is the meaning of it?" Updike said that the myth about Chiron, a version of which he came across in an old book by Josephine Peabody, had struck his imagination both as a story in itself and for the deep, purely personal associations the story aroused. These concerned the writer's father—a teacher of mathematics, his father's life and the part he played in his son's life, and the years of his own childhood and youth. The writer saw his own past, his parents and teachers *as a myth:* that is to say, enlarged, "more than life-size," somewhat mysterious and fantastic—just as grown-up people appear to a child and a young boy.

That was his answer to the first question, but then came the second question—what was *the meaning* of the mythological element in the novel—and here widely differing interpretations were possible. The origin of a work's mythological kernel, and the result of it are two entirely different things. In the author's own words, his intention in his book was for reality to be the "modern wrapping" of the myth. But it must be admitted—and I am probably not wrong in supposing many readers of the novel say the same—that from the start one views the mythological episodes not so much as something strange (it is hard to amaze the mid-20th-century reader) as dispensable. The sad, frightening and wonderfully warm-hearted tale of the ill-starred George Caldwell is of such overwhelming authenticity and the monologue of Peter's recollections fits so well into the author's narrative, that everything else seems superfluous. It cannot be denied that it is picturesque, intriguing, and brilliant but...it is not essential and therefore unnecessary. But perhaps the writer here was deliberately taking a risk for the sake of experiment? No, although Updike is a very bold writer, he is not attracted by irresponsible experiments as ends in themselves. If you read the book closely, you see that in the main, if not in all its ramifications, the mythological element is organic—if George Caldwell were just a school-teacher, we would be faced with a novel of an entirely different spirit, different inner rhythm and, naturally, different philosophical overtones.

As we try to discover the meaning of the novel's mythological element, we may note the use of satirical parody on the one hand and a certain romantic "escape-valve" on the other: the ugly, vulgar and dull reality of life in a small American provincial town is contrasted very sharply with the grandeur, beauty and harmony of the world of ancient myths... Such a view of John Updike's work is expressed in Anna Elistratova's article "The Tragic Animal, Man," published in *Foreign Literature* magazine (No. 12, 1963).

But I think this is not the main point. In the first place, is the world of gods and titans that emerges in Updike's novel all blue skies and grandeur? Fantastically refined cruelty, cunning, violence, lust, vengeance, envy —all this is very characteristic of the sky-dwellers of the ancient myths, and even such a picturesque scene as Chiron's lessons with his pupils in the Arcadian grove (Elistratova contrasts this with the bedlam and disorderliness reigning in Caldwell's real-life lesson) is idyllic only in appearance. Here, too, there is a canker—there is a point in Chiron recalling with his pupils the blessed times when Love ruled the world, but later the scepter passed to Uranus.... There is an obvious contrast between the bourgeois dullness of Olinger and the picturesqueness of the myth, but, in my view, the essence of the allegorical turn of the plot does not lie here.

It is intriguing, of course, to try to see a little Zeus in the sensuous petty despot, the headmaster Zimmerman; a Minos in the cafe proprietor Minor Kretz, a spiteful grumbler with clear fascist sympathies; a Mars in March, the glossy priest and ex-serviceman; a Hephaestus in Caldwell's sullen but loyal friend, the lame Hummel, a car mechanic with golden hands; an Aphrodite in his seductive wife Vera who teaches the girls gymnastics. All this is intriguing, though far from always convincing: not for nothing and not without humor did the author ("on the advice of my wife") supply the American edition of the novel with a profoundly academic index of mythological characters, with page references to where they appear both in their Olympian and Olinger embodiments...

All this is trimming, a more or less successful construction of the brain. Only one character, George Caldwell, proves in the reader's eyes to be the very heart and sole "justification" of the allegorical element in the novel. It is no accident that *all* the mythological scenes are not only bound up with the Chiron's presence, but are also presented, as it were, through his eyes. The very device is typical by which the writer "welds" the myth to the present age and fantasy to everyday life. The teacher, George Caldwell, is stepping with heavy tread along the school corridors; a metal dart is sticking in his ankle, thrust by one of his dear charges—the cruel blockheads of the Olinger school. A few more steps and, instantly, without any warning, he is already an unfortunate wounded Centaur—a fantastic monster, half-man, half-horse. He enters Hummel's garage, where the wretched dart is extracted with great difficulty. While this operation is under way, Hummel and his assistants "turn into" Hephaestus and the Cyclops, making magic at their forge. The same thing happens at the end of the novel. The Centaur approaches the edge of the precipice. Spiritually and physically tormented by the last three days which seem to have concentrated all the tension, anxieties and pain of his hard-working life. Caldwell walks along the road in the early frosty morning to his old snow-bound car. He sees the black Buick ahead of him like a hearse sent by Zimmerman. Caldwell has suspected that he has cancer; he has spent all the recent period preparing for death, trying to bring some order into his confused affairs and thoughts. But now it turns out he hasn't got cancer; he's been given a reprieve. He faces the same grind at the school where his heart, mind and nerves are battered every day: the clumsy maneuvering among those who possess power: the hourly fear of Damocles' sword—of being sacked (there emerged many young teachers after the war) and he still has ten years to go to his pension. Caldwell's tired heart cannot stand the strain. And Chiron welcomes death on the spot. "He died like any wearied man...."

The nature of the story's "mythological element" is clearly apparent in a brief summary of the plot and its denouement. Updike could have written: "Like the Centaur which...." But "like" and all its synonyms are omitted. Basically we are confronted with an extended simile, with a metaphor which has become action, an imagined boundary of real human existence, thus presenting it in relief and in a generalized form. Compared with this character, all the other allegorical similes seem a capricious scattering of bright stones which glitter in the solid realistic ore of the narrative.

But why does the writer—and subsequently the reader—see George Caldwell as a Centaur?

"...I miss only, and then only a little, in the late afternoons, the sudden white laughter that like heat lightning bursts in an atmosphere where souls are trying to serve the impossible. My father for all his mourning moved in the atmosphere of such laughter. He would have puzzled you. He puzzled me. His upper half was hidden from me. I knew best his legs," thinks the grown-up Peter. This bright, "white" laughter of a man whose head touched the stars and who bore in himself and inexhaustible store of wonder at life's secrets and of human warmth which he was ready to share with literally the first person he met—this laughter Peter really heard only many years afterward. While he was living with his father, he only heard it vaguely—probably that was why he loved him, but what he much more sharply perceived was something else: his father's laughable clumsiness in everyday affairs, his ridiculous clothes, cheaply obtained, his morbid suspiciousness, his occasional meek abasement before the people upon whom Caldwell was somehow dependent....

Yes, the head of Chiron may enter the clouds but with all four hooves he is stuck in the hateful everyday struggle for existence, in the struggle which, sooner or later, must break his back. There is something of the melancholy jester, something of Dostoevsky's meekly drooling officials in this tall narrow-shouldered figure in his short jacket and child's knitted cap. But just look at Caldwell in the classroom—the very same room where darts and notes are flying and cheeky well-fed youngsters, versed in school sex and pornographic postcards, squeeze the giggling school-girls in front of everybody! Listen to his story of the origin of the world, which is of quite amazing intellectual clarity and force of artistic imagination—a veritable hymn in praise of the eternal matter. Observe with what penetrating, sad and kind irony he talks after the lessons with those same boys who torment him despicably and are at the same time drawn instinctively toward him, as toward a real and a wise man—and you become aware that Chiron—the tutor of the children of the gods and titans in the Arcadian groves—is also George Caldwell, the Olinger teacher, that the essence of the matter lies not in the outward contrast, in the contrast of the setting, but in the inner similarity.

"Such is Caldwell—this modern Centaur," the critic B. Pankin writes in an interesting and enthusiastic article published in *Komsomolskaya Pravda* on April II, 1965. To him Caldwell's main feature is a noble stoicism dictated by love for his family and his anxiety for it; almost nothing else seems to exist for him "Like the long-distance runner, he gives the last ounce of his strength to the track and to the track alone," writes Pankin.

It is true there is a stoicism and love for his family. But is that the whole truth? No, I think the character has many more aspects. *The Centaur* is a work with precise tokens of the time and place, the social environment and political atmosphere. Everything described in it sticks firmly in the memory.

Quiet, sleepy Olinger and neighboring Alton—a small "capital," with its neon-lit center and frighteningly dark suburbs; the school with its many faces; the sports matches; Hummel's workshop, mysterious and dark like a forge in a grotto; Kretz' cafe; the shabby hotel where Caldwell and Peter stay overnight after the car breaks down; Hummel's sparkling and empty home, bathed in morning sunlight, where the shelterless travellers spend the second night, the night snow fell; and finally, the "family estate," the Caldwell's farm, a cold comfortless home belonging to his father-in-law near the small town of Firetown, with acres of neglected, unproductive land and the family dog Lady shivering in its kennel....

This is a typical Updike setting, with its Chekhovian suggestiveness and its details selected in Chekhov's manner; the night street in the suburbs of Alton where Caldwell left his broken-down car; "The Buick still alone, brooding on its shadow. Its nose was tipped up the slope, toward the unseen tracks. Menthol like a vaporized moon suffused the icy air. The factory wall was a sheer cliff mixed of brick and black glass. The panes of glass were now and then mysteriously relieved by a pane of cardboard or tin. The brick did not yield its true color to the streetlamp that lit the area but instead showed as a dimunition of black, a withdrawn and deadly grey. This same light made the strange gravel here glitter. Compounded of coal chips and cinders, it made a loud and restless earth that never settled, crackling and shifting underfoot as if its destiny were to be perpetually raked. Silence encircled us. Not a window looking at us was lit, though deep in the factory a blue glint kept watch."

The date of the action was not chosen arbitrarily: 1947 was the second post-war year, the first year of the undeclared cold war and the start of the Truman administration. Only in one episode of the novel is there direct talk of politics: Peter Caldwell enters in an argument with Minor Kretz about Communism, the Russians, Roosevelt and Hitler. Into their dialogue—which is fairly incoherent but very temperamental—burst the tart exclamations of the grown-up idiot Johnny Dedman, the supporter of the atomic bomb, who is impatient for war to break out.

This small episode contains a great deal: the mental outlook of one of the philistines who later swelled the ranks of "madmen" (Kretz cannot forgive Roosevelt for the fact that the Americans halted on the Elbe, instead of advancing straight to Moscow), and the mental outlook of the very young man with spontaneously Leftish sympathies which undoubtedly sprung up in Peter under the influence of his humane and democratic father. To Peter Communism was not a scarecrow but the natural future of mankind, the only way to save the world from misery. But the bitter political argument of the two antagonists has a very ordinary and rather sorry ending: George Caldwell, calling for his son at the cafe and hearing Minor Kretz' complaint about the young "atheist and communist," hastens to smoothe over Peter's vehemence with some clumsy and unlikely flattery, with a declaration of his own political loyalty. Caldwell cannot permit himself the luxury of annoying an honored figure in Olinger with heretical views. The headmaster, Zimmerman, has only just noted in his inspection report on Caldwell's lesson that, in speaking of the history of Creation, the teacher said nothing on the question of Divine Providence. The school is a source of daily irritations, but the school is also a source of livelihood for Caldwell the teacher, for his wife, his son and his old father-in-law, and Caldwell will hold on to his post whatever it costs him in effort and humiliation.

The Olinger high school is depicted by Updike with truly savage and Hogarthian strokes. Yet Caldwell understands that even Zimmerman's pupils are, essentially, unfortunate children, the "natural product" of Olinger, of its stupidity, cruelty and the bold bragging of businessmen grown rich during the war, of its dirty morals and its hypocrisy, which has permeated their flesh and blood. And while Peter is full of quarrelsome outbursts, while he seethes and occasionally taunts the bosses, George Caldwell finds some escape and consolation in his work itself. Fairly often, in an ironic and somewhat theatrical tone, he declares himself no better than a slave bound to a galley for life, yet he loves some of the children, feels sorry for others and his heart is in the school. The author conveys with delicacy and truth this outwardly contradictory but very real situation.

The episodes of Caldwell's home life possess the same psychological authenticity. It is a family little acquainted with peaceful well-being, it exists with clashes and friction—tensely, on its nerves. Yet it was a good life, the grown-up Peter recalls. There was sincere and kind love of each other, respect for human personality, humor, generosity and the unpretentious spirituality which Peter noticeably lacks now that he is well-versed in the ways of the bohemian intelligentsi, in the artificial life with "its rather wistful half-

Freudian and half-Oriental sex-mysticism...." "Was it for this that my father gave his life?" Peter asks himself on sleepless nights. This rhetorical question is not self-accusation, not even self-reproach—it is simply an attempt to compare the moral values of two generations. Nevertheless the strange man, seen in retrospect and in some respects ridiculous, in others pitiful, rises before us, not against the author's will, as a more integrated and more valuable person than the unfulfilled Prometheus—Peter.

However paradoxical it may be, Caldwell turns out to be just such a man as he appears in his own obituary, set in the middle of the book. It is an emotional and eloquent obituary—a sarcastic parody of the saccharine style of the samples of a highly developed genre in the United States—it traces the hard road in life of an honest American citizen, a talented teacher and a selfless good man. The son of a poor preacher, he worked his way through college, wandered from town to town, worked as a mechanic, a bus driver, a trainer, an attendant in a hotel, a dishwasher in a restaurant and so on—an almost classic selection of trades and occupations of a young American without his parents' check book in his pocket. All these facts are scrupulously set out in the obituary and all the remarkable traits of Caldwell's character are shown in a benevolent light. It is only the *fate* of the man that is falsified, his place in society, the attitude of the small Jupiters to those very qualities which so move the author of the obituary—one of Caldwell's former pupils.

In his social life George Caldwell did not go beyond municipal and charitable "small deeds" and he was never a fighter or a rebel—simply a very honest, very kind and very conscientious toiler who did not spare himself for the sake of others. But, though alien to the great social movements of his day, he was nevertheless a true son of the 1930's with his instinctive democratic spirit and bitter contempt for the local Jupiters, and with unbounded sympathy for all the disinherited and homeless.

Peter's further career is only hinted at, but its outlines are familiar: it is the generation of the cold war and McCarthyism, of the beatniks and Salinger's frail heroes, a confused and egocentric generation. George Caldwell, worn out by the life of a provincial teacher, would feel cramped and stifled in Peter's New York attic.

Very much in his own way and very boldly but still in the traditions of his country's great literature, John Updike has created yet another character which will remain alive and true for readers along with the most vivid characters of American literature. This is a great deal to have achieved. What more, in fact, could a writer, and a young one at that, dream of? But it is precisely Updike's youth and resilent creative energy that, naturally, immediately prompt one to think about his future. However much we may be dispirited by the "leaden abominations of life" which he touches with a surgeon's light and sure hand, John Updike remains fundamentally an artist with a joyful and poetic view of the world. *The Centaur* confirms this, although in this sad Odyssey (one may give this name to Caldwell's three-day roamings and to the wanderings of the author's thought which embraces a whole human life) the only joy, perhaps, is the sparkling morning of snowfall in Vera Hummel's house. But in order to convey this as he does, one must know what joy is.

For all its originality Updike's work is in the mainstream of mid-century American literature: the writer examines the standpoint in life and the social bonds of his contemporary and fellow countryman. The future of the author of *The Centaur* promises to be of great interest.

Only concern for the integral composition of this article made me leave to the end an estimation of the work of the novel's translator into Russian, Victor Hinkis, although really one should have begun with it. It is a triumph of the same order as Rita Rait-Kovalyova's translation of Salinger's *Catcher in the Rye*, and Faulkner's trilogy translated by her, Victor Hinkis and Simon Markish.

Technical virtuosity, inventiveness, richness of vocabulary are absolutely necessary qualities for a translator tackling prose which is almost as hard to translate as good poetry. But that is not all: one must be able "to swim with the current" of the story's rhythm and intonation which is bound up with the innermost secret of the author's individuality—to swim along with it, while remaining on the surface all the time. This the translator has succeeded in doing.

M. Landor

TRUMAN CAPOTE IN RUSSIAN

Truman Capote's works have recently begun to appear in Russian translations here. However, our critics expressed their opinion about this writer
even earlier. One of the most interesting statements was made by Inna Levidova in her comprehensive article "Restless Souls" devoted to the hero of
postwar American prose. The critic does not hide the fact that she prefers
other postwar writers, as Kerouac and Salinger, but she also gives due credit
to Capote's talent. She says that the author of *Other Voices, Other Rooms*
"very effectively creates an oppressive heavily charged atmosphere going into
very tangible details of the life of the provincial outskirts of the American
south." She considers this novel, which is full of "Gothic" passions and horrors, against the background of postwar prose. Its denouement reminds one
of Salinger's story: After a crisis a youth parts with his childish fantasies and
enters the "adult world."

However, this excellently written book is not regarded as great literature: it lacks depth. "Capote's narrative style is simple and charming; it is
both subtle psychological writing and fantastic grotesque. But the grotesque
is not a means of revealing and intensifying the *essence* of things, as is the case
with writers who inwardly tend towards realism; it is a reflection of the
author's own view of the world."

Inna Levidova proves her point in an analysis of Capote's later novel-
ettes, *The Grass Harp* and *Breakfast at Tiffany's.* Both are woven skillfully,
intricately, and are rich in excellent details. But the author, while supple-
menting his collection of grotesque characters, does not reveal the essence of
the human nature, of the human drama.

In the first novelette, about eccentrics who have fled to the forest away
from the mercantile life of a southern city, the stylization dominates: "Everything here is soft, transparent, and even the grotesque itself is well-intentioned
as in a fairy-tale."

As for the second novelette and its main character Holly Golightly,
Levidova considers them the highest achievement of the writer. "This is an
Americanized and modernized Manon Lescaut—an outwardly carefree waif,'
but subject to grim moods. Her image is full of vigor, humor, and irresis-
table charm." But even Holly Golightly has not become a flesh-and-blood
character. In this case too, the author contents himself with keen but fleeting
impressions instead of profound investigation.

The critic, while noting the author's sensitiveness and ingenuity, comes
to the following conclusion: "But all his characters, men and women, thuogh
incomplete and devoid of authentic qualities, occupy a special place in contemporary American prose. They signal like twinkling night lights in a swamp:
'It's unsteady here!' "

"Master Misery" was the first story by Capote to be translated into
Russian.

It was published in the weekly *Nedelya* and aroused the lively interest of the readers.

The choice was by no means an accidental one: of all the stories in Capote's collection *A Tree of Night and Other Stories* this is the most realistic one. In translation this story was called "Sold Dreams." The grotesque to which the author resorts here, is not perceived by the reader as an aim in itself. It compels the reader more deeply to feel the hopeless loneliness of an unfortunate girl and her friend, a crazy old man with the traits of a tragic clown.

In April 1965 the literary monthly *Moskva* published Victor Golyshev's translation of *Breakfast at Tiffany's*. It produced a very great impression. The readers regarded Holly as a real character amid the polished nonentities, such as Jose, a person who is inwardly honest among hypocrites and the dregs of society. The heroine does not pose when she says: "Be anything but a coward, a pretender, an emotional crook, a whore. I'd rather have cancer than a dishonest heart."

She evokes deep sympathy: the Holly singing freedom folk songs on a fire escape, the Holly so used to deceit and disappointment, the Holly who in a moment of despair throws her favorite cat—homeless like herself—to the ground in the slum quarter.

The first thing our readers detected in the story was its tragic, melanchloy note. The comment with which *Moskva* accompanied the translation seemed to have been written on their behalf. The heroine wants to be her own self, the magazine writes. "But everything about her is borrowed, temporary, unstable as a soap bubble, even her name. She seeks her place in life absurdly, agonizingly, understanding that it is not easily to be found but that it is something which every person needs. She seeks, stumbling, tormenting herself, but she cannot agree to compromises. She suffers one wreck after another, receives blow after blow, and flees from this life, from her misfortunes into the unknown, to the end of the world; she flees only to vanish, to disappear in the cold, hostile, egoistic world."

However, the heroine suffers a certain sentimental simplification. Her character lacks inner contrasts. For Holly the luxurious breakfast at Tiffany's is a symbol of success in life. The author admires her carefree state and her changeability. For him Holly in not only a tragic heroine. She is an exotic flower that has grown up in the field of city vice.

In Victor Golyshev's translation, the accent is placed somewhat differently than in the original. Throughout the story one feels a keen sympathy for the heroine. Nevertheless, this somewhat free translation accurately conveys Capote's wit and vividness. In the Russian text Holly's speech sounds sufficiently caustic and unrestrained. The speech of the episodic characters is also excellently individualized—take for instance, Holly's sly girl friend Mag and the Hollywood agent O. D. Berman.

The magazine *Foreign Literature* has announced that it plans to publish *The Grass Harp*. It will probably get an equally warm reception: Capote tells about the strange people of a small town vividly and with humor. *Nedelya* already introduced the reader to this aspect of his talent when it published his story "Jug of Silver." However, his writings of another type, such as "Master Misery" and *Breakfast at Tiffany's,* evoke greater response with our public.

If we were to compare Inna Levidova's article with the comment in the magazine *Moskva* we would get the impression that these are two different interpretations of Capote. And indeed, the opinions expressed are different, although only one criterion has been used. When reviewing the entire work of this writer Levidova finds that he lacks depth and compassion. The magazine highly evaluates his best story, that in which there is more compassion and depth. And whereas the item in *Moskva* is somewhat simplified, Levidova's article appears to be too severe and categorical.

Those works of Capote's which have attracted the attention of the Russian reader are associated by them with the best traditions of American prose. Capote's best works reflect not only his outstanding ability, but also the originality of his talent: he has succeeded in telling about the old and the usual in his own particular way.

Raisa Orlova

ABIGAIL HOWLAND GUARDS HER HOUSE

Can you call this modern prose? The book has none of the passionate temperament of Baldwin's screaming novels, or the angry lyrical publicist style of Norman Mailer, or compressed time, or "black" humor, or a flood of sex—normal, perverted or super-perverted.

It is an unhurried tale, told at the natural speed with which a family grows, the embryo develops in the maternal womb, and seasons melt one into the other. We see the Howland home in all its details, with its additions, verandahs, passages and queer corners; then the author pauses near the center of the town and lovingly sketches various passing persons who actually have no part in the subject development.

The story sets its own leisurely pace. People grow, mature, marry and in turn bring up their own children.

The book is placed in the American South, about which Soviet readers already know something from Caldwell's grotesques, Faulkner's phantasmagoria and Harper Lee's book *To Kill a Mockingbird* which is very popular here.

This modest book does have its own atmosphere and something to say. Many books have been written about the tragedy of the mulatto, the conflict of feeling, the divided consciousness of people born of a mixed marriage. This is the theme of *The Keepers of the House.* Margaret wants to understand who and what she is, what she has from the white father she has never seen and never will see. She opens up a sore place to look for white blood. But the blood is ordinary red, the same that flows in the veins of white and black and yellow.

Abigail Howland, the main character in the novel, stands on the threshold of the shattered house, that house where her forebears lived, generation after generation. The windows are broken. What had happened? She wants to understand, but to understand she must remember.

The history of the Howlands is closely interwoven with the history of the country, their roots are deep, they took part in its wars. The land which they have owned for 150 years holds much of their blood and their sweat. Abigail need but look back and she will see a long line of forebears. this gives her stability, the stability of a brief human life: my forebears lived before me, my descendants will live after me, in this house.

One need not look at the author's name to know that this book is written by a woman—not so much from the woman's details, but by its theme—woman gives life and answers for new lives. Therefore, it is but fitting that she keeps, guards, cherishes the home.

The pace of the story is uneven. The student years of mother and daughter are given in a quick patter, one feels they bore the author as they do her characters. But when it comes to the pranks of William Howland—these are told in detail. How he bet he would find a secret distillery—and found it. He comes to places he did not know and one feels he has been over the whole distict with his gun. It is told with the swiftness of the rivers along which he sailed.

When his granddaughter Abigail married she did not want her house. It wasn't modern, wasn't the American style. Hardly any Americans stay rooted to one place, they move from town to town, from state to state. But in the south there is a tendency to stay put, even now. After her grandfather's death Abigail returns with husband and children to her childhood home, the old Howland house, and is glad. Her children will be able to look back, as she can, and draw calmness from the past.

Not only calmness, though, and not only gladness. She is caught up in what they did—they, her forebears, near and far. And in particular, what Grandfather and Margaret did.

William Howland, long past his youth, met on his travels a Negro girl of 18, as though risen from the ground. He took her to be housekeeper in his bachelor home. Then she became his mistress. She bore him children. A very ordinary story, repeated time and again in the South. But it is only at first glance it appears ordinary; look more deeply and it is unusual, unique. William and Margaret loved each other for all the 30 years they lived together. Naturally, they wanted life to be good for their children—that is, that they should be regarded as white and enjoy all the privileges of white people. Howland flew in the face of all the prejudices that surrounded him, prejudices more powerful then any law—actually, went against the Howlands: he secretly married his mistress and legitimized their children.

It turned out, however, that this decision helped only them; for the children things turned out tragically.

It is difficult to leap out of one's own story, especially for a woman passive and weak-willed, as Abigail appears almost to the end of the story.

"We're all together, you and me and Crissy and Nina," Abigail says to Robert, Margaret's eldest son, at the end of the book. But it is not only the Howland children and grandchildren who are fastened: it is Americans—black, white and of mixed blood.

And Americans have roots irrespective of the color of their skins. Shots, pogroms, riots may kill a few or many. But the roots cannot be dug out, history cannot be changed.

The Keepers of the House is far from being a thesis-novel. The acute very contemporary problems in this far from modern novel come from within, It is not a book "about" integration. It is a book about life, and how things are in this life. And how things are, is tragically unsettled. The drugged, sleepy submission of small Southern towns with customs going back to the slave-owning days is sometimes explosive. Shots, demonstrations. Marches. Murders. The quietness of the Howland house is shattered, too. After his parents' death Robert, the son of William and Margaret, publishes their marriage certificate in the newspaper, to strike a blow at Abigail's husband John Tolliver who is making anti-Negro speeches. And Tolliver has a good chance to become governor of the state.

Tolliver left and ordered his wife to come with him. But she remained in her grandfather's house. And with great courage beat off the attack of racist savages with the help of one old Negro and William Howland's old guns. The cowshed burned down. Windows were smashed. Abigail Howland-Tolliver stands in the doorway of the shattered house remembering, asking.

It was the Howland house they attacked—not Communists. not atheists, not Negroes. A house belonging to white people, wealthy Americans, protestants of Anglo-Saxon descent, WASP; in the USA that means belonging to the highest aristocracy. How could this have come to pass? Shirley Ann Grau is a writer of the Faulkner school. One of the key words to understanding both the epos Yoknapatawpha and the novel *The Keepers of the House* is community.

William Howland flew in the face of the laws and customs of this little American town, he went against the "community." And for this, the punishment fell upon his granddaughter.

The attackers drove to the Howland home in cars. These were no anonymous monsters, the mistress of that house knew practically all of them by sight, and each of them as an ordinary man. Some are better, others worse. But not criminals, not murderers. Yet together, egging one another on, drunk with mob frenzy, they are capable of anything. They cannot let their "sacred" laws be flouted. Nobody can be allowed to do this, not even the wealthy William Howland. To marry a Negro—no, this is intolerable.

Too much importance must not be attached to Abigail Howland's rebellion. She has little likeness to Yegor Bulychov; she has lived all her life on this street, alongside the rowdies. Too much importance must not be attached to this single nocturnal fight in defense of her home; yet she, too, is a symbol of the times, an indication that the very street itself is changing.

She is the true descendant of her grandfather even in the way she decides to punish the town for the attack. Not with a protest demonstartion, not with the help of the law. by economic sanctions. She orders the doors of the Washington Hotel to be nailed up—that hotel where strangers to the town sit for hours. It is her property, she can do what she likes with it. For her this, too, is one way of preserving her home.

Alexei Zverev

SOVIET LITERARY SCHOLARS ON THEIR AMERICAN COLLEAGUES

Soviet readers have long been quite fully acquainted with American literature from Benjamin Franklin to John Updike. But until recently the broad public knew considerably less about American literary criticism.

To some extent this is natural: in the Soviet Union, as everywhere in the world, writer's books are, of course, much more widely read than books about writers. Quite a considerable number of Soviet researchers and critics are engaged in studying and elucidating literary life in America, so it has not been difficult for readers to learn from a Soviet author's preface, critical article or monograph about the literary career of a particular American writer who interested them. From these studies, by the way, one could also get a clear conception of the battle of ideas which has developed in American literary studies round the work of the particular writer.

Nevertheless until very recent years it was very noticeable that the history and contemporary state of literary criticism in the United States were insufficiently known in the Soviet Union. Literary criticism is just as full-fledged a branch of literature as prose, poetry and drama; without studying the history of literary criticism, one cannot grasp the history of literature. And it is far from a matter of indifference to the reader how particular literary events are judged by the author's contemporary critics, how people in the author's own country view the author catching the reader's attention— Faulkner or Jack London, for instance. It has long been observed that readers in general like to know about the literary life of another country at first hand, so to say—from the statements of writers and critics in that particular country.

The literary surveys, articles and reviews by a number of American critics—Herbert Aptheker, Maxwell Geismar, John Howard Lawson, Sidney Finkelstein—published in Soviet journals, have invariably aroused special interest among Soviet readers. Two years ago Progress Publishers issued a Russian translation of Finkelstein's book *Existentialism and Alienation in American Literature.* Then a translation appeared of all three volumes of Vernon L. Parrington's monumental work *Main Currents in American Thought.* Then there appeared Van Wyck Brooks' book *The Flowering of New England,* generally acknowledged to be the best of his five volumes embracing the century and a half of the history of American literature.

So Soviet readers now have an opportunity of acquainting themselves with the work of the two major American democratic critics of the 20th century. They esteem, as it deserves, Parrington's democratic spirit, his profound understanding of the fact that art is determined by history, his striving to show the vitality and fruitfulness of the realist tradition in American literature.

Soviet readers are also impressed by Brooks, by his rare ability to re-create in full detail the atmosphere of the ideas and literature of a long past age, his burning interest in its problems and conflicts, his knack of seeming to relive, together with the reader, the events of the distant past and the feelings of the people of those days, who have left their mark in American culture.

But time races ahead: both Parrington and Brooks have already departed from the American literary scene. Among contemporary literary scholars in the United States there are not very many like them, who are still inspired by their ideas and, following in their footsteps, frankly struggle to preserve and advance the traditions of realism and the social "commitment" of art—traditions upon which more than one generation of the best American literary craftsman have grown up. Many American literary scholars regard Parrington, Brooks, and also Frank Otto Matthiessen, who met an untimely tragic death, and other representatives of this school, as hopelessly outdated.

The picture of contemporary American literary studies is quite complex and much specialized work is needed to find one's bearings. The first attempt in Soviet literature to tackle this important task was a book published in the spring of 1969 by the Nauka Press, Moscow, entitled *Contemporary Literary Studies in the United States.* It is the collective work of staff members of the Institute of World Literature of the U.S.S.R. Academy of Sciences.

It is not difficult to conceive the difficulties which confronted the authors of the work—experienced scholars Moris Mendelson and Alexander Nikolyukin and their younger colleagues Maya Koreneva and Alexander Mulyarchik. The postwar period witnessed a real "boom" in American literary studies. It seems it was only recently that there were still too many blank spots on the American literary map; even in respect to classic authors it was in several cases difficult to find any more or less full study, even of a purely biographical nature, while hardly any serious literary studies had been written about modern writers, and judgement of them was left only to newspaper and weekly magazine reviewers. Today practically no blank spots remain. Every more or less prominent American writer attracts the very close attention of critics. There is a stream of monographs and books devoted to entire periods in the history of American literature, there are studies of particular works, writer's biographies and collections of articles about their work.

Not only the growing quantity of literary studies is an eloquent fact. Even more significant, in my opinion, is the appearance of a number of truly profound and valuable studies both of particular periods in the growth of American literature and of the works of particular authors. There are also attempts to restore historic justice with regard to certain writers, who were either ignored by American critics until recently or subjected to groundless attacks.

Thus for many years American scholars showed no interest at all in such a figure as Theodore Dreiser. There were many reasons for this, including, of course, reason of by no means a literary nature: the evolution of Dreiser, who arrived at a communist outlook at the end of his life, did not win the sympathies of American critics during the "cold war" years. Ten years ago, if there was any mention of Dreiser in studies of literary history published in the United States, it was invariably from the point of view that Dreiser was a very poor artist, almost a second-rate chronicler of everyday life, who had by accident been elevated momentarily to the summit of world-wide recognition. Time has proved, however, that any honest history of 20th-century American literature is inconceivable without Dreiser, and in the sixties one book after another began to appear about him: *Th. Dreiser: Our Bitter Patriot* by Ch. Shapiro, in 1962, *Theodore Dreiser* by P.L. Gerber in 1964, *Dreiser* by W. A. Swanberg in 1965....

This fact in itself does not, unfortunately, mean that the injustice with regard to Dreiser, which prevailed in his own country for so long, has at last been fully eliminated. For instance, the very detailed biography by Swanberg is imbued with a striving not to expose but in fact to perpetuate the legends which were created round the author's name during the period of McCarthyism, and the work has been justly sharply criticized by Soviet literary scholars in the book under review. At the same time it is difficult not to agree with them that the growing interest of American critics in Dreiser is one of the "signs of a healthier state of American literary research, which have appeared in recent years."

One may trace similar tendencies in the attitude of American scholars to some other writers who have kept to the traditions of social criticism and realism. For instance, all the major studies of Carl Sandburg belong to the last decade. It is only in recent years that the portrait of Richard Wright as a creative artist has begun to be reconstructed in its true outlines. It was also in the sixties that the first comparatively full critical studies of Sinclair Lewis appeared, although they show signs of a clear prejudice against the writer, as M. Mendelson notes on the basis of a convincing analysis of these books. This is particularly evident in Mark Shorer's book: *Sinclair Lewis, An American Life*.

There is a certain regularity to be observed in the fact that works which obviously strive towards an unprejudiced analysis of the work of writers whose names were until recently never mentioned in America, should alternate with works like those of Swanberg and Shorer. One has the impression that American critics are today going through a period of gradual emancipation from the anti-democratic, anti-historical trends which were very widespread in quite recent times. The process of renewal, of a return to the really fruitful trends developed by Parrington, Brooks and Matthiessen is proceeding not without difficulty, so it is not surprising that it is not often that studies of genuine scientific and literary merit appear in America. There are many more books whose authors follow ready-made comparativist, Freudian, formalist and other patterns and sometimes even deliberately distort the meaning of a writer's work in an endeavor to dampen the critical ring of his books.

The Soviet literary scholars, naturally, pay attention to such attempts in their analysis of recent American literature about writers of various trends and eras: Whitman, Mark Twain, Arthur Miller, Saul Bellow and many others. It is no accident that their book bears the sub-title "Arguments about American Literature."

Although American critics rarely enter into direct polemic among themselves, it is hard not to sense the inner polemical character of many of their studies. For instance, diametrically opposed to each other are such works as L. J. Budd's study *Mark Twain—Social Philosopher* (I962), which contains utterly unfounded claim that Mark Twain was only a conservative liberal, and the book, published by the young scholar B. M. French three years later, *Mark Twain and the Gilded Age,* in which he shows that, even when Mark Twain was starting to write, "social anger" was a far from transient mood of his.

The overall picture in American literary studies is of a sharpening polemic between the upholders of formalist and aesthetic schools and the supporters of a genuinely historical estimate of literature. This is the conclusion reached by A. Nikolyukin, who reconstructs the history of the arguments about when American literature acquired its national character, and by M. Koreneva, analyzing critical literature on postwar American drama, and by A. Mulyarchik, examining American critics' views on the fate of the novel. The authors of the book consider that in American literary studies the sixties began a time of renewal, there was a fresh wind blowing, a new generation of critics was formed who are ever more actively departing from the anti-historical principles, deep-rooted in academic literary studies in the United States, and are arguing with the authorities of yesterday.

This argument is ever more frequently revealing the correctness of many of the ideas put forward by Parrington and Brooks, and for this reason it is no accident that one of the main chapters in the book by Soviet literary scholars deals with the democratic traditions of American literary studies.

Assessing very highly the work of Parrington, Brooks and Matthiessen, the author of this chapter, M. Mendelson, rightly says that their heritage is alive even today. An affinity with Brooks may be sensed in some of the studies of so eminent an American critic as Malcolm Cowley; direct continuation of the democratic tradition is to be found in the literary activity of Maxwell Geismar. The same continuation is found by M. Koreneva, too, in her analysis of the statements of the eminent American theater critic Harold Clurman. Particular studies by Alfred Kazin, of which A. Mulyarchik writes in detail, are consonant with this tradition.

The best modern literary scholars in the United States display an insistent striving to restore to criticism its most precious qualities, those which were characteristic, for instance, of Brooks—a historical spirit, depth of analysis, profoundness of judgement and loyalty to democratic ideals. In this

Soviet literary scholars see a promise of the further successful advance of literary research in the United States. Of course, far from all the tendencies which had a negative effect on American literary criticism in the forties and fifties have yet been overcome. But, as facts show, there is a change for the better.

The need for renewal is the first sign of the crisis of those trends which were until recently the most active in American literary studies: the Freudian, mythological, and comparativist trends. This crisis is only natural. Van Wyck Brooks, in his polemic with representatives of the "new criticism," many years ago foretold the lack of prospects along that path. Today his forecast is being justified in full measure, and he has found new supporters and followers.

Analyzing the works of leading American critics, describing the argument about the work of major American writers, the authors of the book *Contemporary Literary Studies in the United States* reach the conclusion that in recent years beneficial changes have been taking place in American literary research and this, naturally, pleases all friends of American culture.

INDEX OF NAMES

Numbers in italic are from the prefatory material, non-italic are from the text.